THE NAME
OF THE POET

THE NAME
OF THE POET

Onomastics and Anonymity in the
Works of Stéphane Mallarmé

Michael Temple

UNIVERSITY
of
EXETER
PRESS

First published in 1995 by
University of Exeter Press
Reed Hall, Streatham Drive
Exeter, Devon EX4 4QR
UK

British Library Cataloguing in Publication Data
A catalogue record of this book is available
from the British Library

ISBN 0 85989 431 2

Typeset in Palatino
by GreenShires Icon, Exeter

Printed and bound in Great Britain
by Bookcraft Ltd, Bath

Table of Contents

Acknowledgements

I should like to express my gratitude to Professor Malcolm Bowie for his patience and supervision over the years; to Nena Roy for her editorial rigour; and to Roland-François Lack for his generous assistance in preparing the final version of the text.

Note on Abbreviations

When referring to works by Stéphane Mallarmé, I have used the following simple abbreviations: extracts from prose texts are followed by the sign *'Pl.'*, meaning 'Pléiade', i.e. the 1945 edition of the *Oeuvres complètes* edited by Henri Mondor and G. Jean-Aubry (Paris: Gallimard); poems or extracts from poems are followed by the sign *'O.C.'*, meaning the first volume of the projected *Oeuvres complètes*, edited by Carl Paul Barbier and Charles Gordon Millan (Paris: Flammarion, 1983).

I must never be joking, for example, or writing a poem

J.L. Austin, *How to do things with Words*

1

Introduction

*Ces noms, j'espère que personne ne les contestera, dans
leur simplicité, dans leur évidence, dans leur clarté.*[1]

My concern in this introduction will be to address two preliminary questions regarding the present project. Firstly, why write a
book about names? And secondly, why study the names and
naming of Stéphane Mallarmé?

1.1 The Name and the Author

The study of names in literature, or what we might call 'literary
onomastics', has of late provided critics an occasion to reconsider
the figure of the author, a problem which, in the past twenty years
or so, had become something of a taboo subject in literary theory.
Recent works by Geoffrey Bennington and Peggy Kamuf have
shown that the author (someone we call by convention 'Jean-
Jacques Rousseau', for example, or 'Charles Baudelaire') may
today return to the fold of theory, but only on condition that when
speaking of that person we disdain the old rags of 'intention',
'personality' and 'style', in favour of terms such as 'signature',
'trace', and of course the most seductive of all: 'the name'.[2] The
new terminology is unmistakably Derridean, so it should come as

no surprise that both the studies referred to were published under the auspices of the Collège International de Philosophie. I propose, then, as a means of responding to my first question, to turn to a contemporary work written in the name of Jacques Derrida, and to ask how we may imagine the name and the signature to exist in theory today. I am thinking of *Jacques Derrida* by Geoffrey Bennington and Jacques Derrida in the series 'Les Contemporains'.[3]

At the entry for 'Le Nom Propre', Bennington first presents us with the name as philosophy has traditionally conceived it:

> Le nom propre devrait assurer un certain passage entre langage et monde, dans cette mesure où il devrait indiquer un individu concret, sans ambiguïté, sans avoir besoin de passer par les circuits de la signification. Même si on accepte que le système de la langue est constitué de différences et donc de traces, il semblerait que le nom propre, qui fait partie du langage, pointe directement vers l'individu qu'il nomme. Cette possibilité de nomination propre doit être le prototype même du langage, et comme tel peut prescrire au langage son telos: pour compliqués que soient devenus nos besoins en matière de langage, l'idéal régulateur peut et doit rester celui d'une nomination propre, éventuellement de la vérite elle-même. (100–1)

For Bennington, such a representation demands to be problematized, as he proceeds to demonstrate:

> Mais il n'y a pas de nom propre. Ce qu'on appelle du nom commun générique 'nom propre' doit bien fonctionner, lui aussi, dans un système de différences: tel ou tel nom propre plutôt qu'un autre se désigne tel ou tel individu plutôt qu'un autre et donc se trouve marqué par la trace de ces autres, dans une classification, ne fût-ce qu'à deux termes. *On est déjà dans l'écriture avec les noms propres.* (101–2, my emphasis)

The argument is persuasive, and particularly so the final formula, not least because it brings us closer to our domain of predilection and concern — poetry:

> Ce qu'on appelle 'nom propre' est donc toujours déjà impropre, et l'acte de nomination qu'on voudrait comme origine et prototype du langage suppose l'écriture au sens élargi donné à ce mot par Derrida. (102)

We might object at this point, however, that in poetry the rules of philosophy precisely do not apply, and therefore that special attention should be accorded to the name as a specifically literary phenomenon. In other words, the name in literature may be less an innocent and passive object of philosophical enquiry than a knowing and active source of literary speculation, a form of laboratory (to invert the scientific roles) in which the author would work on and experiment with both the name and onomastic theory. The surprising by-product of such a process would emerge as a series of 'signatures' for the enquiring reader duly (and more or less naively) to discover. Bennington appears alert to this distinction in his entry on 'La Signature'. The signature, essentially, has a mission — to represent my name, independent of my presence, and even after my death:

> Mon nom propre me survit. Après ma mort, on pourra encore me nommer et parler de moi. Comme tout signe, 'je' inclus, le nom propre comporte la possibilité nécessaire de pouvoir fonctionner en mon absence, de se détacher de son porteur: et selon la logique qu'on a déjà expérimentée, on doit pouvoir porter cette absence à un certain absolu, qu'on appelle la mort. On dira donc que, même de mon vivant, mon nom marque ma mort. (140)

The signature must be even more proper than a proper noun. It must be something more than a mere name:

> La signature, et c'est justement ce qui la distingue du nom propre en général, essaie de rattraper le propre qu'on a vu se déproprier aussitôt dans le nom. (140)

In order to accomplish this task, the name needs a strategy. It cannot be a simple mark on a page:

> L'acte de signer, qui ne se réduit pas à la simple inscription de son nom propre, s'efforce, par un tour supplémentaire, de réapproprier la propriété toujours déjà perdue dans le nom lui-même. (142)

Bennington develops the simple act of signing one's name into a complex interaction of signature and 'countersignature':

> Toute cette temporalité fort complexe de l'écriture est en principe ramassée, non pas dans une seule signature (par exemple celle du contrat), mais dans ce qui doit être considéré comme une contre-signature ajoutée à celle du contrat: c'est par exemple le moment où, le texte terminé, on écrit, après coup, un avant-propos ou une préface auxquels on mettra, avec une solennité qu'on n'interroge jamais, une date et peut-être une indication du lieu de composition. (145)

Openly paradoxical and open to contradiction, the signature is the name writ large and deep. It has become a metaphor for reading itself:

> On doit alors repenser la lecture comme un rapport de signature et contresignature, ce qui permet de penser ce en quoi un texte reste *essentiellement* ouvert à l'autre (à la lecture). La signature du texte appelle la contresignature du lecteur, comme c'est le cas de toute signature: nous voyons mieux maintenant que la contresignature qu'elle appelle est essentiellement la contresignature de l'autre, fût-ce moi-même. (153)

'Were it myself ...'. This speculative phrase reveals the possibility of imagining the writer as the first reader of his own signature, as the first to bring his counter-signature to bear on the reading of his name. By thus actively participating in the elaboration of his signature, the writer would be preparing his name for eternity, for that thing called ... 'la Gloire'.[4] As Bennington puts it (with a minor correction on my part):

> Mieux, du fait même que toute signature n'est que mémoire et promesse de contresignature, nulle signature n'est vraiment réussie avant la (contre-) signature de l'autre, et la signature de [Stéphane Mallarmé], par exemple, n'est donc pas encore achevée. (154)

The present study will work, therefore, in the openness of Mallarmé's name, and will seek to determine to what degree his signature has achieved success.

As a first step, I have tried here briefly to situate my project in relation to contemporary philosophical debate around the name; but we should not forget a second (and more ancient) strand of onomastic thinking, which should also be considered as part of a response to the question 'Why write a book about names?' I am thinking of the *Cratylus* and its descendants, as traced by Gérard Genette in his remarkable study, *Mimologiques*.[5]

1.2 *Voyage en Cratylie*

He who takes an interest in the name is necessarily a cousin of Cratylus. My own relationship with the legendary onomast is mediated, thanks to my lack of Greek, by Genette's discussion of the Platonic exchange between Hermogenes, Cratylus, and Socrates. Now, Genette himself readily admits that his presentation of the text goes against the traditional grain, especially concerning his interpretation of Socrates' role in the affair. Whereas the accepted reading casts Socrates as the deconstructor of Cratylus' absurd theories, Genette places the philosopher in a median position, siding neither with Hermogenes' rigorously 'conventional' approach to the relation between word and thing nor with Cratylus' celebrated insistence on a 'natural' or indeed 'divine' link between the two. Socrates, according to this version, comes over as a would-be Cratylian, regretting what onomastically might have been, yet too great a sceptic to ignore that nothing in this base linguistic world, not even the name, is perfect.[6] Given the slightly controversial nature of Genette's work, I should declare my sympathies without further ado and state that I happily and blindly follow his representation of the scene and of Socrates' part therein. Three features of that characterization strike me as especially relevant to the elaboration of the current project: credence, fabrication, and gravity. Let us address them one by one.

Firstly, it is necessary to recognize that at the heart of the *Cratylus* lies a question of belief. Thus some readers feel a certain sympathy for Cratylus' obstinate credulity, whilst others merely find it frivolous and unphilosophical. In the course of this study, the reader will have to come to terms with a similar belief and a similar obstinacy on my part. Not only do I share (to a degree that this book will measure) Cratylus' undying faith in 'le mystère d'un nom',[7] but also I go so far as to transfer some of that credulity onto the figure of Stéphane Mallarmé. I maintain that we are two of a kind, and it will be for the reader to decide as the text unfolds whether he or she finds such an identification acceptable.

The second point will mitigate to some extent the extremism implicit in the first. It is important to note that Socrates, in his admittedly sympathetic presentation of the Cratylian case, succeeds in modulating an absolutist assertion of faith into what we might call a quietly mystical and artisanal practice. As Genette points out, Socrates comes to stand on both sides of the nature/convention divide. Even within his exposition of the Cratylian or realist creed, he refers on several occasions to the *fabrication* of the name:

> Nommer, c'est fabriquer un nom, le nom est un instrument de la relation entre l'homme et la chose, nommer est donc fabriquer un *instrument* [...] la nature d'un objet détermine la forme idéale de l'instrument qui servira à le nommer: appelons cette forme le nom idéal, ou 'idée du nom'. L'acte de nomination proprement dit, c'est-à-dire l'acte de fabrication du nom, consistera à *imprimer* cette forme idéale à la matière linguistique, c'est-à-dire aux 'sons' et aux 'syllabes'. (Genette, 14)

To the extent that a craftsman follows rules and conventions, this argument of course undermines the strength of the appeal to a natural or divine link between name and thing. And yet, what a gift for the literary onomast! Inescapably the candidate most likely to emerge as official 'maker-of-names' must be the poet, the worker or *fabbro* of language:

> C'est un travail, c'est donc un *métier* que de faire un nom, et il y faut un artisan spécialisé, comme le menuisier pour la navette ou le forgeron pour la tarière: 'ce n'est pas au premier venu qu'il appartient d'établir le nom, mais à un faiseur de nom (*onomatourgos*)'. (14)

By a curious coincidence, Genette at this point makes what is for our purposes a vital transition — from Socrates to Mallarmé. Who, he wonders, is the onomaturge? Certainly he knows who fails to fit that function:

> Notre artisan de mots [...] est d'une espèce qui ne court pas les rues: l'onomaturge, c'est le nomothète, c'est-à-dire la sorte d'artisans 'qui se rencontre le plus rarement chez les humains'. Autrement dit, tout le contraire de ce 'premier venu' (*pâs anèr*) que Mallarmé, en même propos ou presque, appelera (la traduction est littérale) 'Monsieur Tout-le-Monde'. (15)

Although the name of Mallarmé is frequently cited, for reasons not hard to divine, throughout *Mimologiques*, Genette never really develops the potential of this portrait of Mallarmé-the-onomast. Indeed, the chapter he devotes to the poet ('Au défaut des langues') proves something of a disappointment, limited as it is to a 'theoretical' discussion of *Les Mots anglais* and shying away from any engagement with the name as a poetic phenomenon. That said, it is precisely Genette's lack or difference of ambition that allows the present project to exist. I shall be working in the speculative gap opened up but unexplored by Genette, and shall take the time to focus on Mallarmé the maker and thinker of names. The latter will be portrayed as a poet conscientiously inscribing his name over that of 'Monsieur Tout-le-Monde'; as a certain 'Étienne Mallarmé' patiently working, for the best part of his life, to transform a seemingly unmotivated and arbitrarily given appellation into a veritable 'sur-name' — something more than a name, something which Genette-Socrates might call an 'eponym':

> L'éponymie d'une personne, c'est le fait qu'elle porte un surnom; *l'éponymie du nom*, c'est sa valeur de surnom, c'est l'accord de sa désignation et de sa signification, c'est sa motivation indirecte. Par extension, nous dirons que l'éponymie comme 'science' [...] c'est la recherche de ce type de motivation. C'est donc le fait, devant un nom propre dont on sait déjà *qui il désigne*, de se demander en outre *ce qu'il veut dire*, et d'enregistrer — ou d'imaginer — l'accord de ces deux fonctions. (23–24)

The only thing I should like to correct in this passage would be the phrase 'ce qu'il veut dire', which I shall repeatedly and speculatively rewrite as 'what it might mean', 'what it might be made to mean', 'what it might be made to appear to mean', and so forth ... I choose to follow behind Cratylus and Hermogenes as they continue their talk into a rhetorical sunrise.

The third feature of the *Cratylus* pertinent to this study will raise the question of gravity. Just as the unprepared reader might legitimately wonder if I am wholly serious in devoting a book to 'the names and naming of Stéphane Mallarmé', so the collective Platonic readership has had some doubts as to the seriousness of Socrates' stance in the *Cratylus*: 'Can he really sympathize with Cratylus' absurd theories? Or is he just pretending to be interested in etymology and eponymy? If so, why spend so much time discussing them?' As I have already noted, it is precisely the indeterminacy of Socrates' position that gives rise to much of the fascination of the *Cratylus*. For Genette (and once more I follow his judgement) the philosopher emerges finally in the form of a wistful anti-Cratylus: unable to believe, but free to dream. I would ask the reader of this book to adopt a similar attitude. You will not necessarily be required to believe all of the various 'proofs' of Mallarmé's concern for the name, nor to be absolutely convinced by the diverse 'signatures' I shall reveal in the poet's work. I hope that, like Socrates, the reader will at least tolerate or humour the present Cratylus, will listen to his stories, even the least serious amongst them, and above all will take as much pleasure as the philosopher seems to have done while considering the many and varied etymologies and explanations which passed before his critical eye.[8] The joy of onomastics does not come from the discovery, for the name, of a simple shining essence, but rather from the endless and infinite creation, around it, of a series of illusory essences. I shall now turn our attention to the second of my preliminary questions: 'Why, in this instance, Stéphane Mallarmé?'

1.3 A brief history and outline of the project

I was alerted to the possibility of an onomastic Mallarmé by the title of a dissertation given to an *hypokhâgneux* of my acquaintance. It read: '"La poésie, c'est le nom propre" — Stéphane Mallarmé.' Now, the actual origin of this supposed quotation I have never found, even though the formula would seem too neat and too suggestive not to be well known. I have never come across it in *Propos sur la poésie, Ecrits sur le Livre*, or in my recollection of the *Correspondance*. So I believe it to be either apocryphal or wrongly attributed.[9] As for the dissertation itself, it was of interest in so far as it pointed to some sources of a tentative theory of the name: the text entitled in the Pléiade edition 'Sur Voltaire', and the obituary for Tennyson.[10] The first of these, in its closing lines, evokes the putative existence of something called 'le nom idéal' (executing in this way a *theoretical* onomastic gesture); at the same time it initiates, as it were, a certain onomastic *practice*, through a suggestive little pun on 'Voltaire/vol-taire'. This double movement sufficed to stimulate the ambition of a would-be name-theorist, for the promise arose of a fruitful exchange between a speculative theory and a playful and elusive practice: such stuff, indeed, as theses are made of .... The second text, 'Tennyson vu d'ici', did nothing to dampen my ardour, since here Mallarmé insisted on the name as a potentially essential representation of the poet and his works. Moreover, the following soon-to-be canonical passage announced the emergence of a veritably visionary theory of the name:

> Le nom du poète mystérieusement se refait avec le texte entier qui, de l'union des mots entre eux, arrive à n'en former qu'un, celui-là, significatif, résumé de toute l'âme, la communiquant au passant; il vole des pages grandes ouvertes du livre désormais vain: car, enfin, il faut bien que le génie ait lieu en dépit de tout et que le connaisse chacun, malgré les empêchements, et sans avoir lu, au besoin. Or, ce chaste agencement de syllabes, *Tennyson*, avec solennité, dit, cette fois: *Lord Tennyson* — je sais que déjà il somme et éveille, à travers le malentendu même d'idiome en idiome ou des lacunes ou l'inintelligence, et de plus en plus le fera — la pensée d'une hautaine tendre figure, volontaire mais surtout retirée et avare aussi de tout dû, par noblesse, en une manière seigneuriale apportée dans l'esprit; ingénue, taciturne: et presque j'ajouterai que le décès serein y installe quelque chose d'isolé ou complète, pour la foule, le retrait fier de la physionomie. (*Pl.* 529–30)

Closer attention to this dogmatic assertion of the power of the poet's name revealed it in fact to be the hyperbolic magnification of a prior 'philosophical' theory: namely, the onomastic doctrine exposed by the character of 'a poet' in the very particular context of 'La Machine à Gloire', a tale written by Villiers de l'Isle-Adam for his friend Stéphane Mallarmé. It was to this fictional source that I traced the necessary if illusory origin of the latter's onomastic theory. From such foundations I have built this book. Allow me now to sketch an outline of its completed shape.

In Part 2, the following question is posed: 'Does Stéphane Mallarmé have a theory of the name?' Firstly, and before coming to the famous origin just mentioned, I consider two seemingly promising sources of onomastic theory: *Les Mots anglais* and *Les Dieux antiques*. Evidence may indeed be found, in these philo-sophical-philological treatises, of a potentially 'theorizing'

Mallarmé: one who would certainly seem to be interested in the name — who would accord it, for example, a special status amongst words; who would take the time to explore a name's history or anatomy or sheer strangeness; who would quite simply appear to enjoy discussing, examining, and even manipulating names for their own sake. The existence of such fragments alone, however, would be too fragile a base from which to construct a sustained enquiry. I must find a source of theory other than the type labelled 'theory'.

The next step, therefore, pursues the story of origins, and leads us, as already indicated, to a complex of texts centred around Villiers's 'La Machine à Gloire'. One of the accomplices in this group turns out to be none other than Mallarmé's commemorative lecture on the death of Villiers — a performance during which he once more cites from 'Tennyson' the passage evoking the name of the poet. The memorial, however, also contains a bitter lesson for Mallarmé the onomast (and for ourselves). It transpires that the friend Villiers, who arrived on the Parisian literary scene 'all-name', so to speak, comes to represent the failure of the theory of the poet's name, when and if that poet should fail, precisely, to write his name *qua* poetry. Fatally Villiers did not know or did not practice 'what it is to write'. And so it now befalls Mallarmé, mortuary messenger and faithful friend, to write his name for him. As we might say, to write in Villiers's name.[11] This has the necessary and significant consequence that the act of writing for all eternity 'Villiers de l'Isle-Adam' shall be credited, ultimately, not to the man or the work designated by that appellation, but rather to the greater literary glory of Stéphane Mallarmé. In the remainder of Part 2, the lesson of 'Villiers' is developed. The name, in order to survive in the theory of the name (and vice versa), must be worked and reworked, poetically, in an illusion of eternity: the infinity of poetry's work on language mimicking a glorious literary posterity. However, this work, which we might with Bennington call the active counter-signature of the poet, will involve important problems of priority and property, when (as in the case of Villiers) it is not directly the poet who is portrayed, but an Other — be it a friend, a rival, or a precursor.

Parts 3 and 4 of the book essentially pursue these two lines of thought. In Part 3, I am concerned with Mallarmé's usage and disposition of his own name: 'What difference does the presence of a signature make to a specific text? What sort of self-portrait did Mallarmé seemingly desire to construct through the practice of his signature?' Then, in Part 4, I address the Other: 'How, through the name, did Mallarmé communicate with such illustrious and influential names as "Edgar (Allan) Poe", "Richard Wagner", and "Charles Baudelaire"? How did he impose on them, and on their representation, his own signature? How did he negotiate, as it were, his literary succession of these glorious predecessors, while at the same time preserving a veil of literary decorum and filial respect?'

Such are the questions I shall attempt to answer in the pages that follow. In the Conclusion, I shall try to bring together my diverse responses into a picture of what we might pretentiously designate '"Stéphane Mallarmé" today'. (With the centenary of his death approaching, I know I shall not be alone.) For the present, though, and before entering into the body of the book proper, let me offer a glimpse of that conclusion by sketching out a rough first draft of what 'Stéphane Mallarmé' may look like in 1995.

1.4 'Près d'un siècle de lecture maintenant'[12]

This cannot be the place to undertake a full review of all that a century of reading has brought to the accumulated literary glory of Stéphane Mallarmé. Such a study would, I believe, be of great use and interest, both to the specialist and non-specialist reading public, but it would have to encompass all the representations of the poet: portraits and photographs and illustrations and caricatures and novels and memoirs and reviews and textbooks ... in addition to the weighty if uneven corpus of critical views.[13] What I wish rapidly to remark here is a certain shift in Mallarmé criticism which I feel to have taken place in the past ten years or so, and in whose wake I happily situate myself and the current project.

That change may be conveniently signalled by reference to a study — Le Livre et ses adresses by Vincent Kaufmann[14] — which, for the reasons I shall now explain, could stand on its own as a form of 'introduction' to my book. Firstly, the book marks a break with two of the familiar representations of Mallarmé dominating in the sixties and seventies: on the one hand, the image of the poet as the tragic figure of a tragic impossibility or impotence of language (Blanchot); on the other, the emblem or symbolic figure-head of a liberated textuality or 'production du sens' (Sollers). As Kaufmann puts it:

> Via son 'hermétisme', Mallarmé a été considéré comme le champion de l'intransitivité, le modèle de toutes les modernités, le patron de l'autoréflexivité, et le naufragé le plus glorieux parmi les explorateurs de la face noire du langage. (Kaufmann, 11)

The pastiche marks the distance. Such representations, moreover, share one striking inconvenience (unless it be for some a convenience). By giving such prominence to Mallarmé as symbolic father, they obscure the chances of a text-by-text, event-by-event, or 'circumstantial' approach to the works. Kaufmann — whose theoretical declared interest is in favour of the role of the reader, and the pragmatic or contractual nature of writing — wishes to correct this tendency, not merely by the way in which he approaches the texts, but also by the very texts he chooses to consider. As he explains:

> Nombreux sont les théoriciens de la lecture qui ont au moins ceci de commun avec les partisans de l'intransitivité qu'ils réduisent l'oeuvre de Mallarmé à quelques-uns de ses poèmes les plus célèbres, auxquels viennent s'ajouter le *Coup de dés, Igitur,* et quelques extraits (toujours les mêmes) de ses écrits 'théoriques'. Qu'on revendique ces textes comme un suicide par et pour l'écriture ou qu'on y repère un sabordage de la littérature, l'accord subsistera pour passer le reste sous silence. Il est rare qu'on évoque un certain nombre de textes qui ne devraient pas manquer d'intriguer quiconque s'intéresse à la question du lecteur. (11)

Those texts (which he goes on to discuss quite brilliantly) are called *Les Loisirs de la Poste*, the *Eventails*, the *Dons de fruits glacés*, the various *Offrandes* — works, indubitably, by Stéphane Mallarmé, but ones which have frequently been marginalized as too trivial or circumstantial to merit serious reflection. Kaufmann's project does not aim (as at first one might fear) merely to rehabilitate a brave band of texts left out in the critical cold to die of inattention or lack of gravity. It seeks rather to reverse the traditional opposition of valorized *Oeuvre* — exemplary of which would be the notorious if non-existent 'Livre' — over and against trivialized *Oeuvres* — those circumstantial texts which nevertheless constitute the actual readable corpus.[15] He rejects what he describes as the 'positivist' interpretation of the projected 'livre total' (whatever such a thing might be), and insists on both the necessary virtuality of the Book and its vital strategic importance to the works of Mallarmé such as they really exist before our eyes and for our greater pleasure to be read. In order to make this point, he refers us to the 'virtual' character of those notes for the Book reconstituted and interpreted by Jacques Scherer, as well as to the following comment or confession, made by Mallarmé to Verlaine in the letter often referred to as an 'autobiography':

> Voici l'aveu de mon vice, mis à nu, cher ami, que mille fois j'ai rejeté, l'esprit meurtri ou las, mais cela me possède et je réussirai peut-être; non pas à faire cet ouvrage dans son ensemble (il faudrait être je ne sais qui pour cela!) mais à en montrer un fragment d'exécuté, à en faire scintiller par une place l'authenticité glorieuse, en indiquant le reste tout entier auquel ne suffit pas une vie. Prouver par les portions faites que ce livre existe, et que j'ai connu ce que je n'aurai pu accomplir. (cited Kaufmann, 23)

Magnificent obsession! Kaufmann, however, significantly decides not to interpret the 'portions faites' as the scraps of paper published by Scherer, but rather as the poems, prose-poems, tales, translations, critical poems, reviews, journalism, and multiple other divagations variously signed by 'Stéphane Mallarmé'. Thus his commentary on the passage just cited:

> Le Livre, semble-t-il, reste nécessairement et irréductiblement virtuel; il ne peut avoir lieu que sous forme de fragments, qui en font miroiter l'existence et la place. C'est un point sur lequel je reviendrai, et dont je tire pour l'instant la conséquence suivante: l'opposition entre une oeuvre circonstancielle et un livre absolu doit non seulement être amendée, mais elle peut encore ne pas se justifier du tout, puisque les textes existants, même circonstanciels, sont la seule réalisation possible d'un tel projet. En reconnaissant le statut virtuel du Livre, on est amené à réhabiliter la circonstance. (23)[16]

It should be remarked here that 'rehabilitating circumstance' does not mean saving some gems from oblivion, but implies a reconsideration of almost everything the poet ever signed (and however he may have signed it). The general direction of such a rethink might be indicated (at least was certainly indicated to me) by a second passage from the letter to Verlaine cited and discussed by Kaufmann. The latter wishes to argue as follows:

> Cette aporie ou cet embarras [regarding the circumstantial] vont de pair, c'est mon hypothèse, avec l'absence de réflexion sur la réalité discursive ou générique des textes de Mallarmé. La notion de circonstance implique en effet une référence à un contexte, à une situation d'énonciation, et à ce titre, elle vient comme remplacer, dans la pratique mallarméenne, le rôle du genre, en une sorte d'épure. Son enjeu n'est donc pas en premier lieu le référent (la chose dont on parle), mais la mise en place d'un espace discursif. (24)

According to Kaufmann, the metaphor Mallarmé found most

appropriate to describe the necessarily cirumstantial status of his works was that of the calling-card:

> Au fond je considère l'époque contemporaine comme un interrègne pour le poète qui n'a point à s'y mêler: elle est trop en désuétude et en effervescence préparatoire pour qu'il ait autre chose à faire qu'à travailler avec mystère en vue de plus tard ou de jamais et de temps en temps à envoyer aux vivants sa carte de visite, stances ou sonnets, pour n'être point lapidé d'eux, s'ils le soupçonnaient de savoir qu'ils n'ont pas lieu. (cited Kaufmann, 24)

Kaufmann comments thus:

> Le genre circonstanciel serait ainsi lié à une conception donnée de l'efficacité du discours littéraire, à laquelle la carte de visite sert ici d'emblème (cette efficacité se réduirait à l'institution ou au maintien d'un lien purement formel). (24)

Here we find a general view of Mallarmé's works — all his works — according to which each individual text would be no more and no less than an elaborate and circumstantially circumscribed rendition of one's *name*. Over and against a representation of 'Stéphane Mallarmé' as identified with a work ('l'Oeuvre', 'le Livre', etc.), and regardless of the interpretation one might give of that work, there would appear a series of gestural 'Stéphane Mallarmé(s)', variously inscribing versions of that name, and in number equal to the number of *works* ('stances ou sonnets', 'études en vue de mieux', etc.) which the aforenamed author diversely produced. Happily for the present project, Kaufmann himself makes an explicit theoretical link between his comment on the calling-card and the name:

> En effet, si la remise de la carte de visite implique une distance (puisqu'on se fait en quelque sorte représenter par elle), elle n'en constitue pas moins une mise en rapport. La carte a une fonction presque

instituante, elle permet de se nommer pour un autre,
à qui on la remet. (27)

And again:

> Le rôle de la carte de visite n'est donc pas seulement
> formel, ou alors ce qui est formel n'est pas gratuit,
> mais lié au contraire à la constitution d'un circuit
> purement symbolique où chacun peut se nommer à sa
> place. (27)

For Kaufmann, this hypothesis will be (persuasively) tested via
an analysis of *Les Loisirs de la Poste* and other 'circumstantial'
texts. Amongst these he includes *La Dernière Mode*, in respect of
which he makes the following highly enlightening remarks
concerning the function of the *name* and the *pseudonym* (it
being clear that, for my purposes, every 'Stéphane Mallarmé' is a
pseudonym, to the extent that the name is reinvented each time
it is signed):

> L'auteur rédigeait les différentes rubriques en signant
> 'Marguerite de Ponty', 'Miss Satin' ou, plus
> ironiquement encore, 'Ix' et 'Marasquin' en tant que
> directeur de la revue (nom où s'entend littéralement
> la mascarade). Cette pseudonymie vient contresigner
> le caractère de fiction du lien ainsi mis en place. Et si
> elle est la condition nécessaire de cette mise en place,
> si elle permet d'éprouver la question de la place du
> lecteur en donnant à l''auteur' la possibilité de jouer
> plusieurs rôles, elle indique aussi la limite d'un tel
> pouvoir de prescription: le sujet, qui est appelé à
> devenir une fiction. La 'réussite' du système
> mallarméen semble exiger que celui qui en est à
> l'origine ne s'y engage pas en son propre nom:
> personne ne saurait instituer un dispositif symbolique
> en le fondant sur son propre nom, toujours donné
> par l'Autre. La pseudonymie apparaît comme
> une stratégie permettant de contourner cette
> impossibilité. (43)

17

One of the aims of this study, then, will be to argue that the 'strategy' indicated here by Kaufmann with regard to *La Dernière Mode* may be seen to pertain to all the works of Stéphane Mallarmé, and that the 'réussite' of the work (or what has often been referred to as 'le bonheur de Mallarmé')[17] may be measured by the degree to which a name — 'Stéphane Mallarmé' — will have been successfully and successively reinvented and transformed, in each specific work, in each specific context, so as to sustain before the reader's eyes the illusion of a felicitous communicative system or series of onomastic acts always and everywhere *taking place*.

2

Does Stéphane Mallarmé have a theory of the Name?

In this section I shall first look briefly at *Les Mots anglais* and *Les Dieux antiques* in order to measure to what degree Mallarmé's apparent theoretical interests in linguistics and comparative mythology might contribute to a hypothetical theory of the name in his works. Then I shall present the complex of texts centred around Villiers de l'Isle-Adam and 'La Machine à Gloire'. Lastly, three short texts — 'Sur Voltaire', 'Manet', and 'Whistler' — will be considered as a form of escape route from the theoretical impasse encountered at the end of the discussion on Villiers and the name.

2.1 Looking for theory in theory

2.1.1 *Les Mots anglais/Les Dieux antiques*[1]

Here are two promising theoretical sources, in part translated, in part rewritten by Mallarmé, the first of which is clearly concerned with linguistics, and with that science considered as the study of *words* reified and isolated in their form and origin from the actions of syntax; the second taking a linguistic approach to

19

THE NAME OF THE POET

mythology which we could happily characterize as 'onomastic', in so far as it consists of an analysis of divine names in various mythologies of the world. Together they seem to offer the possibility of locating, external to the poetry or word-by-word activities of the author proper, a philosophical source, a linguistic *a priori*, a ready-made theory, which we could then observe being applied in the works. The fact that they are translations of a sort does nothing to lessen the charm of this hypothesis. On the contrary, it would help to make the authority all the more external and, as it were, purer. How simple Mallarmé's difficulty would become, if I could show it all to be the application of an arcane and authoritative science! However, the reader tempted by *Les Mots anglais* and *Les Dieux antiques* to look for a key against which to read off rather than read the works of the poet might find himself discouraged by Mallarmé's own description of the theoretical couple in the famous 'autobiographical' letter to Verlaine of 1885. He dismisses them thus:

> J'ai dû faire, dans des moments de gêne ou pour acheter de ruineux canots, des besognes propres, et voilà tout (Dieux Antiques, Mots Anglais) dont il sied de ne pas parler. (*Pl.* 663)

Such a disclaimer could, of course, be a decoy, and certain readers of Mallarmé have acted as if it were.[2] In the current project, it is rather the pair *Les Dieux antiques/Les Mots anglais* which will act as a decoy. It is not here, in these self-consciously scientistic studies, that a full-blown announcement of a theory of the name is to be found: Mallarmé will prefer a fictional source for that occasion (see section 2.2 below). Nevertheless, we may note for the present how he goes about marking off the limits of science's claims to the name, thus preparing the ground for the ulterior situation of his own thinking elsewhere.

2.1.2 A study of Names

> *Ces personnalités anciennes qui, pour nous, consistent notamment dans l'effet familier que nous produit leur nom.* (Pl. 1276)

Les Dieux antiques promises so much because it is quite simply a study of divine names. The highly onomastic theory which it promotes runs as follows. All mythologies, according to Mallarmé out of Cox, spring from one source: primitive man's reactions to and spontaneous explanations of nature, and in particular his imaginative response to the course, diurnal and annual, of the sun. Man first personified, and so named, the various phenomena he was witness or subject to. Then (the argument goes):

> Comme le temps marcha, et que les peuples se séparèrent, le vieux sens s'oblitéra, totalement ou partiellement [...] Quelques-unes [les tribus] errèrent au sud, d'autres au nord et à l'ouest; et il arriva que toutes gardèrent les noms donnés jadis au soleil et aux nuages et à toute chose, alors que la signification de ces noms était presque perdue. (*Pl.* 1164)

Such a thesis appears most stimulating, for it implies that all names (or at least all divine and heroic ones) have a hidden or forgotten meaning. The task of *Les Dieux antiques* would be to correct 'cet oubli de la signification première des mots' (1167). The remaining hundred or so pages of the treatise are devoted to supplying the examples that prove this theory. As the tireless adaptor-translator cries, in that tone of ever-renewable enthusiasm and wonder chosen by Mallarmé for his didactic roles:

> Que d'exemples! c'est en foule qu'ils viennent à la mémoire de qui a étudié les auteurs classiques. Ces noms, Argynnis, Phoronée et Erinys, sont, en grec, des mots qui ne présentent aucun sens. Or, ils s'expliquent dans la vieille mythologie de l'Inde, et l'on voit qu'Erinys est l'aurore lorsqu'elle 'rampe dans le ciel'; Argynnis, un nom du matin, désignant ce qu'il a de brillant; Phoronée, c'est le dieu du feu, Bhuranyu. (1165)

And so, through all the mythologies of the world, the theory proceeds.

21

Have we discovered here a fundamental theory of the name, from which to construct a sustained study of Mallarmé's onomastic practice? At the sight of our poet not just happily translating his way through such a mass of material, but occasionally even adding his personal embellishments, it would be difficult to reply other than in the affirmative.[3] However, such enthusiasm should be tempered in a number of ways. Firstly, in spite of his eager approval of it, the theory is not 'Stéphane Mallarmé's'. This is literally so, in so far as the work remains a translation and reorganization of various works by Cox. But it is also true in that no very convincing link may be made between the intellectual substance of *Les Dieux antiques* and Mallarmé's actual poetic practice. The poet makes an oblique comment on this separation in the following passage:

> Les poètes [faced with mythological material] ne pouvaient apparemment échapper au cercle enchanté dans lequel ils aimaient reproduire, sous le déguisement de noms, de lieux et d'incidents différents, la grande et touchante TRAGEDIE DE LA NATURE. (1178)

We might think this a fatalistic (not to say superstitious) attitude to meaning. But it is also curiously liberating. For if the poet knows that, whether he likes it or not, the meaning of his text is predetermined and always the same ... then surely he may write, indifferently, whatever he please?[4] This intuition of Mallarmé's presumed thought appears more persuasive when we consider the almost total lack of concern for mythology shown by the writer in the rest of his works. Not for him the *Poèmes barbares*, or *antiques*; nor *La Légende des siècles*. Nor, more famously, the grand mythological machinery favoured by Wagner.[5] As for 'L'Après-midi d'un faune' and 'Hérodiade', they show little or no regard for dictionary references. In no way, then, does Mallarmé attempt to 'prove' in his poetry the name-theory of *Les Dieux antiques*. Indeed why should he, when the favourable proofs seem already so abundant?[6] No, the thesis of *Les Dieux antiques* will only have an indirect influence upon Mallarmé's own name-theory. The poet is not terribly interested in gods; but he is certainly

22

interested in names. Thus he may quite happily watch the former disappear from theoretical view:

> Quel plaisir se mêle à notre surprise de voir des mythes connus lentement s'évaporer, par la magie même qu'implique l'analyse de la parole antique, en l'eau, la lumière ou le vent élémentaires! (1276)[7]

But this, on condition that they leave their names behind them: 'car combien de noms charmants nous gagnons!' (1277). When he writes of 'ces personnalités anciennes qui, pour nous, consistent notamment dans l'effet familier que nous produit leur nom', we can see that a line has clearly been drawn, marking ourselves off from the ancient gods, but leaving us none the less impressed by the 'effect of their name'. Such will be the space — the potential effect or aura of a name as perceived and created by Stéphane Mallarmé — in which I intend to operate, having first retained from *Les Dieux antiques* two notions or beliefs which will prove fundamental to this project. Firstly, the mythological treatise guarantees the existence of the 'mystery of a name', and that the latter may always be satisfactorily revealed through its reworking or transformation at the hands of the poet. Secondly, it suggests that this process of transformation may count far more in itself than does the specific 'meaning' duly revealed: thus 'Phoronée' is indifferently transposed into 'Bhuranyu' or vice versa; that either of them may signify 'the god of fire' we may innocently ignore. Moreover, the pleasure derived from the manipulation of the name becomes in prospect infinitely repeatable and inexhaustible, once we have suppressed (or at least parenthesized) the finality towards which it might once have appeared to move. The gods are gone; their names remain, as a source, not of divinity or authority, but of endlessly renewable 'charm'. Thus Mallarmé seems less troubled by an empty heaven than he would be by the prospect of a world onomastically impoverished:

> Car combien de noms charmants nous gagnons, dont plusieurs sont maintenant inhérents à la langue presque usuelle au point qu'il ne serait pas licite de les annuler sans qu'ils y fissent quelque vide regrettable! (1277)

We may detect here the desire for an onomastic theory which will not so much explain names and their origins as provide a space wherein they may, in all their splendour, perform.

2.1.3 A study of Words

Les règles philologiques n'ont à faire avec presque aucun de ces cas. (Pl. 1045)

Mallarmé's sentiment as to where the domain of science ends is even more clearly marked in *Les Mots anglais*. Tongue in cheek, he assigns himself the role of 'le savant et ingénieux professeur du lycée Fontanès' (*Pl.* 1059), and professes in his Foreword a seamless scientistic faith: 'j'attends de ce Traité, placé au début d'une Science, qu'il se perfectionnera autant qu'elle se développera' (897). The interminable list of more or less accurate facts about the English language that constitute ninety-nine per cent of the text of this philological treatise is punctuated from time to time with expressions of narratorial enthusiasm similar to those remarked upon in *Les Dieux antiques*. Disingenuous wonder is tempered by a more than mildly offhand attitude to the business of demonstration.[8] But the demarcation is more explicitly inscribed when a choice must be made between rigour and charm. Consider this methodological aside:

> Ce qu'on nomme du *jeu*, il en faut, dans une mesure raisonnable, pour réussir quelque chose comme ce travail complexe et simple: trop de rigueur aboutissant à transgresser, plutôt que des lois, mille intentions certaines et mystérieuses du langage. (919)

Or again, when speaking of the 'barbarisms' committed in the act of transforming Latin and Greek words into French or English (and sometimes, for example, fusing both elements into one mongrel term), Mallarmé has this comment:

> Que maintenant des confusions, par milliers, se soient produites, quelque bizarrerie ne messied pas dans le

24

Langage: car il ne faut point oublier que tel fait anormal, où s'indigne le linguiste, cause la joie souvent du littérateur, voué à un travail de mosaïque point rectiligne. *Trop de régularité nuit.* (1026; my emphasis)

He reveals his delight in the workings of the linguistic imp-of-the-perverse, for the present expression of which he is happy to adopt the disguise of a linguistician.[9] As regards the name, the whole tendency of the treatise — taking as it does words as objects in isolation, to be manipulated and wondered at, rather than as elements, say, of a phrase — leads us step by step into the belief that names, the most isolated, the most objectified of words, must form a special and we might think superior class of their own.[10] They seem more primitive, more curious, more stimulating, more mysterious, more bizarre. ... They are more than mere words. Thus it should come as no surprise to find at the end of *Les Mots anglais* a special 'Appendix on Names':

L'Etude consacrée aux Mots d'un parler resterait incomplète, ses Noms propres négligés: ils relèvent presque toujours de procédés de composition très primitifs, ce qui les rend curieux à plus d'un titre. Mêlés encore à la Langue, leur sens tient l'imagination en éveil; autrement, incompréhensibles ou anciens, c'est par leur aspect presque bizarre. (1041)

But even before this explicit and carefully situated recognition of the specificity of names, some indication had already been given of their relative superiority: stemming, significantly, from their supposedly greater capacity for 'transposition'. When discussing the 'felicitous plays on words' which occur in the passage from French to English, Mallarmé had remarked that 'aux noms propres seuls appartient une transposition absolue et complète' (997). Thus 'Bellerophon' becomes 'Billy-Ruffian', and 'Le Chat Fidèle', 'The Cat and the Fiddle'. A heightened potential for transposition sets names apart, as a kind of super-word. And Mallarmé no doubt alludes to this special status, when he underscores the 'sur-' of 'surname' in the following passage:

25

> Une appellation, dite aujourd'hui encore en anglais *Surname* parce qu'elle a d'abord consisté véritablement en un Surnom [...] appliquée, comme chez les romains et les grecs, à un personnage dont elle louait les qualités ou raillait les défauts, une même épithète, plus ou moins transparente, se perpétue souvent de père en fils. (1041)

For the name-maker a name is always, or should at least ever aspire to be, a sur-name: that is, something more than, greater than, above and beyond, a mere appellation. In deference to some sort of aesthetic imperative, the name should become what might be called a 'sublime' word, equipped with a special aura able to overwhelm, albeit momentarily, the reader's cognitive faculties. Mallarmé's interest in the name, therefore, appears philosophical or philological only ever in passing or disguise. It forms part of a performative aesthetic or, perhaps more simply, an aesthetic performance, in which the linguistic higher realm that the name appears to attain would command less attention than the act of apparition itself. Although the name might in a sense be seen as the exemplary instance of linguistic illusion and of the power of words to attract and fascinate our readerly eye, such an illusion, Mallarmé knows, must be worked at and sustained in a thousand discreet ways, if it is to 'se perpétuer souvent'. The question of how such an endurance may be attained and of how the fading of the name may be avoided I shall examine in the course of the next section, which first takes us back to the genuine if fictional source of the theory of the name.

2.2 At the source of theory

That source may be found in a curious exchange of texts between Stéphane Mallarmé and his friend Villiers de l'Isle-Adam. In one of his *Contes cruels*, Villiers seemingly announces, through a representation of Mallarmé, a grand onomastic theory and a statement of belief regarding the destiny of the 'name-of-the-poet'. It remains unclear in the immediate context whether this profession of faith should be read as comical or straight, or even whether it might not be a gentle ironic jibe, on Villiers's part, at the pompous convolutions of his friend's aesthetic pretensions. The situation becomes further complicated by the manner in which Mallarmé, on two subsequent occasions, cites the relevant passage, changing in the process the context and the tone in which it might be read. Indeed, the poet appears to rehearse the theoretical fragment in such a way as to transform what began as a mere wink or exchange of glances into a highly serious statement of a bizarre aesthetic doctrine. His gravity seems all the more imposing when we consider that the second occasion on which he recites the theory of the name represents nothing less than the necrological conference given by the poet in honour of his dead and damned friend. Let us now proceed through this territory point by point, beginning with an earlier example of literary 'complicity' between the two writers.

2.2.1 Complicity: 'L'Agrément Inattendu'

This story was published by Villiers in the *Gil Blas* of the sixth of August 1887 and then included in *Histoires insolites* of the following year.[11] It is addressed to 'Stéphane Mallarmé'. The critical notes in the Pléiade edition of Villiers's complete works (1262–64) provide us with some interesting background information to the story as well as a speculatively 'complicitizing' interpretation of the text. The editors propose that the tale be read as Villiers's allegorical response to the famous 'night of Igitur' in 1870, when the unhappy young schoolteacher read his work-in-progress to the somewhat startled company of Villiers, Catulle Mendès, and Judith Gautier, who were passing through the Midi on holiday. Such an interpretation may at first appear improbable, if we consider that some seventeen years would thus have had to pass in order to allow Villiers to formulate his imaginative reply. However, research shows that the project had been on Villiers's mind for some time:

> Sur une liste de 'nouvelles à terminer' établie en 1877, on lit: 'L'étang souterrain (histoire italienne)'. Sur une liste manuscrite de sujets datant de 1883, on lit encore: 'Le lac souterrain'; et sur une autre, de 1885, on relève la mention: 'Le bain dans le souterrain'. (1262)

The text that Villiers finally produced ('récit [...] déroutant dans sa mystérieuse simplicité' (1262)) relates how, at the end of a long and tiring day, the narrator, on holiday in the South of France, discovers a rustic inn ('une maison blanche') run by a rather strange and almost bestial man, who, upon hearing that his guest is of an artistic bent, offers to show him a 'curiosity' of the region. The hero accepts and is led by his guide down into the depths of the cellar, where, at a sign from the innkeeper, a spectacle is revealed:

> O subit panorama, tenant du rêve! Je voyais se prolonger, — presque à perte de vue, — au-devant de moi, de très hautes voûtes souterraines, aux stalactites scintillantes, aux profondeurs qui renvoyaient, avec mille réfractions de diamants, en des jeux merveilleux, les lueurs, devenues d'or, de la lanterne sourde: et, s'étendant à mes pieds, sous ces voûtes, une sorte de lac immense d'un bleu très sombre, où ces mêmes lueurs tremblaient, illusions d'étoiles! — une eau claire, polie, dormante, à reflets d'acier, où se réfléchissaient, démesurées, nos deux ombres. C'était superbe et inattendu. (311)

After a brief moment of contemplation, the narrator, feeling 'malgré moi [...] une attirance vers le ténébreux enchantement de cette onde' (311), strips off and plunges into the pool. He then gives his host five francs and resumes his journey 'd'un pas raffermi et joyeux, l'agrément imprévu de ce bain m'ayant inespérément pénétré de nouvelles forces' (312). Now, according to Jean-Aubry, the tale, as well as discreetly alluding to 'l'événement sans doute le plus important de ce séjour chez Mallarmé: la lecture [...] d'"Igitur"' (1262), operates, in the passage quoted above, a symbolic transposition of the strange effect produced on Villiers by his friend's experimental prose. Certainly one may identify elements in the passage reminiscent of Mallarmé's own representations of what his writing might look like: vaults, scintillations, reflections and refractions, the play of lights and precious stones and stars. However, alongside this imitative flattery appear signs of a more complex literary complicity, and of correspondence conducted through literary effects of a more arcane nature.

We should first note that the story is explicitly addressed to 'Monsieur Stéphane Mallarmé'. Beneath the dedication stands the following epigraph taken from La Fontaine's fable 'Les Deux Pigeons':

> Je dirai: j'étais là; telle chose m'advint;
> Vous y croirez être vous-même![12]

Following Jean-Aubry's reading, we as readers should identify ourselves with the 'vous' of the verse: Villiers, in the double role of witness-messenger, is telling us what it was like to be there on that night in 1870; he is also acting as guarantor, in our eyes, of Mallarmé's genius, of the authenticity of his dazzling but notoriously difficult miracle; most extremely, he would be encouraging us to make the effort, the leap even, necessary to reach and appreciate Mallarmé's superb surprise. It is also possible, however, to read the 'vous' of the epigraph as being addressed to the 'Monsieur Stéphane Mallarmé' sitting just above the citation. In this perspective we might also note that in his 'Notes sur le théâtre' featured in the *Revue Indépendante* of the first of December 1886, that is, nine months before the first appearance of 'L'Agrément Inattendu', Mallarmé had used a balletic representation at the Eden Theatre of 'Les Deux Pigeons' as a springboard for some aesthetic speculations on dance, impersonality, and sexual difference (see *Pl.* 304–5), and had even quoted the opening line of the fable:

> Deux pigeons s'aimaient d'amour tendre.

This clue introduces a new complexity into the exchange. In the fable, the two pigeons are 'frères', one of whom goes a-wandering, while the other stays sensibly at home. The question is posed: 'Is experience worth the effort?' Transposing the problem to 'L'Agrément Inattendu', the answer would be positive: travel, in spite of the wear and tear incurred, may lead to miraculous discoveries. Transposed again to the context of the exemplary friendship, Villiers would be cast as the wanderer, returning to relate wonders to his sedentary brother. Such a relationship may be inferred from the lines which in the fable precede those forming the epigraph:

> Je reviendrai dans peu conter de point en point
> Mes aventures à mon frère.
> Je le désennuierai: quiconque ne voit guère
> N'a guère à dire aussi. Mon voyage dépeint
> Vous sera d'un plaisir extrême.
> Je dirai ...

These verses carry potential reproach: Mallarmé's *travail* — the ever-abandoned and ever-resumed and unrealizable 'Oeuvre' — would figure as the bored poor relation to Villiers's *travel*, whose adventures at least produce something to relate, something, at least, to say.[13] On the other hand, in the fable itself, it is the wandering brother who is duped: after various unhappy adventures he returns, somewhat battered, to the love of his brother. And even in the context of 'L'Agrément', it could be argued that, although Villiers's vagabondage turns up a marvel, the surprise contains in some form the signature of his brother, Stéphane Mallarmé.

It would be foolish to expect this overlaying of texts and intertexts, of intimations and tensions, simply to be resolved into an equation. Yet some kind of happy outcome to the exchange will be reached (an unexpected agreement?), notably in the manner in which the problem of Mallarmé-as-host is managed. According to the logic of the allegory, if Villiers is the narrator of the tale and the 'monsieur qui voyage dans le Midi' (310), then surely Mallarmé must correspond, in some sense, to the rustic hotelier. At first sight, such a thought seems absurd:

> A droite, et bien au fond, dans l'angle, assis à une
> manière de comptoir, l'hôtelier, face farouche, au poil
> roux, — l'encolure d'un taureau, — me regardait.
> (310)

But a perhaps surprising textual parallel between 'L'Agrément Inattendu' and a text of Mallarmé's will help us to see that after a fashion the hotelier is indeed a portrait of the exquisite poet. The prose poem 'Un Spectacle Interrompu' (*Pl.* 276–78) was first published in December 1875 in *La République des Lettres*, but had recently reappeared in *Le Scapin* of the first of September 1886, that is, less than a year before 'L'Agrément Inattendu'. The piece recounts a moment of potential danger that interrupts a vaudeville act ('*la Bête et le Génie*') featuring a clown and a polar bear: as the clown teases the bear by pretending to have caught in his hand something (a fly?) flying through the air, the bear becomes so intensely gripped by the power of the illusion that he grasps his 'brother' ('frère brillant et surnaturel [...] aîné subtil') in a violent plea; this is verbalized by Mallarmé, the superior spectator, as a kind of explanation of what the illusion, and fiction in general, might mean. Things almost turn out nastily for the mime-artist. But our attention should rather be fixed on the wording of this passage:

> L'*ours* rythmiquement et doucement levé interrogeait cet exploit, une griffe posée sur les rubans de l'*épaule* humaine [...] Qu'allait-il arriver? L'autre patte s'*abattit*, souple, contre *un bras longeant* le maillot; et l'on vit, couple uni dans un secret rapprochement [...] (*Pl.* 277)

We should compare it with this, from the moment, in Villiers's text, just preceding the revelation in the cellar:

> A la quarante-deuxième marche, comme j'allais demander combien il en restait encore à descendre avant la 'surprise', une forte main s'*abattit* sur mon *épaule*. En même temps s'*allongeait le bras* tenant la lanterne au-devant de mon *front* [see 'crâne' and 'buste' in 'Le Spectacle Interrompu'], et j'entendis mon guide me dire, à l'oreille, en un murmure assez analogue au rauquement d'un *ours*: 'Hein? [...] Regardez-moi ça, m'sieur?'. (Villiers, II, 311)

It is difficult to ignore the allusion here; but equally the inversion, in so far as in Villiers's story it is the beast who enlightens the

31

genius, whilst in Mallarmé's the genius fails to enlighten anyone (unless, that is, the real genius be positioned, elsewhere, in the audience). In Mallarmé's tale the point of interest is a non-event, the climax collapses; in Villiers's tale, the 'féerique spectacle' is realized, verbalized. This apparent opposition of the two men, their techniques, their geniuses, need not be characterized as antagonistic. Indeed one could read the following sequence as a happy recognition, on Villiers's part, of the two friends' differences:

> J'y pris un bain délicieux — éclairé par la complaisance de l'hôtelier, qui me considérait d'un air de stupeur soucieuse, concentrée même [...] car, vraiment, à présent que j'y songe, il avait des expressions de figure incompréhensibles, ce brave homme. (311)

In Villiers's eyes, the author of 'Igitur' undoubtedly had some 'incomprehensible facial/figurative expressions', and his prose may often have appeared grotesque. But that does not prevent an act of amicable communication taking place:

> Après un bon merci, un bon frappement de ma main sur son épaule, — accompagné d'un coup d'oeil appuyé [...] mais, là, ce qui s'appelle le blanc des yeux. (311)

Given the conventional image of Mallarmé the difficult, the obscure, the impotent, the poet of rupture and failure, it would perhaps seem surprising to argue that he might have shared his friend's belief in the simple efficacy of such direct gestures. But all those 'loisirs de la poste', all those tomes of inconsequential correspondence, all that occasional verse — surely so much felicitous, uncomplicated communication testifies to some sort of pleasure taken in the performance of banal and daily linguistic acts.[14] As we shall see, one such act — naming — an act so banal as to pass almost unnoticed in everyday linguistic activity, will provide not just pleasure but a veritable 'oeuvre de sa patience' for a certain Stéphane Mallarmé, the Mallarmé I have chosen in this study to

32

portray. Let us now consider a further example of complicity between Villiers and his friend, one which will lead us directly to the apparent source of that 'antique soin' for the name.[15]

2.2.2 Exposition: 'La Machine à Gloire'

As was the case with 'L'Agrément Inattendu', an amiable air of complicity surrounds the second tale dedicated by Villiers to 'Monsieur Stéphane Mallarmé':[16]

> Noir et cher scélérat! [...] Ah! mon vieux Villiers, je t'admire! Monsieur Stéphane Mallarmé te remercie spécialement. Au revoir. S.M.

Thus the latter to his friend in 1883, thanking him for a copy of *Contes cruels*, and especially for the story 'La Machine à Gloire'.[17] But the intertextual exchanges woven around this tale prove to be a degree more complex than the knowing intimations of my first example. In this instance, the dedicatee and, to some extent, object of the text, Stéphane Mallarmé, will return the compliment, both by reciting and resituating 'La Machine à Gloire' in his own works and, ultimately, by employing a passage from it in his final act of dedication to Villiers, the memorial lecture of 1889.

How does Villiers present his friend in 'La Machine à Gloire'? The story itself is a straightforward satire of the practice of the 'claque' as a means of promoting theatrical and literary fame. The author imagines a mechanical version of the process, with robotic hands to clap and lungs to cheer, and even tear-gas as a guaranteed means of stimulating pathos. Moreover, the machine, in as much as 'l'Esprit du siècle, ne l'oublions pas, est aux machines' (Villiers, 592), becomes emblematic of Villiers's dystopian vision of an increasingly mechanized, rationalistic, and demagogical future society. But where does Mallarmé stand in such a vision? Firstly, at the epigraph:

> La Machine à Gloire/SGDG/A Monsieur Stéphane Mallarmé/'Sic itur ad astra'

33

Several whispers may here be overheard. If the text that follows presents itself as a description of the future path to the stars, then Villiers would seem to exclude from the start the participation of 'Monsieur Stéphane Mallarmé' in such a glory.[18] As if to mitigate any disappointment caused by this remark, he includes an apparent disclaimer of authorial responsibility via the acronym 'sans garantie du gouvernement', as if to say: 'That's just the way things are.' The exchange between old friends would articulate a wry and comprehending 'coup d'oeil appuyé'. Mallarmé's second appearance, however, brings us to the heart of our concern. Although the main body of the story consists of a description of the operation and development of the machine, the text opens with a discussion, in a deliberately pseudo-philosophical tone, of the question: 'Qu'est-ce que la Gloire?' The author consults a journalist, from whom he receives a merely facetious response, and then … a poet:

> Adressez-vous à un poète, voici, à peu près, l'allocution qui s'échappera de son noble gosier: — 'La Gloire est le resplendissement d'un nom dans la mémoire des hommes'. (594)

At first, the imaginary poet, who shall remain for the present nameless, continues in the dominantly sarcastic vein of the narrator. He takes the example of 'SCRIBE (prenons celui-là)', and states that 'l'impression électrisante que causera [au public] ce nom peut, d'avance, être traduite par la série d'exclamations suivantes' (594). There follows a series of clichés: 'Cerveau compliqué! Génie séduisant!' This much is standard nineteenth-century contempt for the bourgeois vulgar. The poet then takes the counter-example of 'MILTON', estimating that out of a sample of two hundred people one hundred and ninety-eight will not have read any Milton, and even the remaining two will have misunderstood him. 'Cependant', he adds; and with this 'cependant' everything, suddenly, changes:

> Cependant, au *nom* de MILTON, il s'éveillera, dans l'entendement des auditeurs, à la minute même, l'inévitable arrière-pensée d'une Oeuvre beaucoup

MOINS intéressante, au point de vue positif, que celle de SCRIBE. — Mais cette réserve obscure sera néanmoins telle, que, tout en accordant plus d'estime pratique à SCRIBE, l'idée de tout parallèle entre MILTON et ce dernier semblera (d'instinct et malgré tout) comme l'idée d'un parallèle entre un sceptre et une paire de pantoufles, quelque pauvre qu'ait été MILTON, quelque argent qu'ait gagné SCRIBE, quelque inconnu que soit longtemps demeuré MILTON, quelque universellement notoire que soit, déjà, SCRIBE. *En un mot, l'impression que laissent les vers, même inconnus, de MILTON, étant passée dans le nom même de leur auteur, ce sera, ici, pour les auditeurs, comme s'ils avaient lu MILTON.* En effet, la Littérature proprement dite n'existant pas plus que l'espace pur, ce que l'on se rappelle d'un grand poète, c'est l'Impression dite de sublimité qu'il nous a laissée, par et à travers son Oeuvre, plutôt que l'Oeuvre elle-même, et cette impression, sous le voile des langages humains, pénètre les traductions les plus vulgaires. Lorsque ce phénomène est formellement constaté à propos d'une Oeuvre, le résultat de la constatation s'appelle LA GLOIRE! (595; my emphasis)

A strange exposition indeed, whose tone, sarcastic or sincere, satirical or mystical, resists interpretation. In the immediate context of the story, one receives little guidance, for the narrator imperiously dismisses the words of 'notre poète' as 'cette phraséologie, où perce une vanité monstrueuse [...] aussi vide que le genre de gloire qu'elle préconise', and goes on to expound the virtues of the machine and its positivistic conception of fame. However, given that the narrator's declared opinions do not necessarily coincide with those of the author Villiers, one could argue that the latter, on the contrary, would more understandably take sides with 'our poet' ... who would of course be none other than the story's dedicatee, Stéphane Mallarmé. For our purposes, it is less important to distinguish between a measure of sympathy and a measure of mockery in the balance of Villiers's mind, than it is to see what happens to the passage, bearing as it does the

35

promise of a theory of the poet's name, when it is transplanted from the satirical-dystopian domain of Villiers de l'Isle-Adam to the very different and mysterious works of Stéphane Mallarmé. There 'our poet' will twice reproduce the very same onomastic discourse, but with certain important contextual changes.

2.2.3 Citation: 'Tennyson vu d'ici'

The first instance occurs in Mallarmé's obituary for Tennyson,[19] written in 1892 for the English review *The National Observer* and then reprinted five years later, with a few alterations, in *Divagations*, as one of the 'Médaillons et Portraits en Pied'. The passage quoted from 'La Machine' is the following:

> En effet, la Littérature proprement dite n'existant pas plus que l'espace pur, ce que l'on se rappelle d'un grand poète, c'est l'*Impression* dite de sublimité qu'il nous a laissée, par et à travers son Oeuvre, plutôt que l'Oeuvre elle-même, et cette impression, sous le voile des langages humains, pénètre les traductions les plus vulgaires. Lorsque ce phénomène est formellement constaté à propos d'une Oeuvre, le résultat de la constatation s'appelle LA GLOIRE! (*Pl.* 529)

How does Mallarmé resituate the extract? The evident context in which the citation finds itself has shifted, radically, from satirical tale to death-notice. The question of the name-of-the-poet will presumably be treated here with solemnity, care, respect. Solemn indeed is the tone upon which the obituary opens:

> Maintenant que tout est dit [...] voici une piété à ressaisir [...] avant leur dispersion, la tourbillonante et volante jonchée de regrets, le jugement et l'émotion; autour du vide, que marque Tennyson. (527)

The singularly tight phrasing of the last clause almost succeeds in producing ghostly quotation marks around the name 'Tennyson': the regrets, judgements, and emotion of those who read, along with the incompetence and curiosity of the illiterate, will soon disperse; within that void lies another, where Tennyson was; and where now there is nothing, except the name 'Tennyson'. It is that name which Mallarmé wishes to contemplate. He first pushes aside all attempts to translate the name across cultures:

> Et on cita Cabanel, quant à la galerie peut-être des fascinants portraits féminins dans les premiers poèmes, lorsque l'occasion s'offrit de taire le nom de ce seul peintre. (528)

He rejects equally the desire for facile equations:

> [On pourrait] peut-être et le temps que tout de suite se dissolve ce propos fugitif, énoncer, au sujet de Tennyson, les noms d'un Leconte de Lisle, tempéré par un Alfred de Vigny et celui aussi quelquefois de Coppée: soit, mais que c'est faux! (528)

For the poet there is no such thing as translation, especially, it is implied, as far as names are concerned. This curious linguistic nationalism represents a 'nécessaire infirmité peut-être qui renforce [...] l'illusion qu'un objet proféré de la seule façon qu'à leur su il se nomme, lui-même jaillit, natif; mais, n'est-ce pas? quelle étrange chose'. Nor may one simply equate the name with the sum of the works it signs. As the theory of 'our poet' states, in the lines preceding those actually quoted in 'Tennyson':

> L'impression que laissent les vers, même inconnus, de [TENNYSON], étant passée dans le nom même de leur auteur, ce sera, ici, pour les auditeurs, comme s'ils avaient lu [TENNYSON].

Having dismissed these various methods of considering the name, the necrologist must find a way of countering so much negativity. He opts for a combination of cheap trickery, dubious authority, and shameless hyperbole: in short, the rhetoric of the dandy. Time, he says, will form its own sentiments regarding 'Tennyson', but 'l'éloignement, de telle façon, joue les siècles' (529). The 'vu d'ici' of the title takes on a cheeky self-importance, when Mallarmé asserts that: 'Un recul à quelques heures de wagon ou de mer, commence l'immortalité' (529). In order to conceal this sly transition (which, incidentally, destroys any credit for gravity he may hereto have earned), Mallarmé now switches pseudo-scholastically to the authority of one Villiers de l'Isle-Adam, and produces the passage cited ('En effet, la Littérature …'). But we should note that a set of inverted commas has gone missing here, since it was not Villiers who spoke in 'La Machine', but 'notre poète'. The suspicion that our poet might in truth be called 'Stéphane Mallarmé' is confirmed by the proprietorial rights which that person now feels free to exert over the quotation. Thus he simply removes, along with the quotation marks, any traces on Villiers's part of ironic distancing such as we may have detected in the original context. Our poet acts as if the original address 'à Monsieur Stéphane Mallarmé' had implied a waiving of any authorial rights to the meaning of the tale. Then, again acting as if to forestall objections, this time against his little theft, Mallarmé, far from excusing or explaining himself, instead further inflates his pretensions. The Name as concept may not figure in the extract quoted, but now it emerges in all its glory:

> Le nom du poète mystérieusement se refait avec le texte entier qui, de l'union des mots entre eux, arrive à n'en former qu'un, celui-là, significatif, résumé de toute l'âme, la communiquant au passant; il vole des pages grandes ouvertes du livre désormais vain: car, enfin, il faut bien que le génie ait lieu en dépit de tout et que le connaisse chacun, malgré les empêchements, et sans avoir lu, au besoin. Or, ce chaste agencement de syllabes, *Tennyson*, avec solennité, dit, cette fois: *Lord Tennyson* — je sais que déjà il somme et éveille, à travers le malentendu même d'idiome en idiome ou des lacunes ou l'inintelligence, et de plus en plus le fera — la pensée d'une hautaine tendre figure, volontaire mais surtout retirée et avare aussi de tout dû, par noblesse, en une manière seigneuriale apportée dans l'esprit; ingénue, taciturne: et presque j'ajouterai que le décès serein y installe quelque chose

> d'isolé ou complète, pour la foule, le retrait fier de la
> physionomie. (530)

Thus the theory is exposed. Quietly, magnanimously. But no
sooner does it reach this apparent summit of exposition than
already it finds itself threatened by exposure. For the veritable
explosion of epithets (a dozen from 'la pensée' down to 'phys-
ionomie') provoked by the mere utterance of the syllables of the
name will not long suffice to hold our attention. Too much disper-
sion, however energetic it be, undermines the essentialist drive of
onomastics. So, before it should fade, Mallarmé acts quickly to
minimize (not to say negate) the importance of this adjectival
apparition, with the elliptical phrase: 'Aucun de ces termes … [ne
suffira]'. Such self-denial ensures retained control over the theory,
suggesting that beyond the immediate effect of the display lies
something else (more essentially 'Tennyson', onomastically more
powerful) to be revealed at a later point.

   In the meantime, Mallarmé proposes two possible strategic
solutions to the problem of exposure and fading. The first recommends repetition, or the recitation, with minor variations, of the
name, in the simple belief that the charm will never wear off, that
the miracle will always be renewed.[20] In a sense this would be the
method already applied to the passage from 'La Machine', which
is rehearsed with no questions asked (indeed, with hyperbolic
additions). As regards 'Tennyson', we can hear — in addition to
the seminal but chaste 'agencement de syllabes, *Tennyson*, avec
solennité, dit, cette fois: *Lord Tennyson*' — the following variants:
'tennysonienne […] Alfred Tennyson […] Tennyson […] Lord
Tennyson […] Tennyson […] Tennyson'. But hand in hand with
repetition comes the second support to the spectacle of the Name:
it is the force lent by 'work-on-language' or, more simply, poetry.
In order not to fade, the name, throughout its repetition, must be
constantly and poetically worked and reworked, and thus
renamed into renown. Discreetly identifying 'naming' with
poiein, Mallarmé perhaps alludes to this notion at the close of the
death-notice:

> Et je pense qu'un considérable deuil flotte à la
> colonnade suave du temple de la Poésie, édifice à

> l'écart. Que son ombre y soit reçue avec les termes mêmes de l'hyperbole affectueuse qu'au temps de jeunesse, à lui illustre mais encore futur, dédia l'enthousiasme de Poe: 'l'âme poétique la plus noble, qui jamais vécut'. (531)

The referee is impressive, for not only is Poe the exemplary poet, but 'Poe' is also the exemplary name-of-the-poet. The terms 'Poésie [...] Poe [...] poétique' afford a glimpse of a poetic labour (an edifice or 'temple-building') which otherwise would remain undeclared. And it is as if some of the depth of the poetry of the name had been uncovered, this time, behind the single epithet 'noble', when we recall the following definition from the 'Appendix on Proper Nouns' to *Les Mots anglais* (*Pl.* 1043):

ALFRED, ou le NOBLE.

Despite the self-assurance and modesty of such a gesture, already the beginning of a doubt has appeared that, however convinced or convincing it may sound, maybe something more than the mere assertion of the name-theory, such as we found it firstly in 'La Machine à Gloire' and now in 'Tennyson vu d'ici', will be required, in order finally to persuade not just the sceptical eye of the curious onomast, but even its first prophet and practitioner, our poet Stéphane Mallarmé. We shall see this tendency confirmed in the following section with the drama of Villiers de l'Isle-Adam.

2.2.4 Citation: 'Villiers de l'Isle-Adam'

> *Le nom de Villiers de l'Isle-Adam, à votre attention proposé.* (Pl. 507)

The commemorative lecture for Villiers de l'Isle-Adam,[21] written and performed within six months of the latter's death in 1889, has something of the status of a text abandoned. The original version, which runs to some twenty-nine pages in the Pléiade, represents the longest piece of prose, barring translations, that Mallarmé ever wrote; but when it reappeared in *Vers et Prose* (1893) and again in *Divagations* (1897), it was cut down to about a quarter of its initial length. A similar process of scaling down seems to have been applied to the projected series of which the text would have been part, since the manuscript of 'Villiers' bears the general title 'Les Miens, no.1', as if to announce Mallarmé's intention of writing a series of studies-cum-portraits of artists he had known particularly well. Now Mondor, somewhat strangely, speaks of 'Les Miens' as an unrealized project ('études dont on ne regrettera jamais assez qu'elles ne parurent pas'), but surely one could argue that these studies did appear, only under a different title — *Médaillons et portraits en pieds* — and in a considerably revised and reduced format. The *Médaillons*, such as it exists, seems to correspond perfectly well to the description Mondor gives of the abandoned 'Les Miens': 'une suite [...] d'autres conférences ou études [consacrées] à des hommes qu'il avait particulièrement aimés'. However, what has changed between the idea of 'Les Miens' and the actuality of *Médaillons* is the manner in which Mallarmé attempts to commemorate the name of the friend-artist. In this process the lecture on Villiers may be seen retrospectively as a prototype, necessarily to be abandoned therefore, but from which Mallarmé would have learnt how to perform, in this celebratory-necrological genre, the shorter, sharper, and more successful gestures that figure in the rest of the sequence. Such will be my argument in the following pages.

The passage from 'La Machine', again with just the one set of quotation marks, is cited near the beginning of the lecture, from 'Au nom de MILTON, il s'éveillera' down to 'le résultat de la constatation s'appelle la Gloire!' It is offered as an example, amongst others, of the textual memories that might be evoked by the enunciation of 'Villiers de l'Isle-Adam'. The choice and situation of the extract would suggest that the name, in this commemoration, is going to count. Throughout the lecture, in effect, Mallarmé will insist on foregrounding Villiers's name, not merely via its repetition, but by the repeated suggestion that his name had, or should have had, some special power or mission. We might say that Villiers is represented 'as' rather than 'by' his name. To give just one example of this dramatization, we can highlight the manner in which Mallarmé continually returns to what he calls the *arrivée* of Villiers, denoting both his literary

41

arrival in Paris and his sudden apparition or announcement, out of the general mystery of his life, at a social gathering or simply on the street: 'un de ces abords subits sur le trottoir, bris ainsi que d'une vitre, d'où s'écroulait la joaillerie'. Let us consider more closely these different manifestations of Villiers-the-Name.

Firstly, then, as regards the repetition of the name itself, we may note a play of repetition and variation similar to that remarked in 'Tennyson'. Given that Villiers's full name was 'Jean-Marie Mathias Philippe Auguste de Villiers de l'Isle-Adam', we can understand that Mallarmé had a considerable number of variants to play with. But he shows restraint. The longest version he allows is 'Philippe Auguste Mathias comte de Villiers de l'Isle-Adam'. Otherwise we find 'Villiers de l'Isle-Adam' (ten times) and plain 'Villiers' (seven). Related to the presence of the name itself is the genealogy from which it grew. This Mallarmé refers to — hinting implicitly at the enormous onomastic weight Villiers felt himself to bear — in the following passage:

> Il avait atterri (à Paris) d'autant mieux qu'à de hauts *noms*, comme Rodolphe-le-Bel, seigneur de Villiers et de Dormans, 1067, le fondateur. (490)

The list continues, and is immediately followed by a description of Villiers's other genealogy, namely his intellectual references:

> A tant d'échos, après tout qui somnolent dans les traités ou les généalogies, le dernier descendant vite mêlait d'autres *noms* [...] Saint-Bernard, Kant, le Thomas de la Somme, principalement un désigné par lui le Titan de l'Esprit Humain, Hegel, dont le singulier lecteur semblait aussi se revendiquer entre autres cartes de visites ou lettres de présentation. (491)

There is no lack of names, then. But in addition to the weight or number comes the self-conscious dramatization of the name *qua* name. Thus Villiers is made to say: '"Vraiment, je porte un *nom* qui rend tout difficile"' (490). Or of his friend's youth Mallarmé remarks: 'indéniablement que des circonstances préparaient, hérédité, éducation par soi et les grèves, un *nom* à lancer aussi haut que sa pensée' (496). Or of his arrival on the Parisian scene: '[Villiers] qui venait tout conquérir avec un mot, son *nom*, autour duquel déjà il voyait, à vrai dire, matériellement, se rallumer le lustre, aujourd'hui discernable pour notre seul esprit' (492). In this last example may already be heard a certain doubt on Mallarmé's part, a doubt as to the material realization of the name's promise; as to whether it is really sufficient, in order to secure one's fame, to have, on the one hand, a polysyllabic appellation, bathed though it be in historical and intellectual recommendations and tradition, and, on the other, to insist, simply, upon the effect which that name is going, so it promises, to produce. Mallarmé even has his subject share this doubt, when he makes Villiers declare:

> 'Avec l'ambition — d'ajouter à l'illustration de ma race la seule gloire vraiment noble de nos temps, celle *d'un grand écrivain*'. (489; my emphasis)

Something — *writing* — must be added to the name, in order for the latter to find itself transformed into the name-of-the-poet. But, from the start of the conference, writing itself has been in doubt. The lecture opened with surely the most doubtful of writerly questions:

> Sait-on ce que c'est qu'écrire? (481)

The doubt as to whether 'le jeune Philippe-Auguste de si prodigieux nom' succeeded in *writing* his name, as to whether he had that extra something which separates mystery from dupery ('avait-il été joué, était-ce cela?' (496)), begins, with the unfolding of the lecture, to turn the exposition of the name, its proud enunciation and future promise, into its exposure, or the revelation of Villiers's failure 'to add the only true glory of our times'. This turning may be traced through the obsession of the arrival.

The arrival goes hand in hand with the name. It is Villiers's presence summoned by the magic of his name. Thus Mallarmé, ever seduced by onomastic charm, claims of Villiers's life that two events essentially resume it:

> Je veux dire l'*arrivée* de Philippe-Auguste Mathias
> comte de Villiers de l'Isle-Adam, à Paris, vers 1863; et
> cette fin, août 1889. (489)

At first the arrival is portrayed in glowing terms:

> Nul, que je me rappelle, ne fut, par un vent d'illusion
> engouffré dans les plis visibles, tombant de son geste
> ouvert qui signifie: 'Me voici', avec une impulsion
> aussi véhémente et surnaturelle poussé, que jadis cet
> adolescent. (489)

But there are also certain niggling qualifiers, such as, here, 'que je
me rappelle', which we can easily miss on a first reading, and
which compromise to some degree the speaker's declared
credulity. For example:

> Je ne sais pas mais je crois, en réveillant ces souvenirs
> de primes années, que vraiment l'*arrivée* fut
> extraordinaire. (489)

His appearance amongst the Parnassians is presented in
spectacular terms:

> Un groupe [...] au milieu de qui exactement tomba le
> jeune Philippe-Auguste Mathias de si prodigieux
> nom. Rien ne troublera [...] la vision de l'*arrivant*.
> (490)

The imagery remains consistent:

> Certainement, il surprit ce groupe où [...] il avait
> atterri d'autant mieux qu'à de hauts *noms*. (490)

But so does the possibility of doubt. Consider, for example, the
following oneline paragraph (of which device Mallarmé makes
ample use in this text):[22]

> Un génie! nous le comprîmes tel. (490)

44

This proves, on examination, a somewhat double-edged compliment, since in the space around the phrase might arise the question: 'Is it a "genius" — or is it rather, somewhat absurdly popping out of a bottle at the mention of his name, a "genie"?' And likewise we may detect, around 'comprîmes', some doubt as to the quality of 'our' youthful understanding. With the passing of time, what was once the sign of his promise becomes the mark of his evident failure. Mallarmé accordingly switches tone from reverential recollection to pity:

> Ainsi il vint, c'était tout, pour lui; [...] et toujours, des ans, tant que traîna le simulacre de sa vie, et des ans, jusqu'aux précaires récents derniers, quand chez l'un de nous, le timbre de la porte d'entrée suscitait l'attention par quelque son pur, obstiné, fatidique [...] invariablement se répétait pour les amis anciens eux-mêmes vieillis, et malgré la fatigue à présent du visiteur, lassé, cassé, cette obsession de l'*arrivée* d'autrefois [...] . et maintenant ce devenait plus beau peut-être, plus humblement beau, ou poignant, cette irruption, des antiques temps, incessamment ressassée, que la première en réalité. (494)

And again:

> L'évanouissement tardif, jusqu'à l'espace élargi, du timbre annonciateur, lequel avait fait dire à l'hôte 'C'est Villiers' quand, affaiblie, une millième fois se répétait son *arrivée* de jadis. (495)

Finally, we find the exposure of the name as the symbol of Villiers's failure summed up in the brutal one-line paragraph:

> Villiers de l'Isle-Adam se montrait. (494)

The whole disaster may be perceived in the juxtaposition of that one-liner with this one, taken from the opening of the lecture:

> Qui l'accomplit [écrire], intégralement, se retranche. (481)

45

'Se montrer: se retrancher'. Writing, completely, demands first the complete suppression of the writer. He cuts himself out for writing by cutting himself out of writing. Indirectly and mysteriously, however, the name 'se refait avec le texte entier' (*Pl.* 529); that is, far from showing itself, from exposing itself — as Villiers exposed himself trailing genealogical and intellectual calling cards of glory — it retreats radically into the work, reworking itself into the work as writing, so that, at the end of this onomastic process, the work, eventually and eternally, becomes the name:

> Le texte entier [...] de l'union des mots entre eux, arrive à n'en former qu'un, celui-là, significatif, résumé de toute l'âme, la communiquant au passant. (529)

The specificity of Villiers's failure may be seen in a passage from 'Villiers' very similar to the one from 'Tennyson' just cited. Mallarmé is describing his friend's relations with the Parnassians, for whose poetic efforts Villiers had little time or sympathy: poetry itself is '[un] souci qui [fut] moindre pour un prince intellectuel [...] pesait peu [...] ne signifiait guère' (491). The only thing that might have interested him in the poetic debates or efforts of the Parnassians would have been:

> La particularité peut-être que nous professâmes, le vers n'étant autre qu'un mot parfait, vaste, natif, une adoration pour la vertu des mots: celle-ci ne pouvant être étrangère à qui venait tout conquérir avec un mot, son *nom*. (492)

This attempt to bring Villiers and poetry together in fact serves only to expose the crisis more flagrantly. Villiers was not a poet: the examples given of his early efforts in verse are followed by a quotation from Poe — in theory or at least by name the exemplary poet — where even the master confesses that, circumstance having got the the better of him, he has failed truly to be a poet.[23] This is not merely a question of writing or not writing verse, for poetry, we know, is simply writing taken to a higher degree of consciousness or conscientiousness, in that 'toutes les fois qu'il y a effort au style, il y a versification' (*Pl.* 867). Rather, Villiers's indifference to verse signifies his failure to grasp the true importance of writing in all its intimate mystery. The name of Villiers will suffer thereby, since only through the 'ancienne et très vague et jalouse pratique' (481) of writing may the mystery of the name be accomplished. Villiers failed to 'intégralement se retrancher' within that practice; rather, 'il vint, c'était tout, pour lui [...] Villiers de l'Isle-Adam se montrait'.

2.2.5 *Salut*: 'Mon dessein [...] ce Message'

The salvation of Villiers and his name must nevertheless be seen to take place for appearance's sake. This Mallarmé achieves, at the close of his performance, by effectively ignoring and turning away from the double disaster — the death of Villiers the friend, the failure of Villiers the artist — the news of which he has just communicated to his audience.

The fourth and final section of the lecture opens, it would appear somewhat desperately, thus:

> Tout cela n'est pas, que ce penseur ait succombé [...] à la monotonie, qui verse la fatigue, et à l'écoeurement [...] n'importe, tout cela n'est pas, les maux [...] n'importe! (502).

And further on:

> Je dis: il faut que rien de cela ne demeure, car ce serait l'irréparable! sauf pour quelques-uns. (502)

Then Mallarmé appeals, again with an air of seeming desperation, to the doctrine of the name: when we say the name of Villiers de l'Isle-Adam, his whole work will appear before our startled eyes:

> Je voudrais [...] je voudrais [...] que cette oeuvre, à vous qui la savez, la feuilletez, tout de suite apparaisse, ainsi qu'après les siècles de littérature elle doit persister. (503)

But at the evocation of the name, in these final pages, all that appears is a handful of quotations from the collected works. Is that all the theory will amount to? The speaker himself seems a little perturbed by this doubt when he admits that 'j'avais [...] supprimé ici toute lecture' (504). Something more than the edited highlights of Villiers's works must be produced in order firstly that his reputation may be saved and secondly that the theory of the name retain its power to attract and mystify. What Mallarmé effectively opts to do is to substitute the failure of Villiers's life and literary performance with the success of his own present rhetorical gesture. Thus it is that, having read the extracts from Villiers's works ('Tel', he resumes, 'l'Oeuvre qu'évoquera le nom de Villiers de l'Isle-Adam'), he simply turns his back on them and draws our attention to something quite different, namely his own works and concerns and current performance.[24] What, according to Mallarmé, is the *impression* created by the evocation of Villiers's works? The impression which, 'étant passée dans le nom même de l'auteur', will count for all eternity? The answer to that question both shifts the debate from Villiers's to Mallarmé's world, and at the same time allows the latter to present himself definitively as the new guardian or bearer of the name. Here it is:

> L'impression, somme toute, ne ressemblant à autre chose, choc de triomphes, tristesse abstraite, rire éperdu ou pire quand il se tait, et le glissement amer d'ombres et de soirs, avec une inconnue gravité et la paix, remémore *l'énigme de l'orchestre*. (507; my emphasis)

Suddenly, surprisingly, we find ourselves removed to a familiar and favoured battleground of Mallarmé's, namely that which opposes music and letters. Villiers (who, incidentally, would have been just another Wagnerian foot-soldier in this battle) has disappeared from sight. The passage continues:

> Or mon avis suprême, le voici. Il semble que [...] au moment exceptionnel où la musique paraît s'adapter mieux qu'aucun rite à ce que de latent contient et d'à jamais abscons la présence d'une foule, ait été montré

que rien [...] n'existe que ne puisse [...] rendre la
vieille et sainte élocution; ou le Verbe, quand c'est
quelqu'un qui le profère. (507; my emphasis)

The debate over Villiers's eternity may only be continued through
the works — the words and concerns — of Stéphane Mallarmé.
This transfer is confirmed by the ambiguity of the term
'Quelqu'un'. For the awful question arises: 'But was Villiers really
"someone" to proffer the word?' Have we not just read an
account of his failure as a writer? Mallarmé responds very simply
by himself arising into the space left by Villiers and offering
himself as the answer:

> Mesdames, Messieurs,
> (prononcé debout)

By standing up in order to pronounce the closing section — the
resolution, as it were, of the conference — Mallarmé identifies
himself as the 'someone' to proffer the word concerning Villiers.
Thus, in the long, syntactically complex and wholly and typically
'Mallarmean' last phrase of the lecture, the author casts himself in
the role of the messenger, the happy purveyor of a successful
communicative act:

> Mon dessein se forma dès ce temps [Villiers's death]
> de vous parler, ici, un jour, de lui: et ce serait à ma
> présomption un motif suffisant, ou plausible, n'eussé-
> je pas, en des minutes comptées, à souhait évoqué un
> si lumineux fantôme, que d'apporter, en son *nom*
> désormais imprimé seulement — du pays prestigieux
> toujours par lui habité et maintenant surtout, car ce
> pays n'est pas — comme une bouffée unique de joie et
> une exaltation suprême — à la terre amicale qui, un
> moment, se mêla à ses rêves, ce Message.

Stéphane Mallarmé, unlike his friend, is an authentic poet, who
knows therefore that, for the name and the theory of the name to
survive, work, *poiein*, poetry, must be brought into play. The safe
arrival of that message in a sense succeeds in saving even Villiers

49

de l'Isle-Adam. Although it is true that the latter, as a writer, failed to make a literary name for himself, Mallarmé, his friend and memorialist, by preserving and pursuing the onomastic theory which in its origins stemmed from the name of Villiers, proves himself sufficiently generous in his own triumph to shed some glory on his dead friend's renown.

The experience of 'Villiers', then, the lesson so to speak of the lecture and its performance, tells us that, in addition to the theory of the name as discovered in 'La Machine à Gloire', a complex poetical and rhetorical *practice* of the name must be developed — a practice which would be less an application of the theory than its necessary and vital extension or expansion. The theory will only work if the name is poetically kept working. It is with the full range of effects and consequences provoked by such poetic labour that the remainder of this study is concerned.

2.3 Working theory

Jeu (avec miracle, n'est-ce pas?)

In the opening paragraphs of the conference on Villiers, the speaker, in response to the self-consciously naive and absolute question 'Sait-on ce que c'est qu'écrire?', invoked the possibility of a now familiar 'doubt':

> C'est, ce jeu insensé d'écrire, s'arroger, en vertu d'un doute — la goutte d'encre apparentée à la nuit sublime — quelque devoir de tout recréer, avec des réminiscences, pour avérer qu'on est bien là où l'on doit être (parce que, permettez-moi d'exprimer cette incertitude, demeure une incertitude). (481)[25]

We might now call on this combination of doubt and duty — of virtuality and labour — in the present context of our theory of the name. The daily task of Mallarmé the onomast will be to work on and encourage our doubt that a name-theory might indeed exist, while certainly doing nothing to confirm the doubt that it may not. In the following pages I shall take three examples that run counter to the unhappy experience of 'Villiers'. They resemble the latter text in that each addresses the works, but above all the name, of a fellow-artist (one writer and two painters), and tries to convey some of the mystery surrounding the enunciation of such terms as 'Voltaire', 'Manet', and 'Whistler'. But the strategy employed in these cases differs greatly from the one adopted for the conference. The onomastic gesture has become much briefer, more elusive, more suggestively essential. Equally, any attempt to represent the works themselves of the artist has disappeared, in favour of a subtle and underhand nagging at the reader's credulity. To put it simply, the technique has become Mallarmean: the reader of the poetry recognizes himself in the reader of Mallarmé's rhetorical and theoretical strategies. This last point raises a further question, which in a sense will prepare us for Parts 3 and 4 of the present study by obliging us to ask ourselves to what extent the name of, say, Voltaire, once reworked and reinvented by the hand of 'Stéphane Mallarmé', must necessarily bear the latter's paraph or signature. The name of the namer will at that point have to be addressed

2.3.1 'Sur Voltaire': *le nom idéal*

This short text of uncertain name and origin may be seen as an antidote to 'Villiers'.[26] After the long, rambling, and sombre conference, this fragment by contrast appears brief, casual, and even slightly giddy. The very idea of bringing onto the same page the names of Mallarmé and Voltaire might suffice to raise a smile, and it is in just such a smiling spirit that the former ('ici entre une cigarette et l'autre') adopts his strategy of reply to the question of 'Voltaire's significance' today.

As a first step, the works themselves ('il faut exclure, avec la fumée, presque les vers, tragédies, poèmes épiques') are all but banished from our minds. Secondly, we find that the very quali-ties Mallarmé claims to admire in Voltaire's philosophical stories and letters bear an uncanny resemblance to those on display in the present critical performance: 'un négligé [valant toute nudité]'; and 'le concis, ou le dégagé'. The first may be seen as the veil of smoke in which Mallarmé clouds his reflections — a veil borrowed, incidentally, from a similarly posed occasion of contrived spontaneity and felicitous obfuscation, namely the sonnet 'Toute l'âme résumée' of 1895 (*O.C.* 432); the second quality deriving from the brief and relaxed style of the reply, and the way it appears to show a clean pair of heels to the massed volumes of Voltaire's literary production.

Having thus disengaged himself from any obligation seriously to represent Voltaire and his works, Mallarmé is left with nothing but the name; which is where our attention is alerted. He declares himself to be in tune with the present age, in that the latter

> substitua [à l'oeuvre] l'attitude personnelle et générale de l'esprit, abstraitement: à faire plafonner, aux olympes, comme archer dévoré par la joie et l'ire du trait qu'il perd, lumineux. Jeu (avec miracle, n'est-ce pas?) résumé, départ de flèche et vibration de corde, dans le nom idéal de — Voltaire. (872)

The works may be replaced by an abstract image. But is it an image of 'the spirit of Voltaire'? Or rather: 'the wit that may be exercised about "Voltaire"'? Given the clearly advertised indifference of the present writer to the dead one's labours, the second possibility seems the more likely. So the name is turned into 'voltaire', and the image developed from that gesture. Now almost immediately Mallarmé waves away any desire arising at this point to take him too seriously ('Tout ceci en vue de causer'), and disappears; but in the interval of his performance he has 'caused' the trace of a doubt — '(… n'est-ce pas?)' — that a miracle may have taken place. And the doubt persists in the image traced of the archer, for the writer is there represented as being consumed in the act of making, a phenomenon which leaves behind it the fading trace of his name. The ideal spiritual gesture suggested here would be a signing trait (of wit, of genius, of the writing hand), on condition that, no sooner traced, it disappear into an illusory depth (not unlike the *trompe-l'oeil* of a ceiling), where it may just still be perceptible to the discerning eye. The importance of the illusory nature of the name's performance is underlined by the fact (which, it is true, goes unmentioned in the text, but which every schoolboy knows) that 'Voltaire' was not merely not Voltaire's real name, but was itself a hastily but brilliantly improvised invention, a transposition of 'Arouet, l.j.'.[27]

So, in this seemingly spontaneous and reactive move on Mallarmé's part, many new 'performative' features have suddenly, if only partially, appeared around what was previously the mere assertion, the declaration, the *theôria*, of the name's mysterious qualities. Now we must contend with speed, spontaneity, lightness, play …. Furthermore, an indication has been given of the importance of depth in the representation or illusion of the name, and of the concept of the signature. In the latter case, a new problem arises: namely, 'Whose signature, in the act of signing, for example, the name "Voltaire", is in practice being signed? The subject's or the signer's?' This question, along with that of the almost painterly nature of the representation of the name, may be pursued through the examination of two 'double' or 'reflecting' portraits: on the one hand, Manet's and Whistler's renditions of their friend the poet; on the other, Mallarmé's 'médaillons [ou] portraits en pied' of the two painters.

2.3.2 Manet: depth, *durée* [28]

> *J'ai, dix ans, vu tous les jours mon cher Manet, dont l'absence aujourd'hui me paraît invraisemblable. (Pl. 661)*

How, then, to give depth to the illusion of the name?

Mallarmé's response to 'Voltaire' suggested a strategy combining spontaneity and contrivance, high theory smuggled in under the casual veil of humour. We find a curious reflection of this in one example of Manet's own portraiture of a name-artist. His 1868 picture of Emile Zola represents, according to one critic, the painter's response, a spontaneous gesture of gratitude, to the defence Zola had made of Manet in *L'Evénement*, and then in the pamphlet entitled *Manet* (which we in fact see, on the writer's table, in the portrait itself).[29] Despite the occasional nature of the painting, Manet worked fast and hard to give its illusion a kind of spiralling, abysmal 'depth' similar to that which I have been discussing: depth around the name. Rather than put his signature where we would expect to see it, in the bottom righthand corner of the canvas, Manet chooses to place it in the background, on the wall of Zola's study. It is an allusive signature formed by the representation of a reproduction of *Olympia* (reputedly Zola's favourite painting by Manet). However, at the very point where we might again expect to see the signature on the reproduction, Manet once more conceals it, by arranging two other reproductions, one of Velasquez's *Les Buveurs*, the other of a print by Utamaro, in such a way as to cover up the bottom righthand corner.[30] Yet the signature, in spite of or with the additional complexity provided by this game of hide-and-seek, does appear in the portrait, cleverly integrated into its texture: on the writer's desk lies the pamphlet, whose title (written, incidentally, in exactly the same manner as the artist used to sign his own name) reads 'Manet', and whose author, since it is in fact the very study which inspired the painting, reads 'Zola'. This gives us: '""'Manet" by Zola' by Manet" in "Zola" by Manet'. A simple handshake of gratitude indeed! The *trait* of the archer-artist shoots off into illusory depth.

The portrait of Zola by Manet forms an interesting precursor to Manet's 1876 portrait of Stéphane Mallarmé. Firstly, the circumstances of its creation are similar, since, like Zola some ten years earlier, Mallarmé had taken up his pen, on two occasions, in order to defend his friend's name.[31] The picture, executed in the same year as the article in the *Art Monthly Review*, would seem again to convey a simple expression of gratitude. But do we find also the same striving after abysmal complexity? At first sight one would think not, in so far as the canvas is free of the informational clutter of *Zola*. The wall in the background bears no references; merely a pattern of unreadable flecks. The paper, bottom left, over which hovers the poet's smoking hand, remains blank. Perhaps it is Mallarmé's famous inscrutability that Manet is seeking to express? Or might it not be the infinite potentiality of the white sheet, from which, like the smoke drifting towards and into the specks of 'writing' on the wall, endless future poems will be born? There can of necessity be no answer to these emblematic questions. At best, a riposte may be discovered, some twenty years after the execution of the painting (which had, in the interval, sat on Mallarmé's salon-wall, rue de Rome), when we consider the ironic self-portrait, once more fake improvisation or fake statement-for-eternity, contained in the sonnet 'Toute l'âme résumée'. 'Et voici des vers que, par jeu, le poète voulut bien écrire à notre intention pour cette enquête', wrote the *Figaro* journalist of the day in presenting to his readers the following (*O.C.* 432):

> Toute l'âme résumée
> Quand lente nous l'expirons
> Dans plusieurs ronds de fumée
> Abolis en autres ronds

The sonnet virtually writes itself back onto that empty page on the painting on the wall.[32] And the signature detected in the opening line ('Toute l'âme résumée' yielding by transposition of sounds: 'mal-ar-mé') returns to rest, in the old painting, just above the name of 'Manet' (which, as signature, lay beneath the blank page of 1876). The names do, then, come together, as did 'Manet-Zola'. But, all along, had not both the names been there, together? For if we scrutinize sufficiently closely, and with a certain interpretative desire, the shape traced on the canvas by the smoke of Mallarmé's cigar, we may distinguish (or imagine so) firstly the letter *S*, for Stéphane; then, in exactly the shape used by Manet to sign, when he included it, the initial of his first name, *E*; and lastly, bringing the names together, *M*, as in Mallarmé-Manet.[33]

Depth, in this latter case, derives not merely from work on the name, nor from an interplay of references-within-references, but above all from the very time (*durée*) through which the various and complex relations between the two names have evolved. This persistence or endurance comes itself to be emblematized in the word 'Manet', in the text by Mallarmé of that name. First, however, we should note that persistence had been present as a theme, and almost redundantly so, in the English text of 1876.[34] Likewise, in the later text, Mallarmé insists on this quality, adding to it this time an autobiographical touch: 'enseignement au témoin quotidien inoublieux, moi, qu'on se joue tout entier, de nouveau, chaque fois'.[35] But he also shows fidelity to the very terms in which he describes his friend's magic or method. The latter would stem from a double source: the reserve of skill, study, and technique acquired over the years, and then the sudden and forceful execution of the specific work in hand. In 1876 — ambient *Japonisme* being all the rage — Mallarmé had described this dynamic fusion (which may remind us of the spontaneity and contrivance of 'Sur Voltaire') in quasi-Zen terms:

> The hand, it is true, will conserve some of its acquired secrets of manipulation, but the eye should forget all else it has seen, and learn anew from the lesson before it. It should abstract itself from memory, seeing only that which it looks upon, and that as for the first time; and the hand should become an impersonal abstraction guided only by the will, oblivious of all previous cunning. (Florence, 12)

When it comes to 'Manet', he remains true to the hand-eye combination, condensed into the formulaic: 'L'oeil, une main'. But now this formula plays also a structuring role in the text, dominating *à l'attaque* the two phrases forming the second half of the text. 'Cet oeil — Manet', the second paragraph opens; and then: 'Sa main'. The violent incision of the name ('— Manet —') effects an equally violent identification of the name with the agents it inspires: 'main-oeil' blurs into 'Manet', and vice versa. The ear will just have to adjust to the fact that the pseudo-orientalism of fifteen or twenty years ago has become the name as illusory essence of the work. Essence, or rather essences, since the yoking together of 'Manet/main-oeil' is not left as illusion, to stand or fall, alone. In support, alternative or alternating 'Manets' duly appear. The name MANET may claim at least two etymologies (etymology being a science which is never less than generous): the first, if the French name be an adaptation of an Italian one, MANETTI, finding its roots in 'magin', meaning 'forza, potere'; the second (although they seem to overlap) tending more towards the Germanic 'man', that is, man.[36] Now, both of these sources accordingly reappear in the prose portrait. Amongst the sadness and regret that he feels for his lost friend, Mallarmé also remembers 'une ingénuité *virile* de chèvre-pied au par-dessus mastic' (532); and it is this virility, pushed almost to the point of animality, of ferocity, that forms, along with his urbanity, the *force* or *power* of Manet:

> Bref, railleur à Tortoni, élégant; en l'atelier, la furie qui

56

le ruait sur la toile vide, confusément, comme si
jamais il n'avait peint. (532)[37]

The dynamic fusion of hand and eye, cunning and power, gener-
ates a force which is the very essence 'Manet'. But there also exists
an even simpler identification, encapsulating all that has been
said in the preceding pages. The 'Manet' we see on all Manet's
paintings, including naturally the portrait of Stéphane Mallarmé,
spells, to the scrutiny of even the weakest Latinist: 'il reste'. The
whole thematics and *mise en scène* of persistency in a sense stares
back at us from the signature on each canvas. But it also appears
on the page of '"Manet" by Mallarmé', when the poet says (with
regard, precisely, to the artist's effort of will to be, daily, such as
eternity will make him): 'qu'on se joue tout entier, de nouveau,
chaque fois, n'étant autre que tous sans *rester* différent, à volonté'.
This is how 'Manet' persists and signs.

2.3.3 Whistler[38]

Nous ne pouvons chanter tout le temps.[39]

A certain depth may be given to the illusion of the name by a
shuffling or shifting of references and relations. This sleight of
hand and eye, however, takes place in time, and thus the
reworking of the name may be seen to foreshadow its illusory
appearance in eternity. In the exchange between Whistler and
Mallarmé, we shall witness a different technique of magnifying
the name, involving an insistence not on depth and endurance
but rather on the seemingly opposite concepts of surface and
interruption. The signature, as practised by Whistler, operates less
as the unremarkable guarantor of the painting's market value
than as a wilfully eye-catching decoration, come to disturb
(although not to destroy) the blandly contemplatable surface of
the illusion. Stéphane Mallarmé, after his fashion, theorizes this
strategy and transfers it to his own domain of poetry, bringing out
as he does so the much more aggressive character of this technique, and contrasting it sharply therefore with the serene fidelity
of the work around 'Manet'. The two strategies should not for
all that be perceived as competing or contradictory: they are

alternating operations rather than alternative options. The more techniques for glorifying the name, the happier our enterprise.

The signature represents a problematic 'remainder' in the theory of artistic anonymity with which Mallarmé is famously, and quite accurately, associated.[40] After all, if we follow strictly the notion that the author, in ceding the initiative to words, literally disappears, or even commits suicide, into the text … what then becomes of the name? And yet it refuses to fade away, and, as we have begun to see, remains vital to Mallarmé's concerns. In the text entitled 'Whistler', we find at first the theory of authorial anonymity dogmatically reiterated. Responding to the question (journalistically posed, I assume) as to whether the celebrated American dandy and artist is 'l'homme de sa peinture', the poet feigns some irritation at the indecorous demand and then explains that a work such as Whistler's 'joue au miracle et nie le signataire'. The signatory may be negated, but the name persists. As if conceding this point to the obstinacy of the name (or is it to the interrogator's incomprehension before the miracle?), he then gives himself over to a more complex reflection on the nature of this remainder. For he admits that, undeniably, there exists 'un Monsieur […] Whistler'.

As in the case of Manet, the 'Mister Whistler' concerned had his own thoughts on the matter, and these need to be taken into account, by ourselves as they were by our author. How did James McNeill Whistler 'désigne[r] que c'est lui'? The answer comes very simply: he did so in the form of a butterfly. This was so, at least, from 1873 onwards:

> In each of the plates made at Speke Hall in 1873, Whistler employed his new signature for the first time. His rectilinear monogram which resembles a butterfly was composed, like that of Millais, of his interlocking initials, and was given an oriental shape which recalls the seals on Japanese prints. This heraldic device, which evolved in the late 1870s into a small and sprightly butterfly, was placed with infinite care in different areas of the composition, its location dictated by Whistler's sense of oriental balance and placement.[41]

Like many other artists of the period, Whistler was interested in making his signature into a decoration, an additional motif to be all but integrated into the canvas. The signature, conventionally invisible, or rather ignored, comes to receive careful painterly attention, and may even find itself, as if it were a painting within a painting, sealed off from the rest of the picture surface. But Whistler seems to have pushed his thought at least one step further than did his contemporaries. The signature-as-ornament steps outside the illusion and points necessarily to the latter's artificiality: that much remains quite in accord with the modernist or decadent tendency to which Whistler owes allegiance. But the game may be rendered one degree more complex if, having made an object of the name, he then virtually reintegrates it, with a feigned naivety, into the scene depicted in the painting. This is in effect what Whistler does — and 'with infinite care'. As a result the spectator is caught in his contemplation, hesitating between the butterfly as 'butterfly', as something fluttering in the illusion before our eyes, or as 'Whistler', the author, transformed into his signature, and momentarily alighting on his own canvas. In addition, the butterfly itself (which we alternately see and now we don't) emblematizes the process. Such scrutatorial hesitancy occurs, for example, as we consider *Speke Hall I* (1870), where the woman pictured in the left foreground of the composition appears to be looking at something on the ground: it is the butterfly signature. In *The Gold Scarab* (1879), the butterfly has a long tail, tipped with an arrowhead: this is clearly pointing at the devilish figure, sitting at the piano, over which the signature hovers. A final example of this potentially comical use of the signature would be *Lady with a Fan*, a drawing from the early 1870s. Here the butterfly signature seems to be pursuing the said lady: one wonders whether she is not going to swat it. Now, in the famous lithograph of Mallarmé of 1893, the spectator may likewise speculate as to the relationship between the butterfly and, in this instance, the poet.[42] The subject appears vaguely uncomfortable and as if he were trying deliberately not to look at the butterfly-signature flitting around him. Is he attempting to 'deny the signatory'? The poet, so to speak, would be experiencing some discomfort at the thought that, in his present position, he is little more than the product of a butterfly called 'Whistler'. When we go on to read Mallarmé's medallion or portrait of Whistler, however, we realize that the poet's apparent unease has been transformed into nervous but intense reflection. Retrospectively, '"Mallarmé" by Whistler' finds itself re-entitled 'Stéphane Mallarmé thinking about the signature': for the prose counter-portrait reveals that Mallarmé could respond in kind, notably by folding the image of butterfly-and-poet back into his own more elaborate onomastic project.

The very act of writing a 'Whistler by Mallarmé', a counter-portrait, contributes to the debate around the signature, in as much as it helps to produce a mirror-effect — 'Mallarmé by Whistler'/'Whistler by Mallarmé' — in which we are obliged to reflect upon the significance and interchangeability of those names. But the text itself shifts the emphasis of the discussion away from the potentially rather sterile insistence on representation — the question, as it were, being: 'Who is who? Who does the signature refer to? To whom does that which it signs belong?' — and towards a new query, which would rather ask: 'What does the signature do?' The reply to such a question comes, not surprisingly perhaps, between two verbs:

> Un Monsieur [...] *désigne* que c'est lui, Whistler, d'ensemble comme il peint toute la personne [...] et *rentre* dans l'obsession de ses toiles. (*Pl.* 531, my emphasis)

The presence of the name is an interval, a flash in the spectator's mind, creating the suspicion that the name may indeed be up to something worthy of closer attention. But what happens in that flash? The answer is suitably elliptical:

> Le temps de provoquer! (532)

One could read this provocation as specific to the author of *The Gentle Art of Making Enemies* and of paintpots in the face of the public. But Mallarmé makes it clear that he considers Whistler's case to be exemplary and of theoretical import, for he asserts that 'l'enchanteur [...] a compris le devoir de sa présence'. The role of the signature, acting somewhere between (over there) the infinite, impersonal operation of the work and (over here) the dumb contemplation of the viewer, must be to 'interrompre cela' with its necessary flicker. The illusion — be it that of the work-in-hand or of the ineffable work-in-progress — must be broken in order to live and, in the long run, to survive. The name, appropriately dressed, may perform this function marvellously well, flitting between the public's reference, the canvas, and the destiny of the work. Little surprise, then, that at this point in the text Mallarmé should introduce the 'signature' of his subject:

> Cette discrétion [...] pour peu [...] éclate en le vital sarcasme qu'aggrave l'habit noir ici au miroitement de linge comme *siffle* le rire et présente, à des contemporains devant l'exception d'art souveraine, ce que juste, de l'auteur, eux doivent connaître. (532)

Now, the actual play on 'Whistler' had been waiting in the wings for some time, and on several occasions Mallarmé had flirted with the idea of revealing it. But, in the various addresses he made to his friend, he generally refrained from blowing the whistle. The dedication in Whistler's copy of *L'Après-Midi d'un Faune*, for example, hints at the tune the Faun might play ('Tu peux, Faune, oui c'est l'air/Le jouer à Whistler.' (O.C. 567)). The famous 'Billet' presents the extravagant closing name-rhyme as a flash of the tutu ('Sinon rieur que puisse l'air/De sa jupe éventer Whistler'[43] (O.C. 384)), but in fact diverts onomastic attention onto a different, although in a sense equally whistling, name, *The Whirlwind*.[44] When we come to the prose portrait, with its now explicit pun on the meaning of the name, the whistling laugh of Whistler appears to fulfil the function of the signature as I have just described it. The presence of the artist is virtual, intervallic: 'siffle' is and at the same time isn't 'Whistler'. The appearance is a provocation: the whistle attracts the attention — or rather breaks the inattention — of the regarding public, but also mocks the latter's dumb suspension of disbelief, in as much as 'siffler', by a happy inversion, implies also the act of booing or hissing at someone's performance. Such aggression may again be read as specific to Whistler the provocative artist, but might also remind us of the high standards Mallarmé himself expects of his readership. Finally, the signature does in a sense come to assume the role of guarantor (as any signature would), but this it does more in the spirit of aesthetic guardian than professional connoisseur. Protecting the mystery of the work and the name, alert to the approaches of the curious public, the signature alternates signals of ferocity and fascination. It is 'le ténébreux d'autant qu'apparu gardien d'un génie, auprès comme Dragon, guerroyant, exultant, précieux, mondain' (*Pl.* 532). Situated relative to the illusion in a position we might describe as 'in' but not 'of', the signature occupies a privileged and magical space. And around it, if Mallarmé's work on the name succeeds, there would appear a kind of sublime aura — of the sort, perhaps, we momentarily perceive in that celebrated passage of sublime magnification from 'Prose pour Des Esseintes':

> Oui, dans une île que l'air charge
> De vue et non de visions
> Toute fleur s'étalait plus large
> Sans que nous en devisions
>
> Telles, immenses, que chacune
> Ordinairement se para
> D'un lucide contour, lacune,
> Qui des jardins la sépara. (*O.C.* 248)

Thus it is that, here, the little butterfly finds itself magnified into a dragon — a splendid and imaginary beast.

3

What is — Stéphane Mallarmé?

We are now going to examine the manner in which Stéphane Mallarmé wrote his name into his writings. I should not like the reader to take the third section of this book, however, as the practical application, so to speak, of the second. It should be clear by now that the theory of the name, far from being set in stone, needs itself to be insistently practised and worked over in order to survive as a theory. So any simplistic division of practice from theory would be inadvisable. The present chapter could almost stand on its own as a series or collection of readerly observations regarding the name 'Stéphane Mallarmé' — whether the latter take the form of a pair of initials, a play on the meaning of the forename or surname or indeed of parts thereof, an anagram of the letters of the name, a transposition of its sounds, and so forth. I have tried to present the material in crescendo form: that is, beginning with the most modest examples of a mere *s.m.* or 'paraph' discovered in a poem, and building up to the claim that the name plays an essential role in Mallarmé's conception of nothing less than the sublime. At each stage, my concern will be to show what effect the presence of the name might create, what change it might provoke to our reading of the text in hand; but above and beyond that (and despite my warning against a facile matching up of theory and practice) it will also be to determine to what degree the occasional, unsystematic appearances of the name may nevertheless be fed back into our constant reflection on the onomastics of the poet's mysterious appellation.

Let us begin with the examination of a phrase, the glossing of which will perhaps help us to understand how and why Mallarmé keeps his reader ever alert to the name.

3.1 'un semis de fioritures'

The phrase occurs in the antepenultimate paragraph of the text entitled 'Le Livre, Instrument Spirituel' of 1895 (*Pl.* 381). Having just explained his dissatisfaction with the current state, the physical form even, of both the book and the newspaper, Mallarmé switches exceptionally into italics in order to add:

> *Mais ...*
> — J'entends, *peut-il cesser d'en être ainsi*

And then, in a sentence which to a degree acts out the very process it is describing, he goes on to sketch out a hypothetical text, which the reader will recognize as a projection of 'Un coup de dés', published just two years later in 1897:

> *Pourquoi* — un jet de grandeur, de pensée ou d'émoi, considérable, phrase poursuivie, en gros caractère, une ligne par page à l'emplacement gradué, ne maintiendrait-il le lecteur en haleine, la durée du livre, avec appel à sa puissance d'enthousiasme: autour, menus, des groupes, secondairement d'après leur importance, explicatifs ou dérivés — *un semis de fioritures*. (381; my emphasis)

Many aspects of this sentence make it typical of the late speculative style of *Divagations*. First, the very fact of describing in one actual text another imaginary one, but in such a way as to make the current performance (here, for example, its syntactical suspense) foreshadow or reflect that which the later and probably unrealized project might become. We could equally choose to highlight the ambiguity of the question-form ('Pourquoi [...] ne maintiendrait-il'), hovering in aesthetic abstraction, somewhere between naive interrogation and breathless affirmation. Then again we might stress the appeal to the reader, whose intelligence, if it is to accede to this hypothetical sublime, will be required to 'mettre les choses en scène, elle-même' (cf. 'Igitur', *Pl.* 433).[1] But beyond all that, at the close of the phrase, curiously isolated from it by the dash, and yet by the same means cleverly linked to the very first term — 'Pourquoi' (which suddenly, as if now meaning 'in order to achieve this', appears split in two) — we read also the phrase which concerns us: 'un semis de fioritures'. What does it mean? And why should we now call attention to it?

In response to the second question, we could say that it draws attention to itself. To bring 'semis' and 'fioriture' together in this manner and in this context isolates the enigma at the sentence's close. And given that the phrase reveals nothing less than a vision of Mallarmé's late sublime, the mysterious terms call for closer examination. The *hypsos* that Mallarmé hypothesizes would derive its power essentially from syntax: the reader's awe will be inspired by the sheer effort of lungs that the phrase requires of him. Thus it is probably less the 'grandeur' (indifferently 'de pensée ou d'émoi') which Mallarmé qualifies as 'considérable', than the 'jet' tracing the *hypsos* across the page. This trace, or perhaps the reader's breath, Mallarmé knows will fade. And so, around and about, there must be something else: something sustaining or supportive, or simply distracting. This he describes at first somewhat abstractly as 'des groupes'; but then gives way to the phrase I have highlighted. The latter would thus seem to indicate a key point in Mallarmé's sublime strategy. Now, the primary meaning of 'semis' is, of course, the casting of seeds. In the poetic context, it is tempting to want to blur 'semen' with 'sema', in order to produce 'dissemination', or a broad casting of senses. This would tie in both with the 'fiore' in 'fioriture' and with the notion of a 'flourish' as something excessive and super-fluous. But the term 'semis' conceals another meaning, and one which pulls in quite another direction. Complementary to dispersal, dissemination, and what we might characterize as 'hazardous semantic reproduction', there is another voice to be heard:

> 3. Fig. Ornement fait d'un petit motif répété. 'Reliure ornée d'un semis de fleurs de lis'. (*Petit Robert*)

The *Grand Larousse de la langue française* gives a fuller entry:

> 6. Décoration appliquée sur les reliures de la fin du XVIe et présentant sur les plats la reproduction régulière et symétrique d'un même motif de petite dimension: symbole, initiales, etc.

The dispersal ceases to appear aleatory. It becomes something more like 'disposition'.[2] Far from hazardously scattering meanings or flourishes around his central grand thought or emotion, Mallarmé projects a careful planting and laying out of symbolic flowers or flourishes ... or initials. Surely 'un semis' might also mean the discreet disposition of an infinite number of signatory *s.m.*s? The name, probably in its abbreviated form or 'paraph', would appear as a kind of watermark behind every text. However, as Mallarmé the linguistician at this point might have said, 'trop de régularité nuit' (*Les Mots anglais*, Pl. 1026). The 'semis' of the name must also have its flourish. Which is exactly what the phrase, if read in a different sense, is signalling to us, since 'fioriture' also signifies that additional and supposedly inimitable trait that one gives to one's signature in order to forestall forgery.[3] The phrase 'un semis de fioritures' would therefore come to signify, in Mallarmé's projected sublime, at once the careful, regular planting of his name in the background of his works, a labour of patience and endurance; and yet also its random dispersal, here and there, in the wilder and more spectacular form of an onomastic flourish. In both these activities, stemming from 'un semis de fioritures', we may recognize the authentic presence, the living signature, of Stéphane Mallarmé. Let us now proceed through this disposition of signatures, variety by variety.

3.2 Paraph: 'Monsieur S.M., 29 rue de Moscou'

I shall now consider some examples of texts in which Mallarmé would seem to be alluding to his paraphic *s.m.*. But first some words of caution:

> Les bons sentiments apparaissent fréquemment par le fait de *sm*, ceux qu'impliquent le sourire et le travail honnête. (*Pl.* 948)

Can it be reasonable, when reading this sentence from *Les Mots anglais*, whose status as a source of theory I questioned in section 2.1, boldly to carry one's interpretation beyond a simple reflection on 'smile' and 'smith'? Surely the very choice of those terms, which combine to form a certain image of Mallarmé the crafty poet, would suggest that something other than 'linguistics' is being addressed here. The merest appearance of *s.m.*, it is claimed, will set off certain associations and amongst these must inevitably figure 'Stéphane Mallarmé'. What difference does such a coincidence make?

As we reflect upon the figure *s.m.*, we may first note that the poet made considerable use of his monogram in various communicative situations. We notice it imprinted on letters, gifts, and texts. As such it represents a detail which, without perhaps going to Whistlerean lengths, he thought deserved a certain writerly care and attention.[4] It is tempting, therefore, to bring together the 'theoretical' reflection quoted above with a passage, such as the following, in which Stéphane Mallarmé identifies himself as 'S.M.':

> Les livres de rentrée? Nous sommes prêts à recommander tous les ouvrages adressés à ces initiales: Monsieur S.M., 29 rue de Moscou, par les auteurs ou les libraires, autant qu'indiqués par les familles elles-mêmes; mais en gardant, toutefois, une complète liberté de jugement. (*Pl.* 759)

This juxtaposition of *s.m.*s may, for a while, hold our attention. In this instance the appearance of the paraph indeed evokes work, good feelings, and a polite smile. We may go further, however, and ask whether such a coincidence might in every occurence of the letters *s* and *m* authorize us to see a signature, as well as the tacit, smiling approval of our honest onomastic labour. Therein we evidently run the risk of amassing a somewhat obsessive collection of *s.m.* 'signatures', the vast majority of which, it would be reasonable to suppose, might offer little or no value, either locally — that is, in their immediate poetic context — or more generally, in terms of what they might contribute to a theory of the Name. We should therefore retain at all times a sense of the limits — of plausibility and of interest — traced around our reading of minimal signatures. In the following examples, the highlighting of the paraph will both nuance the immediate reading of the text, and further evoke the possibility of correspondence with the general theory sketched out in the first part of this study. The proposition that such communication exists — between the poetic occasion, the onomastic instance and the virtual existence of our theory — will be confirmed in the following quatrain, which could stand as a kind of garde-fou for this section of our argument:

> Un beau nom est l'essentiel
> Comme dans la glace on s'y mire
> Céline reflète du ciel
> Juste autant qu'il faut pour sourire. (*O.C.* 653)

We look into our names as we look into a mirror. We find ourselves, or rather an image of ourselves. There is room for distortion, for selection. There is certainly a measure of the viewer's imagination in the image ... So we look, as Céline, at 'Céline', and we see 'ciel' (thus neglecting the negative 'ne', which might be sounding a note of caution). What we see is true. But only just. With this joke, and the smile it provokes, Mallarmé disclaims responsibility for any unhappy consequences or excesses his theory might encourage, and the philosophical *agent provocateur* disappears behind a disarming smile. But this closure should be read as a feint, for in the wake of his disappearance the onomastic poet cum Cheshire cat leaves a suggestive theoretical trace. Good feelings, we know, appear frequently by the agency of *s.m.*, those implied by the smile and honest labour. So when we look at the rhyme 's'y mire/sourire', is it not the smile of Stéphane Mallarmé we see reflected there, and especially in the striking initials: 's ('y) m (ire)'? Our suspicions are confirmed by the testimony of the second rhyme pair 'l'essentiel/ciel', since together they (just) write '*S* in the sky', an imaginary apotheosis through the name whose success, to the extent that its effects derive from poetic labour, would seem to conform more convincingly to Mallarmean principles of onomastic glory than did the explicit and exposed apotheosis envisaged by 'La Machine à Gloire'. Just at the point where Mallarmé appears to adumbrate limits to the theory of the name (let your smile of common sense be your measure), the imp-of-the-perverse incites him not only to defy those limits, but also to maintain, serenely smiling, that no such thing as limits may exist where *s.m.* and the greater glory of the name are sovereign. So much for our *garde-fou*!

3.2.1 'Toast': 'dix ans d'avance'

> Rien, cette écume, vierge vers
> A ne désigner que la coupe;
> Telle loin se noie une troupe
> De sirènes *m*ainte à l'envers.
>
> Nous naviguons, ô mes divers
> Ami*s*, *m*oi déjà sur la poupe
> Vous l'avant fastueux qui coupe
> Le flot de foudres et d'hivers;
>
> Une iv*resse* belle m'engage
> Sans craindre *même* son tangage
> De porter debout ce salut
>
> Solitude, récif, étoile
> A n'importe ce qui valut
> Le blanc souci de notre toile. (402)[5]

This is an occasional poem, and a performance. Whatever

meanings or effects it may create, 'Salut' or, as it was first known, 'Toast', signifies primarily what it does: to toast and salute the company gathered for the banquet organized in 1893 by the revue *La Plume*, and presided over, that year, by Stéphane Mallarmé:

> Un fin sourire sur les lèvres, l'oeil tant soit peu extatique, ému, tremblant ainsi qu'une jeune vierge sur qui pèsent les regards de toute une assemblée, le président du septième banquet, ce pur poète, cet homme délicieux, Stéphane Mallarmé, se lève, prend sa coupe, et d'une voix sonore, quoique mal assurée, dit l'exquis poème qui s'inscrit au fronton de cette revue. (*O.C.* 403)

This most self-effacing of texts, this exquisitely blank poem, beginning with nothing and gradually folding itself back into the page and into the infinite potentiality of language, we may nevertheless fix firmly to a precise time and place in the real world. Within the space of the sonnet, Mallarmé pursues and develops this paradox of virtuality and presence in diverse ways (like so many tumbling mermaids). For example, the 'nothingness' ('rien') of the text is also a 'thing' (*res*). The virgin verse still maculates the page. The form that the poem would indicate — the 'coupe' surrounding the bubbles, the blank around the words — exists only thanks to the material cut ('coupe') of the text, or even as the sensible gap ('coupe') between the measures of verse. But the paradox is heightened, and to a degree difficult to surpass, by the intervallic presence of the name. When we hear (line 9, third syllable) '*esse*', and then find our attention rewarded (line 10, fourth syllable) with '*ême*', do we not at that point witness the disappearance of the whole immense theory of impersonality, of anonymity, of a certain textuality, in favour of the initials *s.m.*? The words cede the initiative to the author:

> Une iv*resse* belle m'engage
> Sans craindre m*ême* son tangage

The paraph 'S ... M ...' sings out clearly at the very moment of the salute to 'le blanc souci de notre toile'. The signature (which did

indeed sit like an anchor beneath the text in its original publication, but which inevitably would have to be suppressed in the
book of *Poésies*)[6] now resurges into view, and in such a way as to
suggest that Stéphane Mallarmé was quite happy to carry out 'the
duty of his presence' (cf. 2.1.3 above).

The remaining paraphs (lines 4 and 6) confirm such a commitment, both attaching *s.m.* even more firmly to the circumstance of
February 1893, and also bringing a slight qualification or adjust-
ment to what, in the perspective of literary history, we might call
the 'situation de Mallarmé'.[7] In line 4 the following twinkling of
the initials catches our eye:

De sirènes *m*ainte à l'envers

We see its reflection, with a slight variation, two lines later:

Ami*s*, *m*oi déjà sur la poupe.[8]

In the latter instance, the pause imposed by the comma assures
the variety-in-repetition of the three paraphs: *s m; s, m; esse … ême.*
Equally, it introduces a palpable gap — similar to that moment in
'Tennyson' when Mallarmé asks us to say again ('cette fois, dit,
avec solennité') the name of the poet mysteriously reworked into
the text — into which space the reader's onomastic awe and intelligence are invited to plunge. Lastly, it signals the separation artic-
ulated between the speaker and his public, and more specifically
between 'mes amis' and 'moi', thus raising the doubt of
Mallarmé's positioning relative to the actual audience at the
banquet. He assumes the role of captain, leading them in this
toast, his glass raised at the head of the table towards the imaginary sail-text at the other end; but, as is stated in the poem, this
position of authority ('la poupe') places him behind his young
friends ('l'avant'). In other words, the split of 'Amis, moi' doubly
marks out Mallarmé's separation from his hosts, signalling first
the age gap which necessarily distinguishes the young as the
future generation of poetry, but equally the very special and
specific 'advance' that Mallarmé considers himself to have stolen
not just on the poetry of his time but also on that of the future.
Such an ambiguity admirably expresses Mallarmé's role as false

chef d'école. As he put it more prosaically, and yet to my mind less persuasively, on a different occasion:

> Très affiné, j'ai été dix ans d'avance du côté où les jeunes esprits pareils devaient tourner aujourd'hui. (*Pl.* 664)

3.2.2 'Sainte': 'ténébreux d'autant qu'apparu'

> A la fenêtre recélant
> Le santal vieux qui se dédore
> De sa viole étincelant
> Jadis avec flûte ou mandore,
>
> Est la Sainte pâle, étalant
> Le livre vieux qui se déplie
> Du Magnificat ruisselant
> Jadis selon vêpre et complie:
>
> A ce vitrage d'ostensoir
> Que frôle une harpe par l'Ange
> Formée avec son vol du soir
> Pour la délicate phalange
>
> Du doigt que, sans le vieux santal
> Ni le vieux livre, elle balance
> Sur le plumage instrumental,
> Musicienne du silence.

The poem known as 'Sainte' (*O.C.* 198), written some twenty-eight years before 'Salut', stems likewise from a very specific occasion. On the sixth of December 1865, Mallarmé writes to his friend Théodore Aubanel:

> Je te charge en remettant le billet ci-joint à Brunet, de lire à Madame une 'Sainte Cécile' que je lui avais promise. (*O.C.* 199)

The lady in question is 'Cécile' Brunet, who had earlier that year agreed to be Geneviève Mallarmé's godmother. Concerned there should be no delay in the happy comprehension of this grateful message, the paternal author originally entitled the piece 'Sainte Cécile jouant sur l'aile d'un Chérubin/(chanson et image anciennes)', and signed it 'Stéphane Mallarmé'. Furthermore, although the musical element of the title alludes to the wife and principal addressee, the sender took care not to neglect the husband, Jean Brunet, whose craft of master glassworker is represented by the term 'vitrage'. As if to render his communicative gesture even more appropriate and easily understood, Mallarmé attached a note to the poem, explaining that 'c'est un petit poème mélodique et fait surtout en vue de la musique'. We might consider this move at least a little disingenuous, however, since the development of the poem itself goes on to obliterate the visible signs of musical presence. The viola (like the flute or the mandoline) remains untouched, indeed unseen (1–4); the songbook does not lead the Saint in song (5–8); the only instrument we might hear would be an imaginary harp, formed by the Angel's wing, and played, but only virtually, by the touch of the Saint's finger. The text, like 'Salut' considered above, reads as a hymn to silence and to the power of poetry's virtuality, its theoretical theme coming to drown out the banal occasion of the poem's invention. But what part might the paraph sing (thrice present, as indicated) in such a performance?

Firstly, it completes the address of the text: Cécile is there, as is Brunet; so it is only fitting that the sender should inscribe his initials on the message. Secondly, the paraph marks the supremacy, as demonstrated in this instance, of poetry's 'silent music' over any actual 'heard melodies'. At the same time it identifies such superiority not only with that impersonal, anonymous force called poetry, but also with the work of the specific poet recognizable by the sign *s.m.* In each of the three images which he carefully superimposes one upon the other (the first, unseen, concealed by the window, of the musical instruments; the second, at the window, of the Saint and the book; the third, framed by the borders of the text itself, of the Angel and her harp) the artist insists on placing his signature, with its message: '*s.m.* made me'. But the triple paraph does not merely serve to identify, more or less modestly, the products of one's honest labour; equally, it provokes a broader reflection on the peculiar status and situation of the signature. For the latter lies at once within and without each of these images: the 's ... m ...' of the first quatrain quietly refers to the bolder 'S ... M ....' of the second, and so to the paraph, bottom left (as if sealed off in a cartouche) of the third:

S(ur le plumage instrumental)
M(usicienne du silence).

Via the name, the spectator measures the attention, the involvement, the vertigo perhaps, induced by the illusion's play of depth and perspective. At this point you may halt the abysmal game by definitively invoking the 'real' signature, bottom right, of 1865. Relieved of your readerly duties, you close the book reassured that the only s.m. you can reasonably read is the 'Stéphane Mallarmé' on the manuscript. Yet, as in some Borgesian vision, even with your eyes shut the name continues to flicker (following the formula noted in 'Whistler'): 'le ténébreux d'autant qu'apparu gardien d'un génie'.

3.2.3 'Eventail': 'rien qu'un battement aux cieux'

Mallarmé further thematized and developed such a flickering in the third of the 'Eventail' poems, addressed 'A ma femme. 1er janvier 1891' (389), the other two having been presented to Geneviève (1884) and Méry Laurent (1890) respectively. When reading this text, we should not forget that it was first written in red ink on a fan 'de papier argenté orné d'un simple motif de paquerettes blanches' (O.C. 389). Before pronouncing the first 'Avec', one should first listen carefully for the silent dialogue between a 'semis de fioritures' and the monogram s.m. which the actual object bears:

Avec comme pour langage
Rien qu'un battement aux cieux
Le futur vers se dégage
Du logis très précieux

Aile tout bas la courrière
Cet éventail si c'est lui

74

Le même par qui derrière
Toi quelque miroir a lui

Limpide (où va redescendre
Pourchassée en chaque grain
Un peu d'invisible cendre
Seule à me rendre chagrin)

Toujours tel il appar*aisse*
Entre te*s m*ains sans *paresse* (*O.C.* 388)

The background rhythm of the 'paquerettes blanches' Mallarmé
takes up and develops into the conceit of the poem, transposing
the 'battement' (rhythm and interval) of their appearance into a
metaphor for the poem's creation and for the recreation of poetry
in general.[9] The future verse (the moment of inspiration which the
poem dramatizes) figures as the interruption of a divine silence,
or, perhaps, as an interval of a more perfect silence within that
silence.[10] Mallarmé pursues the 'negative' quality of the 'battement' into the second quatrain, the movement of the fan being
reflected (but is it the same as the flash of inspiration?) in a mirror
behind Madame Mallarmé. The rhyme 'lui/lui' acts out this
miniature drama of doubt, with its brief flash of identity and
difference. The fading of that moment of inspiration or poetic illusion is realized (in the parenthesis of lines 9–12), as the conceit
develops into the image of a messenger-bird shot down in
the very moment of delivering its message.[11] Finally, Mallarmé
telescopes this entire theoretical speculation into the paraphic
signature of the closing couplet:

Toujours tel il apparaisse
Entre te*s m*ains sans *paresse*.

Thanks in part to the polyvalent reference of the masculine
pronoun, the poet, literally situated between 'te*s m*ains', identifies
himself absolutely with the 'vers', the 'éventail', and with this
verse and this fan in particular. At the flash of *s.m.* in the final line,
the poem-object momentarily becomes 'Sté-fan' — then fades into
the smile traced by such a thought. That flicker flirts, however,

with eternity. The optative subjunctive of 'toujours tel il appa-raisse' reveals the immense ambitions hidden behind the too small name. And even as the *s.m.* fades from our mind, we find ourselves ultimately and perhaps eternally reminded that all along the illusion was made 'par S'.

3.2.4 *il reste*: the latest style of 'Brise Marine'

In section 2.3.2 I raised the question of *la durée*. In other words, how does the illusion of the name last? This problem may be approached from a different angle by looking at two texts, 'Brise Marine' of 1865, and *La Dernière Mode* of 1874, whose discreet correspondence Mallarmé uses to show how the name, like its author, may evolve through time.

Brise Marine

La chair est triste, hélas! et j'ai lu tous les livres.
Fuir! là-bas fuir! Je sens que des oiseaux sont ivres
D'être parmi l'écume inconnue et les cieux!
Rien, ni les vieux jardins reflétés par les yeux,
Ne retiendra ce coeur qui dans la mer se trempe,
O nuits, ni la clarté déserte de ma lampe,
Et ni la jeune femme allaitant son enfant.
Je partirai! Steamer balançant ta mâture,
Lève l'ancre vers une exotique nature!
Un Ennui, désolé par les cruels espoirs,
Croit encore à l'adieu *suprême des mouchoirs*!
Et, peut-être, les *m*âts, invitant les orages,
Sont-ils de ceux qu'un vent penche sur les naufrages
Perdus, *sans mâts, sans mâts*, ni fertiles ilôts...
Mais, ô mon coeur, entends le chant des *m*atelots!

The poem bears a paraph, bottom right:

Mais, ô mon coeur, entends le chant des *m*atelots!

We should be confident enough by now to call this a signatory paraph, without any need for further explanation. But just above this, in line 15, we read: 'sans *mâts, s*ans *mâts'* — where the *s.m.* is repeated and also reinforced by the initial letters of the figure. And then, in line 13, a variant: 'Et, peut-être, les *mâts'.* Finally, line 12 also bears the author's initials, written into that most curious phrase: 'l'adieu suprême des *mouchoirs!'*[12] Here might be an instance where we should think about the limits of our pretensions. Does not the very abundance of paraphs here work against any attempt to make them all appear of interest? Is it not just a matter of chance? In reply, we might observe that Mallarmé himself seems to have insisted upon rather than diminished the importance of the signature, since in line 15 he changed the original wording from 'sans mâts ni planche' to the striking 'sans mâts, sans mâts' that we read today (see *O.C.* 177). Furthermore, this change, and the repetition of the monogram throughout the poem, may be read in quite another light, if we note that the close of the poem, where the five paraphs appear, draws its inspiration (and heavily so) from the endings of successive poems in *Les Fleurs du Mal.* Thus 'Le Cygne' closes: 'Je pense aux matelots oubliés dans une île' — and 'Les Sept Vieillards': 'Et mon âme dansait, dansait, vieille gabarre/Sans mâts'.[13] The function of the repeated paraphs would perhaps be to stamp the young poet's name on property stolen from his master (cf. 4.3 below). Now, the identity of Stéphane Mallarmé was of course destined to evolve, and the young poet was successfully to rid himself of the overpowering early influence of Baudelaire. Despite that change, Stéphane Mallarmé remained 'Stéphane Mallarmé'. How, then, to negotiate this evolution, while at the same time remaining true to one's name?

A response may be found in the first two numbers of *La Dernière Mode.* It comes, we should note, not from 'Stéphane Mallarmé' as such, but from two individuals named 'Marguerite de Ponty' and 'Ix'. In his first 'Chronique', the latter, given the season, is discovered contemplating a maritime scene, a fact which alerts us immediately to the possibility of a reference to 'Brise Marine'.[14] This duly arrives, albeit in the form of a correction. Whereas the anguished text of 1865 expressed the Baudelairean desire to: 'Fuir! là-bas fuir!' (*O.C.* 176), the fashionable columnist of 1874 has a very different view of exoticism: 'Fuir ce monde? on en est' (*Pl.* 719) Moreover, speaking in the name of his 'lectrices', Ix claims that, even if we go to the sea, it is not to escape, but rather to repose; and as we contemplate the maritime spectacle before us, it is not the thought of exotic, primitive, alien beauties which springs to mind, but rather a vision of urbanity, spirituality and artifice:

> Vous quittez encore le bois et le fleuve, avides de reposer tout à fait vos yeux dans l'oubli causé par un horizon vaste et nu; n'est-ce pas, certes, pour trouver là une nouveauté de regard habile à goûter le paradoxe de toilettes ingénues et savantes, que l'Océan, au bas, brode de son écume? (Pl. 719)

This reflection on the marine topos of 'Brise Marine' reappears, at once more precise and more complex, in the 'Courrier de la Mode' of the following month. There we find 'Marguerite de Ponty' discussing accessories:

> Quant aux Mouchoirs microscopiques faits pour les plus petites des mains, j'en vois plusieurs, dont un hanneton brodé en couleur occupe l'un des coins portant deux lettres entrelacées rose et bleu ou rouge et bronze, ce qui est, au moins, original. (Pl. 746)

She casts a glance back to the poem of 1865 (where the 'mouchoir' had been sublimely expanded into the imaginary 'toile' of existential escape), thereby wittily transforming the s.m. of the final line ('Mais, ô mon coeur, entends le chant des matelots!') into an embroidered monogram on a poem-handkerchief. Such a radical resituation of the young man's desire is confirmed in the next few lines of the article. Recommending to her readers, entre femmes, the truly indispensable accessory of the season, Madame de Ponty subtly pastiches a passage from 'Brise Marine':[15]

> Mais toutes ces fantaisies de bientôt familières à plusieurs d'entre nous s'effacent devant une restée la parure indiscutable de l'heure, après l'avoir été de la saison; que rien, ni les mois employés à regarder la mer, n'ont fait passer de mode, ni les semaines occupées déjà à chasser sur les terres. (Pl. 746)

This echoes unmistakably lines 4–8 of the poem:

> *Rien, ni* [...]
> *Ne* retiendra
> O nuits, *ni* [...]
> *Et ni* [...]

Should we conclude from this parody that the Mallarmé of 1874 simply found ridiculous the 'Baudelairean' Mallarmé of 1865, and wished here to mark the distance he had taken from his former self? I think it more persuasive to speak of readjustment rather than rejection. After all, according to Barbier and Millan, 'Brise Marine', reprinted in *L'Echo de la Semaine* of the fourth of September 1898, represents 'peut-être le dernier poème publié du vivant de Mallarmé, qui est mort le 9 septembre 1898' (*O.C.* 179). No doubt, then, that Mallarmé remained true to his young name: with less than a week to live, he was happy to sign the youthful sea-piece. But in thus authenticating the text, he was now conscious of the fact that, thanks in part to the rewrite of 1874, he had changed the perspective in which the name would be read. As part of the same process we could perceive the following gesture, repeated annually at New Year, of sending a text-and-handkerchief to Méry Laurent's maid:

> Si vous faites naufrage, Elisa, tout nous sert,
> Agitez ces *m*ouchoirs sur un îlôt désert.

And again:

> Celle ici qui ne prisa
> Que l'amitié simple et franche
> Veut pour son nez
>   Elisa
> *Une pure toile blanche.*

And again:

> Quoique à ses pieds une sultane
> Ensemble n'en voie autant choir

Lisa, recevez de *Stéphane*
Mallarmé maint et maint mouchoir.

The monograms of 'Brise Marine' reappear in a new and
sparkling light. And the young text itself has become the hand-
kerchief with which the poet waves goodbye, if not supremely, to
a writer he no longer is.

3.3 Renown: making a name for yourself

Thus far in this section I have been concerned with the disposition
of the minimal signature or paraph, arguing that the planting of the
initials *s.m.*, essentially in a borderline position, neither within nor
without the illusion, may significantly change our conception of the
text-in-hand. We may measure that change in terms either of the
meaning we assign to the latter, or of its situation in the context of
the real world, or indeed of its relation to other texts within the
corpus signed 'Stéphane Mallarmé'. I have also maintained that this
activity contributes in a more abstract way to the theoretical debate
around the name. Now I shall turn our attention to what I described
in section 3.1 as the 'flourish' of the name, which will involve
focusing on what the name itself in certain poetic contexts might
mean or be made to mean. Whereas in itself *s.m.* signified little
beyond 'Stéphane Mallarmé' (unless it be 'smith and smile') — its
function denotative and strategic, as it were, rather than connotative
— the versions of the name I shall presently discuss offer themselves as so many speculative (and by no means mutually exclusive) meanings of the two terms 'Stéphane' and 'Mallarmé'. We
have already seen how Mallarmé endeavoured to rework the senses
of such names as 'Voltaire', 'Manet', or 'Whistler', creating a
complex poetic illusion around those figures. Now I shall ask how
he approached the representation of himself through his own name,
and how he renamed himself in order to attain renown.

3.3.1 Why not — 'mal-armé'?

'What is — Stéphane Mallarmé?' We may find an answer to this direct question, simply enough, in any dictionary of proper nouns. For example:

Malarmé (Est *-ey*), plus souvent *Mallarmé*, 'mal armé'.[16]

This version of the name, along with it associations of weakness, ill-preparedness, and incompetence, appears so self-evident and prematurely definitive that it should come as no surprise to find the poet adopting a strategy necessarily aimed at recasting those associations, eliminating or attenuating in the process the influence of 'negative' elements, and simultaneously inventing new, more subtle, and potentially more glorious aspects of the given appellation. We should note in passing that the young Stéphane had at an early date tried somewhat naively to change his name. Mondor relates how the unhappy schoolboy took the pseudonym of 'le comte de Bougainvilliers', in order to bespeak a more noble lineage, as well as to avoid the mockery he was evidently ill-armed to repel.[17] Although that first attempt may have failed, its fate resembling to a degree that of Villiers de l'Isle-Adam and his intellectual and genealogical calling-cards, Mallarmé (it is the claim of the pages that follow) proved more successful when in later years he devised a more complex and indeed more underhand approach to the matter of renown, applying even in the domain of nomination his declared preference for 'suggérer' over 'nommer'.[18]

Firstly, then, the notion of being 'mal-armé' he will either exclude from consideration or disarmingly recontextualize. We do find a suggestion of the term in these lines, addressed to (and supposedly being spoken by) Méry Laurent:

Mon goût correct s'est *gendarmé*
Contre ces vers de *Mallarmé*. (*O.C.* 391)

On the whole, however, in order to find such references, we need to look outside the works of Mallarmé himself. For example, in a sonnet felicitously described by Mondor as 'facile et gouailleur', Paul Verlaine, having complained in the octave of the description

THE NAME OF THE POET

of himself and his friend as 'décadent' and 'symboliste', concludes:

> Soit! chacun de nous en somme
> Se voit-il si bien nommé?
> Point ne suis tant enflammé
>
> Que ça, *vers les nymphes*, comme
> Vous n'êtes pas *mal armé*
> Plus que Sully n'est Prud'homme. (*Pl.* 1586)

In accord with the editor of the Pléiade, we may judge less than astounding the effects of such a play. More impressive might be the sonnet that the young and admiring Paul Claudel addressed to his master, as part of a celebratory batch, on the occasion of Mallarmé's fiftieth birthday (that is, incidentally, a mere six years before his death). The reference to the name again occurs in the sestet:

> Gardien pur d'un or fixe où l'aboi vague insulte!
> Si, hommage rustique et témoignage occulte,
> Ma main cherche quoi prendre au sol pour *s'en armer*,
>
> Je choisis de casser la branche militaire
> Dont la feuille à ta tempe honore, *Mallarmé*,
> Amère, le triomphe, et verte, le mystère. (*Pl.* 1636)

It may help the reader to know that the author, at the time of composing the poem, wore uniform: courageously breaking with his military allegiance, he comes to the defence of his ill-armed idol, and crowns him with a now poetic laurel wreath. Such glory, and such a glorious transformation of the militarily ill-armed into the poetically triumphant, Mallarmé, for himself, will achieve by other means. As regards the martial metaphor, we might consider the late self-portrait contained in 'Petit Air (guerrier)', in which the poet figures, standing beside the fireplace, as an imaginary 'tourlourou' ('nom donné par plaisanterie aux soldats de l'infanterie de la ligne' (*O.C.* 429)), the heat of the fire momentarily providing the required illusion of red trousers, just as the poker might pass for an officer's 'baguette':

82

Nue ou d'écorce tenace
Pas pour battre le Teuton
Mais comme une autre menace
A la fin que me veut-on

De trancher ras cette ortie
Folle de la sympathie (*O.C.* 428)[19]

The poet is best-armed with a magician's wand, deflecting the sting of criticism, or transforming it with a spell into a mere tickle. At fifty-three, Mallarmé has long found his true pose, from which (well what do you want of him?) he appears untouchable, insensible even to insult or aggression.

3.3.2 *Larme*: 'Oh! je voudrais pleurer!'

Besides the obvious reference to 'mal armé', the name 'Stéphane Mallarmé' may be alluded to in many different ways: by breaking it down into smaller elements ('Mal', 'larme', 'alarmé', 'alarme', 'fan', '-phane', and so forth) and then alluding to one or more of these, we may effectively open up a vast range of virtual and overlapping meanings for the name, from which to select an appropriate sense for a particular occasion. I propose that we now examine which aspects of the name Mallarmé seems to a greater or lesser degree to have favoured at different points of his career, in order to establish how the name evolved, and how that change was related to the development of his aesthetic vision.

As we read, for example, those early poems contained in the exercise book so aptly entitled *Entre Quatre Murs*, we can hardly help but remark the extraordinary quantity of 'larmes' that are shed by and around the young poet. It is true he had an unhappy childhood. But one may wonder what the reader, any reader, and indeed their first reader, Stéphane Mallarmé, should make of such torrents as these:

Et son oeil souriait mouillé de douces *larmes* (*O.C.* 11)

[...] qu'un ange dans ses rêves
Passe, essuyant de l'aile une *larme* en son oeil! (13)

Et l'onde [...]
Murmure son amour aux herbages en *pleurs.* (40)

Ah! cessez de souffler la tempête
Et d'enfanter les *pleurs*! (45)

Et bénir la famille et sécher quelques *larmes* (50)

Et quand je *pleure,* ô Dieu, [...]
[...] on voit, la *larme* à l'oeil, [...]
On ignore pour qui sa *larme* coule — et prie! (52)

'Aujourd'hui, c'est la *larme* à l'oeil!' [...]
'Hier! les *pleurs*! hier, le deuil!' (54)

'De cerceuils pleins de lys, de *pleurs*!' (55)

Oh! je voudrais *pleurer*! *pleurer* sous la feuillée
Pleurer [...]
— Oh! je voudrais *pleurer*! (57)

De ton ciel ris-tu quand je *pleure*? (59)

J'eus des *pleurs* dans les yeux [...]
Sans *pleurs* je dormirai dans mon tombeau fécond (60)

Une *larme* noyée au sein d'un flot géant! (61)

Sur des autans doutex ne verse point de *larmes*! (68)

Qui vend au prix de *pleurs*, hélas! son fatal charme
[...]
Sous chaque baiser une *larme* (73)

Pâle, j'allais — versant des *larmes* sur chacune (80)

Ses *larmes*, ses amours et ses rêves d'azur [...]
Le classique en frac noir, le romantique en *larmes* (81)

And finally, as if the boy had had enough of the same tearful refrain:

Pleurnichons! Pleurnichons! [...]
Pleurnichez! Pleurnichez! [...]
Pleurnichons! Pleurnichons! (85–86)

What impresses here is the sheer quantity of tears flowing through the poet's early verse. Mallarmé himself later described how, as a young man 'd'âme lamartinienne' (*Pl.* 661), he had written with an inexhaustible fecundity and (as he no doubt viewed the matter subsequently) with an utter lack of judgement and restraint, the pen either falling or having to be wrenched from his tireless fingers.[20] The story of that boy's evolution into what we call 'Stéphane Mallarmé' would have to chart — as a first step out of anonymity, and out of the mass of adolescents 'romantically' scribbling through sleepless and tearful nights — the important decision to leave behind the lachrymose effusions of Lamartine, the elegiac soaking of the gravestone, and to attempt, having found new models in Poe and Baudelaire, to condense all that creative inspirational force into tighter, stronger, and more elegant forms. Very rarely, indeed, do we find the trace of a tear in works subsequent to *Entre Quatre Murs*. We may note, for example, the signatory flourish at the start of the abandoned 'Ouverture d'Hérodiade':

Abolie, et son aile affreuse dans les *larmes*
Du bassin, aboli, qui mire les alarmes (*O.C.* 208).

Or indeed this opening gesture, in the highly Hugolian 'Apparition' of 1863 (*O.C.* 290):

La lune s'attristait. Des séraphins en pleurs (290)[21]

But the tear is otherwise redefined in later works. In 'L'Après-midi d'un faune' of 1876, for instance, the weeping, commemorative topos of Lamartine or Hugo having given way to an erotic scene, the tear appears no longer in the adolescent's eye but rather somewhere between the Faun's lip and the bodies of the nymphs:

> Je t'adore, courroux des vierges, ô délice
> Farouche du sacré fardeau nu qui se glisse
> Pour fuir ma lèvre en feu buvant, comme un éclair
> Tressaille! la frayeur secrète de la chair:
> Des pieds de l'inhumaine au coeur de la timide
> Que délaisse à la fois une innocence, humide
> De *larmes* folles ou de moins tristes vapeurs. (266)[22]

Later, in the 'Chansons bas' of 1888, Mallarmé rewrites the figure into an ironic observation on the art, precisely, of the elegy. The second poem of the sequence is entitled 'Le Marchand d'ail et d'oignons':

> L'ennui d'aller en visite
> Avec l'ail nous l'éloignons.
> L'élégie au *pleur* hésite
> Peu si je fends des oignons. (366)

Given that the melancholic and the sentimental, the Hugolian and the Lamartinian, are dried up sources of inspiration, the adolescent tears must be wiped from 'Stéphane Mal-*larme*-é', in order for the bearer of that name to advance in the path of his glory.

3.3.3 *Lutte et rature du 'Mal'*

We shall now see how Mallarmé operated a similar process of elimination and resituation around another element of the name. That first syllable, 'Mal', rings loud with its capital M, resonating deep in associations, this time, with the author of Les *Fleurs du Mal*. As we shall see more fully in section 4.3, it was inevitable that, in order for Stéphane Mallarmé fully to assume his name, the break had to be made with Charles Baudelaire, who much more decisively than either Lamartine or Hugo had provided the true formative influence on the young poet.

The difference between the two senses of the term 'le mal' (illness and Evil) marks neatly the passage from Mallarmé's first to second manner. In the former, the dead or dying mother (or sister, or little English girlfriend …) fades away like a pale, sick flower. Thus, to the opening verse of part III of 'Sa fosse est fermée': 'O *mal* traître et cruel!' (*O.C.* 47) — the author adds the footnote: 'Harriet Smythe est morte de la poitrine.' However, as the young poet falls increasingly under the influence of Baudelaire, so the sense of 'mal' modulates from fatal ill to fatal evil. The transition may be nicely captured in the poem 'Donnez!' (73), whose tears I have already had reason to enumerate. 'Ayez pitié de moi!', the poem opens, before turning pseudo-Baudelairean:

> La débauche aux seins nus […]
> Fit de moi, me glaçant avant la fin du jour,
> Une fleur sans parfum, un coeur sans poésie!
> Pour me ravir au *mal*, pour me rendre la vie,
>   Il ne faut qu'un rayon d'amour! (*O.C* 73)

Although 'mal' is written without a capital M, the two senses, ill and evil, clearly coincide at this juncture. The flower is sick, because no longer innocent; the boy wishes to be saved from sin, and thus cured of his mortal ill. Much the same goes for the poem 'L'Enfant prodigue' (106) of 1862. Having opened on the ever so slightly Baudelairean: 'Chez celles dont l'amour est une orange sèche', the poem concludes with the speaker plunging his head into the Saint/Whore's nervous thighs, where: 'J'endormirai mon *mal* sur votre fraîche chair' (106). It was written in the stars, however, that the great poet Baudelaire was destined to exert a strong, formative but ultimately transient influence on his young admirer (according to one reader, Mallarmé's early efforts could have been signed 'C.B.'). Nor did the notion of evil (or, for that matter, good) have a lasting role to play in Mallarmé's universe. If we further trace the evolution of the term 'mal' in Mallarmé's writing, we find it slowly being emptied of any moral-religious content, in favour, as was the case with 'larme', of something more erotically charged. In the first version of 'L'Après-midi d'un faune', entitled 'Le Faune/intermède héroïque' and dating from 1865, we hear Iane, one of the two nymphs, argue thus:

> Alors si cette flûte a le *mal* adoré
> Qui m'enivre, ce *mal* jaloux, je le saurai,
>   (elle ramasse la flûte) (*O.C.* 181)

The 'mal' acquires a slightly male accent, which would serve to emphasize pleasure rather than sin. In the final, much revised version of 1876, the sense of 'mal' has remained hopelessly amoral:

> J'accours; quand, à mes pieds, s'entrejoignent
>   (meurtries
> De la langueur goûtée à ce *mal* d'être deux)
> Des dormeuses parmi leurs seuls bras hasardeux
> (266)

This erotic recontextualization of 'mal' may be seen (as was the case with 'larme') to veer towards the ironic, if we consider the 'moral balance' sketched out in the following quatrain, accompanying a photograph of Méry Laurent:

> Cette dame a pour nom Méry
> Et tient de tout juste balance
> Déjà son sourire a guéri
> Le *mal* que son regard te lance. (578)

The smile (indicative, we know, of *s.m.*) weighs in the moral scales against an 'ill' which Mallarmé now conceives more in terms of an erotic itch than an evil force, and whose only judge will be the object of its desire.

3.3.4 *Alarmé — moi?*

The term 'alarmé' at the heart of 'Mallarmé' presents us with a paradox, from which we may draw a certain dynamic in the name's evolution. Although 'alarmé' connotes the kind of fear, ill-preparedness, or panic which might lead us to confuse it with 'mal-armé', the word in its origins signifies a call to arms (*all'arme!*), that is to say, a response, a reaction, an attempt to defend oneself and fight back. So we may wonder whether

88

Stéphane Mallarmé was found ill-armed at the moment of alarm, or whether on the contrary he was prepared to join onomastic battle.

In 'Carrefour des demoiselles' (1862), we find the following rhyme, which would seem to confirm the portrait of the artist in a state of panic:

> Fort mal noté par les gensdarmes
> Le garibaldien *Mallarmé*
> Ayant encore plus d'arts que d'armes
> Semblait un Jud très-*alarmé* (O.C. 123)

Similarly, the appearance of the word 'alarmes' in early texts would suggest that the term forms one of those elements which the poet must eliminate or redefine in his name. Indeed, 'alarmes' occurs essentially as the partner of the soon-to-be-dispensed-with 'larme', as, for example, in 'Prière d'une mère': 'Elle vit s'envoler ses pieuses *alarmes*' (11) — and again in 'Réponse': 'Interroger le flot, l'âme grosse d'*alarmes*' (68) — as well as the opening rhyme of 'Hérodiade', already cited. Apart from these instances, where fear induces a tearful outburst, I find no further sign of alarm in Mallarmé: unless it be a feint, which is surely the case, some twenty years later, in the opening quatrain of 'M'introduire dans ton histoire':

> *M'*introduire dans ton histoire
> C'est en héros *effarouché*
> S'il a du talon nu touché
> Quelque gazon de territoire (O.C. 320)

That first *M*, its apostrophe marking an absence, demands of the reader the rest of the name, which is duly supplied at the end of line 2, thanks to the synonym of 'effarouché':

> M' ...
> ... (alarmé)[23]

In the context of the poem, Mallarmé feigns a display of alarm and unconvincing resistance (either before the advances of a lover, or faced with the approaching interpretive ardour of the critic)[24] both of which will soon yield, as the conceit unfolds, to the easy victory of the pretended opponent and the spectacular joy of the closing sunset or sonnet.

3.3.5 *Aux armes!*

Such a reversal — of seeming alarm into jubilant triumph — emblematizes the whole process of renaming-into-renown, under whose sign I have placed the current section. In order fully to experience that renaissance, we must switch our attention from the overdetermined surname 'Mallarmé' towards the forename 'Stéphane': or rather, as we should say, 'Etienne', for such was the forename with which our poet was baptized.[25] The baptismal name 'Etienne' unavoidably carries with it a reference to the story of the Saint and first Christian martyr. I shall now relate that story in a version particularly pertinent to our study, and undoubtedly well known to Etienne Mallarmé. It comes from Hugo's 'Les Malheureux', the poem which closes Book 5 of *Les Contemplations*:

> Une nuit que j'avais, devant mes yeux obscurs,
> Un fantôme de ville et des spectres de murs,
> J'ai, comme au fond d'un rêve où rien n'a plus de
> forme,
> Entendu, près des tours d'un temple au dôme
> énorme,
> Une voix qui sortait de dessous un monceau
> De blocs noirs d'où le sang coulait en long ruisseau;
> Cette voix murmurait des chants et des *prières*.
> *C'était le lapidé qui bénissait les pierres;*
> *Etienne le martyr, qui disait: — O mon front,*
> *Rayonne*! Désormais les hommes s'aimeront;
> Jésus règne. O mon Dieu, récompensez les hommes!
> Ce sont eux qui nous font les élus que nous sommes.
> *Joie! amour! pierre à pierre, ô Dieu, je vous le dis,*
> *Mes frères m'ont jeté le seuil du paradis!*[26]

The poem proposes a procession of martyrs, and an argument

(whose power would derive from the accumulated force of its repetition and redundance) celebrating the reversal of an apparently sombre fate and anticipating the glory found in seeming defeat. A few lines further on, for example, we find:

Eh bien, non! — Le sublime est en bas. Le grand choix,
C'est de choisir l'affront. De même que parfois
La pourpre est déshonneur, souvent la fange est
lustre. (291)

And then the conclusion (which is not to say that Hugo, still good for another two hundred lines or so, will stop there):

L'abjection du sort fait la gloire de l'homme.

So the story of Saint Etienne offers not only an exemplary and sublime martyrdom, but also a splendid appeal to the powers of poetic (and, as we shall see, onomastic) transformation. It is with the very material ('pierre') of his defeat that the Saint will build his victory. Indeed, the entire interminable poem might be restrained to that one rhyme and slight transposition: 'pierre/prière'. In the same fashion, the poet-martyr will construct his glory out of language such as he finds it. More specifically he will take the onomastic material of the name 'mal armé' and transform the ugliness and aggression of the epithet into a sublime appellation.[27] The poem represents an object lesson and a source of inspiration for Etienne Mallarmé, not only convincing him of the potential salvation of his unfortunate surname but also showing him practically how to render his forename more mysterious and powerful. When the martyr cries 'O mon front,/Rayonne!', he is quite simply and literally inciting the name 'Etienne' to assume its mystical form 'Stéphane'. Before our darkened eyes, Etienne adopts the *stephanos*, the Greek version of the name signifying 'couronne' and, more precisely, the laurel wreath of poetic triumph now shining radiantly on Stéphane Mallarmé's forehead. The switch marks the passage from martyr to Saint, from victim to victor, but also the counter-move from one name to another, from the given of language to the sublime surname.

Such an apotheosis — aesthetic, in truth, rather than religious — Stéphane Mallarmé had frequently imagined for himself, as he tells us in that early 'poème critique' entitled 'Symphonie littéraire':

> Dans une apothéose, il siège sur un trône d'ivoire, couvert de la pourpre que lui seul a le droit de porter, et le front couronné des feuilles géantes du laurier de la Turbie. (*Pl.* 265)[28]

But in order that the 'fête du poète' should figure as something more than an ill-armed dream, the laurels must be earned. This will come to pass in the long and daily labour of the poet, working and reworking the illusion of his name, conscientious and conscious that 'on se joue tout entier, de nouveau, chaque fois, n'étant autre que tous sans rester different, à volonté'. In the next section I shall accordingly consider how such a reflection on the nature of illusion may be incorporated into the construction of the name.

3.4 *Phainein:* 'Comme dans la glace on s'y mire'[29]

The preceding section has brought us to an apotheosis of the poet envisaged through the name. 'Etienne' is reborn as 'Stéphane' through the adoption of the *stephanos*, a crown symbolic of a certain triumph over adversity, but also, in more strictly poetic terms, symbolic of the poet's victory over the dull or base of language. This 'sublimation' of the name sees the latter 'surgir à un nouveau devoir', becoming momentarily (and, by ever-renewed labour, eternally) something more than a mere appellation, and finding itself magnified into the illusion of something more than mere appearance. 'Stéphane Mallarmé' itself becomes a sublime illusion. Such an assertion, dressed up though it be in its neo-alchemical robes,[30] begs nevertheless two questions: 'What, in this instance, is meant by 'illusion'? And what, similarly, by 'sublime'?' In the next two sections of this study, I shall consider how these problems may be addressed in the context of the workings of the name.

3.4.1 *bhā*: 'Qu'est-ce qu'une "racine"?'

What happens when we decide to split the name 'sté-phane' in order to bring out the illusory nature ('phainein') of the *stephanos*? We may see such a separation taking place in the following signature, from 'Toast Funèbre' of 1875:

> Une agitation solenelle par l'air
> De paroles, pourpre ivre et grand calice clair,
> Que, pluie et diamant, le regard dia*phane*
> Resté là sur ces fleurs dont nulle ne *se fane*,
> Isole parmi l'heure et le rayon du jour! (*O.C.* 243)

In the context of the poem, the signature serves to awaken (for Stéphane Mallarmé, one might think, rather than the celebrated Théophile Gautier) the mystery of a name (see lines 32–35 of the poem). In more abstract terms, the name 'Stéphane', which our critical eye perceives beneath the transparency of the text, reveals itself as in an x-ray. The '-phane' of 'Stéphane' refers (via 'diaphane') back to the Greek 'phainein', thereby 'appearing' or 'shining' all the more strongly. At the same time the rhyme-partner 'se fane' reminds us of the passing or fading of that same illusion. This would suggest that the action of concentrating or expanding upon the '-phane' of 'Stéphane' may prove treacherous, the very desire to enhance the appearance of the name might finish by destroying it. Something of that doubt arises in the only other instance where 'faner' forms part of the signature, namely in line 12 of 'Don du Poème':

> Avec le doigt *fané* presseras-*tu* le sein? (192)

A slight reworking of the highlighted elements gives:

> … fan … é … s … t …

The father of the poem asks the mother to nourish his monster, but the simultaneous appearance of the paternal 'seing' complicates the giving of the gift, and compromises the familial sentimentality of the scene. As a result the illusion created by this curious 'fragment' of 'Hérodiade' seems already to fade around its closing

question mark.[31] The presence of 'phainein' in 'Stéphane' introduces a potentially destructive element into the complex of signifiers around the poet's name. I shall argue, however, that
Mallarmé succeeds in folding into his signature a sustained and
self-conscious reflection on illusion itself, which ultimately will
add to rather than diminish the accumulated mystery of 'Stéphane
Mallarmé'. Firstly, we might ask ourselves whether any evidence
exists that Mallarmé himself had thought through the problems
posed by 'phainein'. Certainly, had he looked at an etymological
dictionary, he would have discovered that the Greek 'phainein'
(meaning 'briller', 'paraître', 'luire') may be traced back to the
radical 'bhā', which in Sanscrit produces, for example, 'bhā-ti' ('il
luit, il éclaire'); 'bhā' becoming 'bhē' and then 'φαε', which gives
'φαμι', meaning 'briller' etc. However, he would likewise have
found that the same root, 'bhā', lies also at the source of the Greek
word 'φημι', meaning 'dire'. The felicitous confusion of speech
and illusion and a splendid revelation of the poet's mission are
grounded in the notion that to speak is to 'rendre clair par des
mots, annoncer'. The second branch of 'bhā' has also made its way
into French, via the Latin 'fari' and in the shape, for example, of a
word such as 'enfant' (which signifies, at root, 'not speaking'). So
the dictionary would have revealed to an etymologically curious
Mallarmé not only that 'to speak' (to announce, to utter, to explain)
and 'to appear' (to seem, to shine, to show) derive radically from
the same source, but also that those same verbs and sources
appear or speak in his own name 'Stéphane'. One does not really
need, however, to construct such an original scene of discovery:
the poet astounded by the revelation within his name of his life's
work. Harder evidence may be found in *Les Mots anglais*:

> Qu'est-ce qu'une *racine*? Un assemblage de lettres, de
> consonnes souvent, montrant plusieurs mots d'une
> langue comme disséqués, réduits à leurs os et à leurs
> tendons, soustraits à leur vie ordinaire, afin qu'on
> reconnaisse entre eux une parenté secrète. (*Pl.* 962)

In the table that follows, we read:

BHĀ, montrer (φημι, fari, etc.)

Thus Mallarmé the pedagogue and linguistician points us first, with 'montrer', to one branch of the 'bhā'-tree, and then, with the Latin 'fari', switches happily and as if there were no difference to the second, 'speaking' branch. Scientifically speaking, language and appearance are one — and bah! to the non-believer.

We know, then, that the root of both speech and illusion lies in the name 'Stéphane', and we know that Mallarmé knew this. We have also seen how the very act of focusing on this fact might provoke the collapse or fading of our onomastic constructions. Let us now consider how Mallarmé appears to negotiate such a delicate passage, as we examine a pair of texts — 'Fenêtres' and 'Apparition' — both explicitly concerned with the question of illusion and irrefutably featuring the signature of Stéphane Mallarmé.

3.4.2 *fenestra*: 'Mais chez qui le rêve se dore'[32]

A mere glance at the title — 'Les Fenêtres' (*O.C.* 400) — recalls 'phainein' and, by the same token, identifies the poet (who will make a more elaborate appearance in the eighth stanza) with the name of the poem. Indeed, with a little etymological juggling, we may rewrite 'fenêtre' as 'phan-être', and thus neatly represent the split (between being and illusion, spirit and matter) which runs through the text.[33] Moving beyond the title, we find that the poem too is split, namely into two equal parts of twenty lines each. The division occurs with 'Ainsi' in line 21, when the opening description of a sick man turning away from the misery of the hospital in which he finds himself, and experiencing, through the window, a vision of Baudelairean luxury (for example, in line 20: 'Dans un grand nonchaloir chargé de souvenirs!'), gives way (via 'Ainsi') to a parallel evocation of the speaking subject's existential torment:

> Ainsi […]
> Je fuis et je m'accroche à toutes les croisées
> D'où l'on tourne l'épaule à la vie, et, béni,
> Dans leur verre, lavé d'éternelles rosées,
> Que dore le matin chaste de l'Infini
> Je me mire et me vois ange! (*O.C.* 400)

The 'je' turns away from the horrors of matter towards a vision of his transformation into some sort of angel or saint, before the poem closes ('Mais, hélas!') with a brutal return to reality and a cry of despair. Although such a thematic development may, in truth, appear somewhat banal, we shall find, by rereading it through the name, an ulterior train of thought more pertinent to our concerns. In line 21, for example, at the hinge of the poem, the material world on which 'I' turns his back is represented by 'l'homme à l'âme dure'. The suggestion here of a signature ('malâm') introduces a novel element into the play of oppositions and doubles dominating the text. The 'je' of lines 21–40 is assimilable to the 'moribond sournois' of lines 1–20; 'Stéphane Mallarmé' is not assimilable to 'l'homme à l'âme dure' that he stands opposed to, as if in a mirror; but a resemblance exists between the surname and the epithet (as there does between the forename 'sté-phane' and the title 'fen-être'), and it is precisely this resemblance which, in the seventh and eighth stanzas, must be reworked and sublimated into a more fitting self-portrait:

> Je *me mire et me* vois ange! et je *meurs, et j'aime*
> — Que *la* vitre soit *l'art*, soit la *mysticité*
> — A renaître, portant mon rêve en diadème,
> Au ciel antérieur où fleurit la Beauté!

As a first step, 'l'homme à l'âme dure' is recast. The multiple *m's* of line 29 accumulate at the rhyme in 'aime', thus preparing for the full signature of line 30:

> (M) ... a ... l'art ... m ... é

'Mallarmé' thus identifies himself in a sense with the 'je' of the poem, but only at the point where 'je' has become an angel. The name reappears in a splendid vision of rebirth, but on top of that acquires the radiant extra of the *stephanos*. It is indeed in the shape of the stephanized 'Etienne' that 'I' or Stéphane Mallarmé is now reborn, 'portant mon rêve en diadème'.

Faced with such a vision, the reader's intelligence might hesitate: Could life and art really be so easy that one may simply

'renaître' through a 'fenêtre'?[34] Surely the rhyming coincidence of
the two terms, bringing us back once more to the complex around
'phan-être', might just as easily undo what it has so impressively
coupled. The match may well bring 'being' ('être') and 'rebirth'
('renaître') together as one, but by the same token it leaves over
'phan-' as an indeterminable and perhaps disillusioning extra to
the scene. In the immediate context of 'Les Fenêtres', this
consciousness of the illusion causes the latter to crack:

Mais, hélas! Ici-bas est maître

The fading of imaginary splendour may be heard in the
'Stéphane' which fails, just, to materialize in line 32:

Au ciel antérieur où fleurit la beauté.

The forename dies a death:

… s … té … f … a …

Or rather, a suicide, heard falling through eternity in the final
lines:

Et de m'enfuir, avec mes deux ailes sans plumes,
— Au risque de tomber pendant l'éternité?[35]

Against such despair, however, we may struggle, and if we allow
a bit of eternity to pass, we may relativize the 'Mais' of line 33.
Firstly, we should point out that what Mallarmé has failed to flee
or to fly from (in 1865) is the problem of Baudelaire. The scene, the
themes, even certain complete lines, one could mark 'C.B.'. But if
we examine closely the circumstances of 'Les Fenêtres', we shall
see that the poem represents, in a very literal sense, an attempt to
surpass the earlier master. According to Barbier and Millan (*O.C.*
145), the poem actually began as a form of attack on Baudelaire.
In a letter addressed by the poet to his friend Cazalis in 1863,
Mallarmé declares:

La sottise d'un poète moderne [C.B.] a été jusqu'à se

désoler que 'l'Action ne fût pas la soeur du Rêve' [...]
Dire 'Je suis heureux' c'est dire 'Je suis un lâche' — et
plus souvent 'Je suis un niais' [...] J'ai fait sur ces
idées un petit poème *Les Fenêtres* et je te l'envoie.

In line 35 of 'Les Fenêtres', should one therefore identify the
'Bêtise' of this world with the 'sottise' of Baudelaire, and the
'maître ici-bas' with an imaginary 'maître C.B.'? With these questions in mind, we could read the failure or falling away of the
closing two stanzas as the frustrated ambition to write fully and
independently the name 'Stéphane Mallarmé' over and beyond
that of 'Charles Baudelaire'.

Some thirteen years into the long life of 'les Fenêtres', an
answer to this call, and to the question of the final line, may be
perceived in the sonnet entitled 'Une dentelle abolit ...' (*O.C.* 326).
The sestet of that poem sounds an echoing 'Mais':

> *Mais* chez qui le rêve se dore
> Tristement dort une mandore
> Au creux néant musicien
> Telle que vers quelque *fenêtre*
> Selon nul ventre que le sien,
> Filial on aurait pu *naître*.

The final rhyme revives the old pair 'fenêtre/naître'.[36] But the
'mais' does not in this instance represent a conjunction of disaster.
On the contrary, it counters the negativity of the octave, the
'néant' becoming, as it were, 'naissant', and the 'phan-être'
successfully coming into being as a ghostly baby. Mallarmé
succeeds in producing music 'selon nul ventre que le sien', and
accordingly we may conclude that, this time, and firmly *chez soi*,
he has given rebirth to himself as his own man.

3.4.3 'j'ai cru voir': 'Apparition'

As a preliminary step, and as a means of justifying the concentration of so much interpretive ardour on a mere title, we should
first note Mallarmé's fondness for the term 'apparition' to
describe himself, his actions or his way of being. Thus, in a

famous letter of 1867, he portrays himself in the following
manner:

> C'est t'apprendre que je suis maintenant impersonnel
> et non plus Stéphane que tu as connu, — mais une
> aptitude qu'a l'Univers spirituel à se voir et à se
> développer, à travers ce qui fut moi. Fragile comme est
> mon *apparition* terrestre, je ne puis subir que les
> développements absolument nécessaires pour que
> l'Univers retrouve, en ce moi, son identité. (*Corr.* I, 242)

Twenty years on, Mallarmé still sees himself in similar terms,
although the 'philosophical' explanations may have disappeared.
Occasionally, he confesses, one may catch a glimpse of him in
worldly Paris:

> Quelques *apparitions* partout où l'on monte un ballet,
> où l'on joue de l'orgue. (*Pl.* 664)

Or at solitary Valvins:

> Là je *m'apparais* tout différent, épris de la seule
> navigation fluviale. (*Pl.* 664)

And then in the particular context of *La Dernière Mode*, with its
celebrated variety of identities, the following phrase speaks
volumes about how Mallarmé conceived his worldly apparition:

> Nous *apparaîtrons*, partout le même (*Pl.* 718)

A play of names on a backdrop of fidelity. Such constancy is
reflected in the way he remained true to both 'Les Fenêtres' and
'Apparition': the former evolving over a period of some thirty
years, the latter, although first written in 1863–64, appearing as
late as 1898 in *L'Echo de la Semaine*, and even with a minor alter-
ation to the text. It would seem clear, then, that 'apparition' as a
title (and regardless of its evocation of 'phainein') counted for
Stéphane Mallarmé. However, it had also already counted for
someone else, since, just as 'Les Fenêtres' bore strong signs of the

influence of Baudelaire, so we may locate a strong pretext for 'Apparition', but this time in the works of Victor Hugo. Book 5 of *Les Contemplations* includes a poem entitled 'Apparition':

Je vis un ange blanc qui passait sur ma tête

Mallarmé seems incontrovertibly to have drawn inspiration from Hugo's 'Apparition', his own angelic vision echoing the pretext's finale:

Et je voyais, dans l'ombre où brillaient ses prunelles,
Les astres à travers les plumes de ses ailes.[37]

Moreover, the critical tradition — according to which the poem, rather than being a portrait of either of its declared models, Ettie Yapp or Marie Gerhardt (see *O.C.* 291), would represent the evocation of Mallarmé's lost sister, Maria, or of one of his sickly childhood loves — has placed 'Apparition' in the memorializing genre of *Les Contemplations*. However, an even more precise reflection of Hugo may be discovered, not, as we might expect, in *Les Contemplations* (the mood of which, to be sure, dominates Mallarmé's 'Apparition'), but rather in *Les Chants du crépuscule*, and more specifically in the poem entitled 'A l'homme qui a livré une femme'. It is a typical piece of Hugolian occasional bombast, the firepower in this case being directed against a certain Simon Deutz, who had betrayed the duchess de Berry, after the latter's failed attempt at starting a rebellion in the Vendée in 1832. Not a very Mallarmean pretext, you will admit! But the evidence is irrefutable:

Sans qu'un ami t'abrite à l'ombre de son toit,
Marche, autre juif errant! marche avec l'or qu'on voit
Luire à travers les doigts de tes mains mal fermées!
Tous les biens de ce monde en grappes parfumées
Pendent sur ton chemin, car le riche ici-bas
A tout, hormis l'honneur qui ne s'achète pas![38]

With this we should compare the close of Mallarmé's 'Apparition', where in the bottom righthand corner we read the following signature:

100

Et j'ai cru voir la fée au chapeau de clarté
Qui jadis sur mes beaux sommeils d'enfant gâté
Passait, *laissant toujours de ses mains mal fermées*
Neiger de blancs bouquets d'étoiles parfumées. (O.C. 290)[39]

We first note the little run of paraphs:

... s(e)s m(ain)s m(al) ...

But this suddenly expands beyond the 'grip' of the verse into something more conclusive:

... *mal* (fe)-*rmé*-(es) ...
... (p)-*ar*-(fu)-*mé*(es) ...

The young poet simply steals a couplet from '[celui qui] était le vers personnellement' (*Pl.* 360), and turns it into a signature of his own name.[40]

Now, 'Apparition' differs from its partner 'Les Fenêtres' in that it bears no apparent sign of fading or failure. But it does include that necessary reflection on the nature of illusion, as these lines testify:

Quand avec du soleil aux cheveux, dans la rue
Et dans le soir, tu m'es en riant *apparue*
Et j'ai cru voir la fée *au chapeau de clarté*

The recollection of the title at the rhyme might indicate to the reader the limits of his credulity, as does the qualifying 'croire' which precedes the vision. However, such a frontier is abolished at once by the crucial intervention of the 'chapeau de clarté', forming around Mallarmé's forehead and around the text itself the little extra of the *stephanos* or 'lucid contour', where the illusion reflects upon itself as illusion. It remains now to be seen (in the next section) whether that little extra constitutes what we call 'the sublime'.

Before responding to such a question, and before entering into the higher realm it evokes, we could do well to consider the following parody of the *stephanos*, with which Mallarmé was inspired when asked by the *Figaro* in January 1897 for his solemn opinion on the 'chapeau haut de forme' (*Pl.* 881). 'Monsieur,' he begins, 'vous m'effrayez de toucher à un sujet tel'. Why such horror, albeit feigned? Because the top-hat is the *stephanos*, and its mystery something to be protected from the vulgar! Thus, not only does Mallarmé reproach the journalist for his audacity in trying to resume the latter 'dans la colonne d'un quotidien', but he must also describe his own efforts (to comprehend the top-hat) in terms similar to those used to evoke that most sublimely unrealizable of projects, the 'Livre':

> Moi, il fournit, presque seul, voici des temps, ma méditation, et je n'estime à moins que plusieurs tomes d'un ouvrage compact, nombreux, abstrus, la science pour le résoudre et passer outre. (*Pl.* 881)

The top hat is projected as the future *stephanos* or 'chapeau de clarté' for the future work:

> Quoi — il commence, seulement, dans sa diffusion furieuse, à faucher les diadèmes, les plumes et jusqu'aux chevelures; il continuera!

The identification is complete when Mallarmé parodies his most notorious comment on the 'Livre':

> Le monde finirait, pas le chapeau: probablement même il exista de tous temps, à l'état invisible. Aujourd'hui, chacun ne passe-t-il pas à côté sans l'apercevoir?

But the mere fact that the *stephanos* might be invisible does not affect Mallarmé's superior vision:

> Néanmoins je dois dire que je le considère, chez autrui, avec qui il me semble faire un — et, me salue-t on, je ne le sépare, en esprit, de l'individu; je l'y vois, encore, pendant cette politesse. Immuablement.

Which would be a way of showing that fidelity and application to the illusion (be it sublime) of one's name (be it sublime also) do not exclude the recognition of humour.[41]

3.5 Sublime: 'l'attention que sollicite quelque papillon blanc'[42]

A thorough study has been devoted to the question of 'Mallarmé and the Sublime' in the book of that title by Louis Marvick.[43] His analysis is divided into two parts, the first of which presents the evolution of the sublime from Longinus through Kant and beyond; the second focusing on those instances where Mallarmé actually employs the term 'sublime', and examining its evolution in specific and Mallarmean contexts. For the purposes of this section, I shall respect Marvick's method (albeit adapted to our onomastic concern), firstly endeavouring to detach those aspects of the discourse around the sublime which seem pertinent to the interest in the name I have thus far pursued, and then discussing in detail one particular instance (see Marvick, 99–109), where attention to the name and attention to the sublime appear to converge.

3.5.1 *dépassement* and *praeteritio*

'En parlant du sublime, Longin est lui-même très sublime.' Boileau's memorable remark (see Marvick, 14) sums up much of the paradoxical charm of the sublime. The recognized founder of that discourse, Longinus, wanted to distinguish clearly and qualitatively between sensation and rhetoric in his presentation 'of the grand'. The sublime effect would have to be more than its rhetorical cause. And yet his treatise is a rhetorical handbook, whose didactic force would aspire to teach access to the sublime. This paradox may also be expressed in terms of a *dépassement*: the sublime surpasses itself, just as it surpasses the figures which seemingly produce it. In order to convince the reader that 'the sublime' is not just another name or critical term, the performance of the writer-about-the-sublime must appear 'itself very sublime'. The Kantian sublime, which is concerned with natural rather than literary phenomena, similarly privileges the notion of *dépassement* (Marvick, 67). In the three stages of the sublime, each phase outdoes its predecessor: thus, the first stage ('the experience of the beautiful') witnesses a balanced, untroubled state of representation and comprehension; this gives way in the second phase to unease, as the experience of the sublime literally overwhelms the mind, which is left, in Marvick's phrase, 'incongruously grappling with too much or too many'; but in the third stage, there occurs a further *dépassement*, as 'reason intervenes and presents the idea of totality or infinitude'. The subject is left to bathe in the 'peculiar state of mind' produced by the 'aggrandizement of reason at the expense of reality and the imaginative apprehension of reality' (see Marvick, 65–67). But Marvick is a literary man, and will only be satisfied by literature. Thus when he turns to Mallarmé, he wants to find rhetorical equivalents to what he felicitously describes as the 'trumpcard-like function [of reason's ideas] in the sublime moment' (Marvick, 67). It is *praeteritio* that reveals itself as the key figure in this domain, pursuing a development similar to that of Kant's sublime: the happy relationship between language (representation) and its object is overwhelmed by an object suddenly beyond the grasp of language (or of the present author's abilities); but the very idea of this incapacity (via the figure *praeteritio*) saves the day and represents the sublime moment in all its lucid complexity. We may add that, in the literary domain, the term 'sublime' is itself transformed: in accordance with the domination of *praeteritio*, the actual appearance of the word 'sublime' must always mark a necessary strategic retreat, to the extent that if we say 'this is sublime', we are in fact saying 'this is an effect which the mere term "sublime" fails to convey'. As a result, the number of stages towards the sublime, far from stopping at three, would be unlimited, and, as in the discourse of the name, the sublime effort must constantly be renewed and the effect infinitely reinvented. In other words, 'when speaking of the sublime …'.[44]

3.5.2 'cette lecture trop sublime'

Marvick's analysis of 'Symphonie littéraire, I' provides an excellent demonstration of the sublime in action.[45] He declares that 'this text is constructed entirely under the sign of *praeteritio*' (103),

the latter being considered as 'a means of protecting one's enthusiasm from ridicule — a means that permits one to name things
while protesting that one is not naming them' (101). He shows
how Mallarmé, as an opening gesture, takes pains first to abase
himself before the impossibility of his subject, the suite opening
with an appeal to the 'Muse moderne de l'Impuissance', and
describing the present writer as 'une âme purement passive qui
n'est que femme encore, et qui demain peut-être sera bête' (Pl.
261).[46] The young Mallarmé takes self-abasement to an extreme,
insisting upon his inability to express anything at all, let alone the
three 'sublimes' which are to follow. Then, in the first twist of
praeteritio, he calmly ignores this self-condemnation, and
proceeds, in the second paragraph, to describe nothing less than
a 'Paradise'. Such an idyllic and (one would think) 'sublime'
moment, however, must be sustained, if it is not to fade. Where
might we find a language more sublime than the sublime?
Mallarmé again proclaims himself unfit for the task, turning
instead to the poetry of one of his senior predecessors. It is
Théophile Gautier's verse which will bring us to a second
strategically placed peak:

> Bientôt une insensible transformation s'opère en moi,
> et la sensation de légèreté se fond peu à peu en une de
> perfection. Tout mon être spirituel, — le trésor
> profond des correspondances, l'accord intime des
> couleurs, le souvenir du rythme antérieur, et la
> science mystérieuse du Verbe, — est requis, et tout
> entier s'émeut, sous l'action de la rare poésie que
> j'invoque, avec un ensemble d'une si merveilleuse
> justesse que des jeux combinés résulte la seule
> lucidité. (*Pl.* 262)

But then arises a second crisis (in truth, a simple repetition of the
first): how to maintain, or respond to, such perfection with such a
poor instrument as language? The reply found to the terrible
question 'Maintenant qu'écrire?' should be familiar to those who
frequent the sublime topos and the figure of *praeteritio*: 'Donc je
n'ai plus qu'à me taire'. But the withdrawal into silence constitutes a second tactical retreat, behind which appears the

inevitable 'toutefois' (or 'mais' or 'cependant' etc.) and the final *dépassement* that it introduces:

> Toutefois, — au bord de mes yeux calmes s'amasse une larme dont les primitifs diamants n'atteignent pas la noblesse; — est-ce un pleur d'exquise volupté? Ou peut-être, tout ce qu'il y avait de divin et d'extra-terrestre en moi a-t-il été appelé comme un parfum par cette lecture trop sublime? De quelle source qu'elle naisse, je laisse cette larme, transparente comme mon rêve lucide, raconter qu'à la faveur de cette poésie [...] une âme dédaigneuse du banal coup d'aile d'un enthousiasme humain peut atteindre *la plus haute cime de sérénité* où nous ravisse la beauté. (262; Mallarmé's emphasis)

The tear will nevertheless speak, and that which it relates will take us beyond the sublime, or at least beyond the mere term 'sublime', since the reading of Théophile Gautier represented already a point qualified as 'trop sublime'. Such is the essence of the sublime, always seemingly grander than the apparently present 'sublime', the true sublime being to the term 'sublime' what the 'sur-name' is to the mere epithet. Now, in that final *dépassement*, may we also detect an 'extra' of the name? It would be very tempting to highlight 'larme' as the vehicle of the sublime in the passage just cited, especially if we add that in 'Symphonie littéraire, II' and 'Symphonie littéraire, III' tears appear again,[47] and that, in 'Symphonie littéraire, I' itself, we may read the following signature:

> ... au bord de *M*es yeux c*AL*mes s'a*MA*sse une *LARM*e dont l*Es* ... (262)

One might conclude that the young Mallarmé was quite simply asserting: 'le sublime, c'est moi'. A case may indeed be made out in that sense, but we shall discover that the strategy adopted involves more twists than we may at first imagine.

Let us consider the relationship of these three texts, and of

106

their three sublimes, one to the other. Although it would be possible to imagine each piece isolated on its own sublime peak, the fact remains that the three form a sequence and indeed a 'symphony', in which each phase, according to the logic of the sublime, should in turn signal a *dépassement* of its predecessor. When we consider the workings of 'Symphonie littéraire, II' (the text devoted to Baudelaire), we might at first be persuaded that it repeats rather than surpasses 'Symphonie littéraire, I', since the same rhetorical pattern presents itself: abasement ('l'hiver, quand ma torpeur me lasse'); vision ('Mon Baudelaire à peine ouvert, je suis attiré dans un paysage surprenant') of an overwhelming sunset; crisis ('Alors, je me voile la face, et des sanglots, arrachés à mon âme moins par ce cauchemar que par une amère sensation d'exil, traversent le noir silence. Qu'est-ce donc que la patrie?') and silence ('j'ai fermé le livre'); and then the more-than-sublime vision ('l'apparition du poète savant') closing with a final pirouette — incongruously 'Catholic', even for the young Mallarmé — upon the negation of the ineffable:

> Et je ne puis regarder plus haut que les vertus théologales, tant la sainteté est ineffable: mais j'entends éclater cette parole d'une façon éternelle: Alleluia! (264)

Surely this conclusion implies that the 'Alleluia' of 'Symphonie littéraire, II' would be more sublime than the 'plus haute cime de la sérénité' of 'Symphonie littéraire, I'? The present sublime moment must always appear greater than the rest. An explicit answer to this problem is provided in 'Symphonie littéraire, III' (the text dedicated to Théodore de Banville), since in this instance the two preceding texts are from the outset represented as the base from which the current sublime will spring. The text itself even opens with the 'mais' vital to *praeteritio*:

> Mais quand mon esprit n'est pas gratifié d'une ascension dans les cieux spirituels, quand je suis las de regarder l'ennui dans le métal cruel d'un miroir. (264)

'Symphonie littéraire, I' and 'Symphonie littéraire, II' are packaged, limited, and labelled, one as the sublime 'serein', the other 'hagard', as if they were an infernal couple, a binary opposition, just waiting for a third term to break the stalemate (be it ever so sublime!) in the act of *dépassement*. The subject, neither serene nor hagard, experiences immediately this moment of euphoria, omitting, as it were, the preparatory steps towards the sublime:

> Fou d'amour, et débordant, et les yeux pleins de grandes larmes de tendresse, avec un nouvel orgueil d'être homme. Tout ce qu'il y a d'enthousiasme ambrosien en moi et de bonté musicale, de noble et de pareil aux dieux, chante, et j'ai l'extase radieuse de la Muse! J'aime les roses, j'aime l'or du soleil, j'aime les harmonieux sanglots des femmes aux longs cheveux, *et je voudrais tout confondre dans un poétique baiser!* (264; Mallarmé's emphasis)

We should remark that in 'Symphonie littéraire, III' no crisis of language occurs, the leap into the sublime being made directly from the base of 'Symphonie littéraire, I' and 'Symphonie littéraire, II', and culminating in the 'apotheosis of the name' that I discussed at the close of section 3.3. At this moment of triumph, everything comes to be confounded in the enthusiasm of the sublime. But might not some confusion also have arisen as to exactly whose name is being celebrated in this process? 'Mon poète' (it is true), 'c'est le divin Théodore de Banville': but by the third paragraph, the latter has lost his name, and is now 'cet homme'; by the fourth, 'l'élu est un homme au nom prédestiné, harmonieux comme un poème et charmant comme un décor'. But which predestined name are we really talking about? It appears in the ecstatic finale:

> Il siège sur un trône d'ivoire, couvert de la pourpre que lui seul a le droit de porter, *et le front couronné des feuilles géantes du laurier de la Turbie.* Ronsard chante des odes, et Vénus, vêtue de l'azur qui sort de sa chevelure, lui verse l'ambroisie — cependant qu'à ses pieds roulent les sanglots d'un peuple reconnaissant. La grande lyre s'extasie dans *ses mains* augustes. (265; my emphasis)

108

The *stephanos* and the paraphic 'ses mains' countersign, as if by miracle, the shadow of a self-portrait which the perspicacious Eugène Lefébure, on first reading 'Symphonie littéraire', had detected back in 1864:

> Oui Gauthier [sic] est bien la perfection grecque, Baudelaire le parfum du péché et Banville la poésie jeune. Toutefois il me semble qu'en peintre ami, vous avez un peu flatté vos portraits. Banville surtout se trouvera grandi [...] S'il y a profusion de lauriers, ils ne s'en plaindront pas, I am sure. *Ils ne se plaindront pas non plus du petit miracle que vous avez fait: je veux dire qu'en les peignant, vous vous êtes peint vous-même et que vous avez mis quatre poètes dans trois* (Pl. 1544; my emphasis)

Four into three will go. In the extra dimension of the name, duly magnified, of Stéphane Mallarmé, mathematical as well as aesthetic miracles may occur.

3.5.3 'ce sylphe suprême'

In part III of 'Symphonie littéraire', the final enthusiastic *dépassement* broke free, we might argue, from any restraining influence exerted by *praeteritio*. Twenty-eight years later, on the occasion of Théodore de Banville's death, Mallarmé revisits and relativizes his earlier triumph.[48] We first recognize a familiar fidelity to his younger self. The text is remembered as 'une des premières pages qu'écolier je traçai dans la solitude' (Pl. 520), and although he qualifies it as 'le pauvre trumeau, suranné; et pardon', he still admits that 'je recueille quelque fierté [...] qu'un sentiment, après un quart de siècle, se reconnaisse'. This careful resituation of the old text should be studied more for its tactical than for its affective content. When, before quoting his early text, Mallarmé remarks that 'pour le célébrer aujourd'hui, [je choisirais] de dire mieux la même chose', he omits to add that this is precisely what he has done, since the supposed exhumation of 'Symphonie littéraire, III' reveals itself to be a subtle and thorough rewrite. Most of the changes to the earlier text could be described as simplifications, the cut often falling, it should be noted, on the divine: for example, 'boire le nectar dans l'Olympe du lyrisme' becomes 'boire à la fontaine du lyrisme'; 'un nouvel orgueil d'être homme', 'un nouvel orgueil'; 'enthousiasme ambrosien', 'enthousiasme'; 'pareil aux dieux', 'pareil aux rois'. Heaven, in twenty-eight years, has been considerably emptied.[49] This tendency — which seems also to have emptied the 'fête du poète' of any social content, in favour of a more playful and erotic fantasy — becomes manifestly clear in the revised apotheosis:

> Dans l'empyrée, il siège sur un trône d'ivoire, ceint de la pourpre que lui a le droit de porter, le front ombragé des géantes feuilles du laurier de la Turbie. J'ouïs des strophes; la Muse, vêtue du sourire qui sort d'un jeune torse, lui verse l'inspiration — cependant qu'à ses pieds meurt une nue reconnaissante. La grande lyre s'extasie dans ses mains. (521)

As regards the paraphic signature noted above, the suppression of 'augustes' apparently gives the *s.m.* of 'ses mains' the final word: the poet thus recognizing himself, albeit in corrected form, across the quarter-century. Such a recognition, however, would require a contemporary version of 'Stéphane Mallarmé' ('pareil mais raffiné dans un sens aigu') in order that Stéphane Mallarmé might unreservedly admire himself in this intertextual mirror. Noticing how the term 'couronné' has been tempered to 'ombragé' in the rewrite, we might at first think Mallarmé has decided to suppress at least partially his younger signature, as if thus to mark a rejection or distancing of the early self-portrait. But we soon see that the crown has disappeared only to resurface all the more spectacularly. Following on from the auto-citation, Mallarmé proposes a closer definition of that 'feeling which recognizes itself', an enduring feeling for poetry, for the sublime, for the name: 'La Poésie', he says, taking as his starting point an opposition similar to that used in 'Symphonie littéraire, III', 'tient au sol, avec foi, à la poudre que tout demeure'; but it is equally strongly driven by a desire to construct, from this ground, from this base, spectacularly upwards. Mallarmé calls this movement a 'cri de pierre', which, against all eternal odds, 's'unifie vers le ciel en les piliers interrompus, des arceaux ayant un jet d'audace dans la prière; mais enfin, quelque immobilité'. He presents this tension — between high and low, between 'hagard' and 'serein', perhaps — as momentarily held in an illusion, and no doubt an illusion of the sublime. But something now comes flying out of the silence with a mission to shake up such a stillness, and surpass it — the sublime edifice is attacked by a bat!

> J'attends que, chauve-souris éblouissante et comme l'éventement de la gravité, soudain, du site par une pointe d'aile autochtone, le fol, adamantin, colère, tourbillonant génie heurte la ruine; s'en délivre, dans la voltige qu'il est, seul. (521)

This figure ('ce sylphe suprême') Mallarmé identifies as Théodore de Banville (or would seem to do so in the immediate context of the obituary, with only the qualifying adverb 'parfois' creating the shadow of a doubt). But in the eternal circumstances of the sublime the true name of the supreme sylph cannot remain long concealed:

> Celui, quand tout va s'éteindre ou choir, le dernier; ou l'initial, dont la sagesse patienta, près une source innée, que des tonnerres grandiloquents, brutaux fragments par trop étrangers à ce qui n'est pas le petit fait de chanter, abattissent leur colosse: *pour, oui! paraître, comme le couronnement railleur sans quoi tout serait vain.* (521–22; my emphasis)

The last-minute appearance ('paraître') of the *stephanos* provides the necessary 'extra' of consciousness (and, incidentally, of humour) without which the authenticity of the illusion would not be guaranteed. And the name glories in this sublime function.

'L'attention que sollicite quelque papillon blanc'
(after a lithograph by Whistler).

4

Writing your name into History

Il gît sous cette pierre! (O.C. 44)

Stéphane Mallarmé. Villiers de l'Isle-Adam. Manet, Tennyson, Verlaine.[1] Edgar Poe. Wagner. And Baudelaire. These are all the names of dead men.

However glorious the projection of the name, however sublime the illusion in which it momentarily appears, Mallarmé the onomast must come to terms with death. As the abandoned project of a text for his dead son Anatole amply testifies, the poet is not always in a position to dictate those terms.[2] However, in the three cases I shall be examining in the final section of our study — those of Poe, Wagner, and Baudelaire — Mallarmé is able to negotiate with Death the conditions of his succession into the gap left by three dead and influential figures. The names of Poe, Wagner, and Baudelaire will find themselves written into the works of Stéphane Mallarmé, and will survive into eternity thanks to those works, and to the name that assures their authenticity. Such an operation will require a particular strategy. It will not be enough simply to name the name, and explicitly to call for its glorification in the common memory of man. This would be to expose the name to the corrosion of irony or ridicule. Nor would it suffice merely to explain and expound the works of the poets in

113

question, with quotations and meanings at the ready. Something more subtle and suggestive will be needed in dealing with Death. As with the signature of Stéphane Mallarmé, the name of the dead will be at once scattered through the text and through the works, to be heard muttered here and there and repetitively;[3] and yet will also appear through certain simple gestures designed to give depth and duration to the meaning of the name. It will be as if the two strands of the strategy were the two halves, for instance, of the question: 'What is — (Edgar Poe)?'.

4.1 Poe[4]

poa, partout et toujours[5]

The first case is exemplary. Poe is the exemplary poet. The absolute literary case.[6] And the poet with the perfect name. Such perfection, however, stems from a minor fault, since if Poe were called 'Edgar Poet', his name would be absurd. The tiny margin (of error or space) allows the name to be perfected in silence, in the poesy of silence. But 'Poe' may also be termed 'exemplary' for the simple banality of its single syllable. Could we not find 'Poe', potentially, 'partout et toujours'? The tension between exception and ubiquity reflects the desire of the Mallarmean project to assume the linguistic given, the commonplace of a name, and transform it into something sublime.[7] The challenge in dealing with Poe would be at once to display the charming banality of a sound, whilst only ever hinting at the perfection of poetry which that syllable might bring into being.

Let us now consider how Mallarmé says 'Poe'.

4.1.1 'Le Tombeau d'Edgar Poe'

Tel qu'en Lui-même enfin l'éternité le change,
Le Poëte suscite avec un glaive nu
Son siècle épouvanté de n'avoir pas connu
Que la Mort triomphait dans cette voix étrange!

114

Eux, comme un vil sursaut d'hydre oyant jadis l'ange
Donner un sens plus pur aux mots de la tribu
Proclamèrent très haut le sortilège bu
Dans le flot sans honneur de quelque noir mélange.

Du sol et de la nue hostiles, ô grief!
Si notre idée avec ne sculpte un bas-relief
Dont la tombe de Poe éblouissante s'orne

Calme bloc ici-bas chu d'un désastre obscur
Que ce granit du moins montre à jamais sa borne
Aux noirs vols du Blasphème épars dans le futur.
                                                    (O.C. 272)

The first thing to remark in this text is that, contrary to Mallarmé's customary practice, the name of the honoured personality does not appear in the rhyme position. This he perhaps does in order to avoid exposing the foreign name — as might happen were it placed at the end of the line — in too openly important a place: apart from the problem of the rhyme for the eye, one hesitates to pronounce on whether Poe really rhymes with, say, 'peau' or 'troupeau' or 'pot'.[8] To place Poe at the end of the line would be to expose it to too many dangers. Besides, the powerful essential virtue of the name 'Poe' means that it should be handled or displayed with modesty.

Where, then, does the name appear? In two places. Firstly in the title, and then in sixth position, line 11:

> 'Le Tombeau d'Edgar Poe'
> [...]
> Dont la tombe de Poe

We may observe that both the title and, naturally, the hemistich consist of six syllables: this serves, while repeating the name, to make of the title itself a hemistich, rhyming, as it were, with that of line 11; but also, potentially, with other points in the text. The juxtaposition brings out the crucial and minimal difference between 'tombe' and 'tombeau'. The difficulty of the task before the speaker will be to create something more than 'tombe'; to add something (namely, one might think, the *beau*) to the mere sad block of stone. It is part of Mallarmé's rhetorical strategy to pretend, in the sestet, that such a complement appears unlikely; but, in matters sublime, modesty is frequently feigned. By establishing as a pair the terms 'beau' (third and accented position, if the title is verse) and 'Poe', the *beau* is incontrovertibly and triumphantly added to the tomb, when we read: '(dont la) *tomb*(e de P)*oe*'. Conversely, something has also disappeared, in the passage from title to sestet: by the time we reach line 11, the name has been refined to pure 'Poe', thus effecting the elimination of the title's indiscreet Franco-English pun: 'le tombeau DEADgar Poe'. But there is a further consequence of the positioning of the name at the caesura: if our eye-ear now runs down that point in all fourteen lines, it will remark two more hemistichs rhyming with the pair we have established:

> Eux, comme un vil surs*aut* [...]
> [...]
> Proclamèrent très *haut*

Now, we could argue that the pursuit of such euphony is firmly inscribed within the traditions of the French sonnet, and does not therefore merit closer attention; or, less kindly, that such a tendency, pushed to the extreme, would seem only the more appropriate in a homage to the author of such classics of over-wrought euphony as 'The Raven' and 'Ulalume'. But the experienced Mallarmé reader, ever in pursuit of significant constellations, will now want to highlight all the points in the text marked 'O', and, having done so, will ask himself whether, for example, in line 6, the words 'aux mots' do not become a means of underlining the dull homogeneity of the mob's speech, out of which to refine poetic difference; or indeed whether, in what becomes the rhyming first measure of line 8 ('dans le flot'), one should not see a somewhat cruel allusion to the *pot* of which the man called Poe was notoriously overfond. However, the most important function of the rhyming hemistichs at 5 and 7 must surely be to prepare, or to give an air of fatality to, the clinching coincidence of 'Poe' and 'Poëte'. Thus, from 'Le Poëte' of line 2

116

emerges a sequence ('sursaut', then 'P(roclamèrent très) haut') leading, as it were inevitably, to 'Dont la tombe de Poe', and then folding back into the title. A discreet circuit of meaning is thus installed. Such subliminal hints — at the name and the significance of the name (Poe as the essence of poetry) — serve to provide a necessary ulterior depth to the representation of Edgar Poe. We have the page, and the words written on it, just as we have the stone ('tombe') and its inscription ('tombeau'); but, in order to break out of the stale opposition of life-or-death, of black-or-white, and at the same time to escape from the timebound linearity of the words across the page, these flickerings of another type of meaning, unextinguished by death because never more than virtually or doubtfully or 'phanetically' present, will retain our attention — as might the points of light left by the passage of the meteor which, for Stéphane Mallarmé, remained the perfect visual representation of the admired poet.[9]

The poem would thus far appear a most sincere homage to Poe and his methods. This impression is confirmed if we consider the sonnet's argument, which *ad hominem* runs as follows: whereas society ignored or slandered the man Poe, to the point of not even knowing he had died, now, and in eternal terms, 'Poe' has justly become 'the Poet' (just as 'le' has become 'Lui-même'); and it will be the gesture of this text both to mark, for ever, the grave movement of the struggle between pure poetry and dull language, between public and poet, and to protect Poe from further calumny in the future. Beyond the argument, however, the intricate *mise en scène* of the name, as seen above, forms itself a practical homage to Poe's famous 'poetic principle': namely, that poetry is language cured of all hazardous indolence and working at maximum efficiency.[10] Mallarmé's idea, as he says himself, would be to build a dazzling tomb *for* Poe; but we could read in a slightly different way the 'de' of line 11, and conclude that in practice Mallarmé has made a memorial 'dazzling *with* Poe(s)'.

I should add a slight qualification, however, to my description of this astonishing tribute. While it is true that the name 'Poe' appears in apotheosis, protected from Blasphemy by the aura of its poetry, one might yet wonder by whose poetic labour such a monument is achieved. Surely not Edgar Poe's. The architect of

117

THE NAME OF THE POET

the memorial is one Stéphane Mallarmé. Such an assertion may seem self-evident, but it raises the following rather Bloomian reflection: 'If I write a sincere homage to my poetic father, am I not at the same time "celebrating" his death, and dancing, as it were, on his grave? And, more importantly, by displaying the virtues of my own poetic efforts, am I not trying in some way to surpass or eclipse him?' The son becomes the guardian of the father's reputation; but he cannot deny that it is he who has made the tomb dazzle and surprise. I shall now try to establish firstly whether Mallarmé was able to resist the temptation of signing the memorial, and secondly how he gently negotiated the delicate passage of succession, into Poe's absent place.

The tension between the artisan and the dedicatee, between the pride of the former and the respect owed to the latter, may be nicely identified in the final tercet. The calm granite block bears, at the heart of line 13, a paraph:

Que ce granit du moinS Montre à jamais sa borne

On the one hand, the initials *s.m.* remind us that Mallarmé has made a promise to protect Poe's reputation from future blasphemies, and the paraph would thus be a signature of authenticity, guaranteeing as it were his commitment to work on Poe's behalf. In order, for example, that the final phrase 'épars dans le futur' will be subtly reworked, from a description of the 'noirs vols du Blasphème' into the simple eternal statement 'e.p.: art dans le futur'. At the same time the initials necessarily indicate that e.p.'s future in art will be lived through the work of Mallarmé, and so we should not be surprised to find in the text further traces of the memorialist's name. Thus, just before the succinct homage of the final hemistich, the 'M' of 'Blasph-*ème*' now takes on a perhaps less respectful and shadier aspect. The doubt is confirmed by the revelation that the final line contains not merely 'M for Mallarmé' but in fact the whole name anagrammatized:

Aux noirs vols du bLASPHèME EpARs dANs LE fuTur

giving:

STEPHANE MALLARME.

One might think this a mere chance formation. But there is no such thing as chance in poetry! Such an assertion finds support in line 4, for example, which anagrammatizes not only the artisan's name, but also that of Edgar Allan Poe:

Que LA MoRt trioMPHAit dANS cEtTE voix Etrange

giving:

STEPHANE MAL(L)ARME

and again:

Que LA mort triomPhait DANs cettE vOix EtRAnGe

giving:

EDGAR AL(L)AN POE.

We should note that this transformation is only feasible because the author deliberately substituted the verb 'triomphait' for the original 's'exclamait' of the 1877 version. Likewise, the change in line 7 from 'Tous pensèrent entre eux' to 'Proclamèrent très haut' allows, in addition to the 'p … aut' mentioned above, a similarly anagrammatized signature:

ProcLAMERENt trèS HAuT LE sortilège bu

giving:

STEPHANE MALLAR(M)E

One might even imagine that the prime motivation for the substitution in line 12 of 'Calme' for 'Sombre' was to set up the progressive apparition of the name in the second tercet, going from the modest 'Mallarmé' of 12:

cALMe bLoc ici-bAs chu d'un dEsastRe obscur

giving:

MALLAR(M)E

via the paraph of thirteen (… moinS Montre …'), to the name's anagrammatical explosion, in fourteen, around the closing formula 'e.p.: art dans le futur'.[11]

Should one consider blasphemous this desire to sign the memorial? We can trace a certain hesitation over this question through a series of changes that Mallarmé made to one detail of the text, as if, precisely, he could not make up his mind. The detail in question is the 'm/M' of 'm/Mort' in line 4:

Que la m/Mort triomphait dans cette voix étrange!

Whereas the *m* is small in all the early versions of the text, from 1889 onwards it suddenly expands into a capital, only to return to its previous state in 1893 for *Vers et Prose*. In *La Plume* of March 1896 it re-expands, while in its final appearance, in the second edition of *Les Poèmes d'Edgar Poe*, it has shrunk once again (*O.C.* 273–78). Now, one could interpret this pattern as a wavering in Mallarmé's desire to assert (M), or to hide (m), his authorial presence, which signals at the same time his subject's death and his own role as death's messenger. This ambivalence before the mortal consequences of one's own triumph may be heard, as an echo, in the note Mallarmé added to the text, when, in May 1891, it appeared on the programme accompanying a theatrical performance of 'Le Corbeau':

A LA MEMOIRE DE BAUDELAIRE/*Que la Mort* seule empêcha d'achever, en traduisant l'ensemble de ces poèmes, le monument magnifique et fraternel, dédié par son génie à EDGARD [sic] POE. (277)

The reminiscence of 'Le Tombeau d'Edgar Poe' in this particular context (a double memorial, so to speak) indicates to what extent Mallarmé's relationship with Poe is mediated via Charles Baudelaire.[12] Nor should one forget that, in order to succeed Edgar Poe, Mallarmé must in the process push aside Baudelaire, who — translator, explicator, defender of Poe — would otherwise appear the ideal candidate for the succession. As we shall see in section 4.3, however, he achieves that aim with all the delicacy and reserve suggested by the hesitating 'm/M' of 'que la m/Mort'. The symbolic death takes place with a minimum of violence. And yet the tribute to the eternal greatness of the predecessor and the respect for the inevitability of his death remain infused with an equally eternal and inescapable desire to assert the great name of the inheritor.

4.1.2 post-Poe

Succession is what comes after. If 'Le Tombeau' represents Mallarmé's attempt to wrest the flame from the dead Poe, while at the same time honouring him, it should not be forgotten that the sonnet represents a relatively early piece, written at a time (the mid-seventies) when he was a long way from becoming the prince of poets. Therefore the 'Stéphane Mallarmé' written into the sonnet was succeeded by a whole series of different 'Stéphane Mallarmé(s)' up to the poet's death in 1898. We might ask how, in the following twenty-one years of living and writing, Mallarmé reacted to or rewrote the text for Edgar Poe, and how he may have sought after the fact to correct the version of himself he had given there. What comes after 'Le Tombeau'?

It is common for a writer to feign embarrassment regarding his early works. (We saw evidence of this, for example, in section 3.5.3) Nor is it uncommon for a poet to rewrite a text of his youth. In Mallarmé's case, one could cite 'Le Guignon' or 'Le Pitre Châtié' as examples of texts which were radically revised at a distance of some twenty years. As regards 'Le Tombeau', it appears clear that, given the sacred or solemn nature of the text, Mallarmé could neither renounce it nor — which would come to the same thing — violently rework it. Some changes, as I have

121

already commented, were indeed effected, and I have suggested why I think Mallarmé made them; but propriety and above all fidelity would demand that the text, and its proud rhetorical gesture of loyalty, should remain largely untouched. And yet, if we read some of Mallarmé's comments around and about 'Le Tombeau', we shall find that his reactions were equally faithful to a certain embarrassment or unease regarding the sonnet — feelings attributable either to the ironic distance offered by the passage of time or to the ambivalence felt by the young as they supplant the preceding dead.

Firstly, then, let us deal with the question of fidelity. Although 'Le Tombeau d'Edgar Poe' probably appeared more frequently and more publicly than any other piece of Mallarmé's, the experience of public exposure did not always prove very memorable. Present, for example, at the dress rehearsal of a recitation of 'Le Corbeau' and 'Le Tombeau' at the Théâtre d'Art in 1891, 'Mallarmé [...] fut tellement choqué "par l'irrespect apporté à la mise en scène" [...] qu'il n'assista pas a cette représentation spéciale' (O.C. 277). This evident failure of the granite to mark the bounds of Blasphemy cannot greatly have surprised its maker, however, since the *mise en scène* of the text had in many ways been wrong from the start. When it first appeared in the *Memorial Volume* of 1877, the author was disappointed to find that the collection consisted of little more than a ragbag of tributes and anecdotes, in which 'Le Tombeau' represented 'presque les seuls vers (et très mal placés): encore sont-ils pleins de fautes typographiques qui les défigurent' (274). As he expressed it, still politely, to the editor of the volume: 'Nous comprenons ce genre de publications en France tout différemment' (274). While it is true that the sonnet had been poorly exhibited in America, one can hardly maintain, given the experience at the Théâtre d'Art, that France proved to be 'a more authentic soil'.[14] In the face of such disappointment, Mallarmé seems to have adopted a strategy aiming, on the one hand, to continue publishing what is still today his most widely known poem, but also to 'correct' the reception of the text by a series of marginal remarks over a period of years. The first sign of this process may be seen in the 'Scolies' accompanying *Les Poésies d'Edgar Poe* of 1888. Mallarmé seeks to confer a certain grandeur and coherence on the occasion of the sonnet's original reading or performance by blindly maintaining that his homage had been 'envoyé [...] lors de l'érection à Baltimore du tombeau de Poe, et lu en cette solennité' (*Pl.* 224). He knew perfectly well that 'la manifestation si noble que fut la fête appelée le POE MEMORIAL, ou l'érection du tombeau' (225) took place in November 1875, that is, before Mallarmé had even put pen to paper. A few paragraphs later, he tries with comparable obstinacy to persuade the reader or himself that, even in America, there is a readerly elite who may successfully receive the poem's message:

> A côté de l'Amérique que vous et moi portons haut
> dans notre estime (il est, hélas! comme un pays dans
> un pays), j'en sais une à jamais offusquée par cet éclat
> trop vif, Poe. (*Pl.* 225)

Despite such determination, Mallarmé still finds it difficult to conceal the disappointment he felt back in 1877. Thus he rather curiously insists on defending himself against the charge of having 'blamed' the organizers of the Poe Memorial for having mishandled the ceremony (and, by implication, Mallarmé's homage). He reproduces (presumably as a form of compliment) the two translations of 'Le Tombeau', written by Mrs Sarah Helen Whitman and Mrs Louise Chandler Moulton, and then proclaims 'me voici abrité contre le soupçon que j'enveloppe des êtres d'élite dans aucun blâme'. One might wonder what suspicion or blame he could be invoking. We begin to suspect that the only elite readership which Mallarmé could really respect would not be practically American but theoretically French. Even that body (given the performance of 'Le Corbeau') would have to be imaginary rather than empirically palpable. In other words, the ideal reader of Stéphane Mallarmé! The following paragraph confirms this suspicion, whilst also ironically undermining the feigned respect that Mallarmé has just claimed to maintain towards the American ladies:

> Aussi je ne cesserai d'admirer le pratique moyen dont
> ces gens, incommodés par tant de mystère insoluble,
> à jamais émanant du coin de terre où gisait depuis un

> quart de siècle la dépouille abandonnée de Poe, ont,
> sous le couvert d'un inutile et retardataire tombeau,
> roulé là une pierre, immense, informe, lourde,
> déprécatoire, comme pour bien boucher l'endroit
> d'où s'exhalerait vers le ciel, ainsi qu'une pestilence,
> la juste revendication d'une existence de Poëte par
> tous interdite. (226)

Six years later, in the Bibliography to the 1894 edition of *Poésies*,
he summed up his feelings (which we could describe as, at the
very least, distant) in the following terms:

> LE TOMBEAU D'EDGAR POE — Mêlé au
> cérémonial, il y fut récité, en érection d'un monument
> de Poe, à Baltimore, un bloc de basalte que
> l'Amérique appuya sur l'ombre légère du poëte, pour
> sa sécurité qu'elle n'en ressortît jamais. (*Pl.* 77)

It could be argued that all we have seen thus far is evidence of a
certain bitterness felt by Mallarmé concerning a botched publication. The presentation of two further texts regarding Edgar Poe
will demonstrate something much more vital to be at stake:
namely, the manner in which the future reading of 'Poe' will
necessarily pass through the name of Stéphane Mallarmé.

Let us consider the introduction to the 'Scolies' of 1888. One
may hardly doubt that the name will here be a subject of importance, since Mallarmé quite simply reproduces Poe's signature,
graphically, as a kind of subtitle to the text. He furnishes an
explanation for this curious act:

> La signature ici montrée a été prise au bas d'une
> lettre, à cause de l'arabesque du paraphe plutôt que
> comme échantillon de l'écriture exquise. (*Pl.* 223)

The term 'écriture' of course reads ambiguously, most probably
meaning 'handwriting', but also suggesting that, at this juncture,
Mallarmé is concerned to set Poe's 'writing' aside, in favour of the
name, and of one aspect of the name in particular:

> Ces deux mots célèbres que lie un trait significatif
> tracé par la main du poète, conservent l'initiale
> parasite de l'autre mot: Allan. (223)

Why should the (adoptive) father's name be qualified as 'parasite'? The argument Mallarmé proceeds to develop (although the
naive reader might well wonder why this argument is relevant
and why it is where it is . . .) states quite plainly that Poe wanted
to recognize his adoptive father by including the element 'A' in
his name (just as anglophones most commonly refer today to
'Edgar Allan Poe'), but that fate has decided otherwise, instead
preferring 'Edgar Poe' as the name (according to Mallarmé) that
eternity will retain. As the text puts it:

> [Allan] jeta dans la vie [...] l'homme jeune qui allait
> devenir Edgar Poe et payer magnifiquement sa dette
> en menant, au sien uni, le nom d'un protecteur à
> l'immortalité: or, l'avenir s'y refuse. (223)

In Mallarmé's version of the future, the 'parasite' will not survive.
In his attempt to suppress the real American genealogy of Poe, by
insisting on the poet's adoption and erasing the name of the
father, he conspires to impose on posterity the French version of
'Poe': the name or the sound that we undoubtedly read or heard
in 'Le Tombeau d'Edgar Poe'. The 'fleur éclatante et nette' of
Poe is transplanted from the 'wrong site' ('para-*sitos*', by a
twisting of roots, becoming 'para-*situs*') — and finds an authentic
soil.

It would be a mistake to imagine that this movement, impressive though it be, merely involves an import to the French canon.
As suggested above, the canon in question is Mallarmé's eternity,
and the reading public his imaginary audience. The true nature of
the transfer becomes apparent in the text he contributed to the
collection *Portraits du Prochain Siècle* of 1894 (*Pl.* 531). The poet has
been asked how he thinks one may best represent 'Poe' for eternity (the same question, essentially, as in 1877). 'Edgar Poe
m'apparaît personnellement depuis Whistler', he opens, only then
to reject as unsatisfactory first Whistler's portrait of Poe, then the

dark dandy Whistler himself, and finally (perhaps unsurprisingly) Villiers de l'Isle-Adam. Eternity will figure Poe differently:

> Cependant et pour l'avouer, toujours, malgré ma confrontation de daguerréotypes et de gravures, une piété unique telle enjoint de me représenter le pur entre les Esprits, plutôt et de préférence à quelqu'un, comme un aérolithe; stellaire, de foudre, projeté des desseins finis humains, très loin de nous contemporainement à qui *il éclata en pierreries d'une couronne pour personne*, dans maint siècle d'ici. (531; my emphasis)

In this fashion Mallarmé rewrites line 12 of 'Le Tombeau':

> Calme bloc ici-bas chu d'un désastre obscur.

The seeming modesty of 1877 has now given way to a discreet but powerful assertion of Mallarmé's succession. The precious stones fallen from the explosion of Poe form no less than a *stephanos* of poetic triumph and continuity. The 'nobody' to wear the crown conceals somebody. And his name is Stéphane Mallarmé.

4.2 Wagner

> *Ricaner quand on entend son nom, et faire des plaisanteries sur la musique de l'avenir.*[15]

In the preceding section our concern was to demonstrate how Mallarmé wrote his name into the line of descent called 'Poe–Baudelaire–Mallarmé', while at the same time redefining the sense of that lineage.[16] In the case of Wagner, we shall see the poet's onomastic talents deployed towards a very different end: firstly, to deny that any common blood might exist between himself and the Teutonic composer, and secondly to suggest the superiority and greater perenniality of his own line over Wagner's. Given the Wagnermania of the period (and particularly amongst those young men at the *Revue Wagnérienne* and elsewhere, whose enthusiasm was equally divided between the two masters), as well as Mallarmé's distaste for the polemical and his respect for literary convention, it will necessarily be an occult strategy that he adopts in order to mark out the difference. His target will be the name. In this case, to the exclusion of any other considerations. Dealing with Poe or Baudelaire (as with Whistler or Manet) the concentration on the name presupposes an intimate knowledge of the subject and his work, of which the 'surname', reinvented by Mallarmé's onomastic genius, would appear as an essence for eternity. By contrast, when Mallarmé looks at Wagner and poses the essential question 'What is that?', his gaze will go no further than the mere appellation. As we shall see, the poet was not only ignorant of the master and his works, but largely indifferent to them as well.[17] The fidelity I have identified as a vital part of Mallarmé's literary personality finds itself here transformed into an obstinate refusal to know of Wagner otherwise than *by name*.

4.2.1 'Hérésies Artistiques'

Je n'ai jamais rien vu de Wagner

This studied indifference first appears in the very early critical text of Mallarmé's — 'Hérésies Artistiques' — rediscovered by Emilie Noulet, who said of her find, although no doubt without the intention of supporting our hypothesis, that Mallarmé was 'fidèle pendant trente ans à cette page première' (*Pl.* 1543). The article is in no sense 'about' Richard Wagner, but it does, at least in its opening paragraphs, seek to oppose music and poetry, an antithesis to which Mallarmé also remained faithful for the rest of his life.[18] Here the young aesthetician is describing the 'mystery' accorded by the vulgar to the former art and implicitly denied to the latter:

> Toute chose sacrée [...] s'enveloppe de mystère [...] La musique nous offre un exemple. Ouvrons à la légère Mozart, Beethoven *ou Wagner*, jetons sur la première page de leur oeuvre un oeil indifférent, nous sommes pris d'un religieux étonnement à la vue de

> ces processions macabres de signes sévères, chastes,
> inconnus. Et nous refermons le missel vierge
> d'aucune pensée profanatrice. (*Pl.* 257)

The name 'Wagner' occurs as an item in a list: 'ou Wagner'. Does it really matter that Mallarmé should have written 'or Wagner' instead of, say, 'or Weber'? As Mondor aptly remarks (*Pl.* 1593), if he did 'cite the name' of this particular Germanic composer in preference to another, it was no doubt because he would have just read Baudelaire's pamphlet of 1861 *Richard Wagner et Tannhäuser à Paris*. But whereas Baudelaire relates in his study how, once touched by the sounds of the maestro, he scoured the streets and salons of Paris for more (information or performance) of the same, his twenty-one-year-old disciple seems to have remained relatively composed before the second-hand revelation. Some twenty-three years later he admitted only half-shamefully to Edouard Dujardin, when requested by the latter to write something for the *Revue Wagnérienne*, that 'je n'ai jamais rien vu de Wagner' (*Pl.* 1592). He had clearly never been tempted to join his friends Mendès or Villiers on one of their yearly pilgrimages across the Rhine. One may wish therefore to reinterpret the paragraph from 'Hérésies' quoted above, this time insisting very literally that it is Mallarmé's own eye which is 'indifferent' to Wagner and to music. The poet disdains to read, other than as pseudo-religious gramarye, the signs on the page, and closes the music-book with indeed 'no thought', profaning or otherwise, in mind. Music interests him only in its opposition to poetry. The latter, he complains, fails to excite in the public mind the same (albeit grossly superficial) respect and awe which music seemingly manages to inspire. Thus a book, for example, although bearing the sacred name of a poet, will provoke a reaction Mallarmé feels to be somewhat over familiar:

> Hasardons, en le mumurant aussi bas que nous pourrons, les noms de Shakespeare ou de Goethe: ce drôle redresse la tête d'un air qui signifie: 'Ceci rentre dans mon domaine.' (258)

With this phrase, the young poet unwittingly parodies his own middle-brow familiarity with Mozart, Beethoven, 'ou Wagner'. But the existence of such a blind spot is more of a help than a hindrance to our cause, since it is Mallarmé's fidelity to a certain form of cecity that I wish to highlight here. His insistence on the exclusive and superior existence of a poetic 'domain', into which Wagner will not be able to enter.

4.2.2 'l'hommage est un peu boudeur'[19]

By 1885, twenty-three years have passed since the name of Wagner first appeared in Mallarmé's works. Then, within the space of six months, the poet is twice solicited by Dujardin for a contribution to the recently founded *Revue Wagnérienne*. As stated above, Mallarmé was far from enthusiastic about the first of these commissions: 'Ne me faites pas de reproches', he asks of his young and demanding admirer:

> Jamais rien ne m'a semblé plus difficile. Songez donc, je suis malade, plus que jamais esclave. Je n'ai jamais rien vu de Wagner et je veux faire quelque chose d'original et de juste et qui ne soit pas à côté. (*Pl.* 1592)

In spite of this part-guilty, part-humble deprecation, he duly produces the 'Rêverie d'un poète français' (*Pl.* 539) (see section 4.2.3). The editor, however, no doubt eager to see the by now prestigious name of Stéphane Mallarmé again associated with his nascent journal, decides to try his chance a second time. He writes to his master in August of 1885 (barely a month after the publication of the 'Rêverie') requesting this time a poetic contribution to the prospective *Hommage à Wagner*, a project featuring sonnets by, amongst others, Verlaine and René Ghil.[20] Mallarmé's response is once again reluctant but ultimately ineffectual:

> Je deviens donc moins que jamais l'homme d'aucune Revue, fût-ce la vôtre! Un quatrain, moi qui suis malade et obsédé de devoirs, me jette quinze jours dans l'âpre sentier que je gravis mentalement [...] mais je ne puis rien promettre, hélas! d'autant mieux que je ne vois pas du tout l'épilogue même banal que

je pourrais ajouter â tant de choses suggestives écrites
sur Wagner chez vous: non, je suis le seul à qui cette
tâche n'incombe pas exactement. (*O.C.* 315)

Although he offers humility and ignorance as the reasons for his
lack of enthusiasm, Mallarmé finds it necessary to insist all the
same on the 'exactitude' of his difference. How does this latter
manifest itself in the sonnet which eventually appeared in the
Revue Wagnérienne of January 1886?

Hommage

Le silence déjà funèbre d'une moire
Dispose plus qu'un pli seul sur le mobilier
Que doit un tassement du principal pilier
Précipiter avec le manque de mémoire.

Notre si vieil ébat triomphal du grimoire,
Hiéroglyphes dont s'exalte le milier
A propager de l'aile un frisson familier!
Enfouissez-le moi plutôt dans une armoire.

Du souriant fracas originel haï
Entre elles de clartés maîtresses a jailli
Jusque vers un parvis né pour leur simulacre,

Trompettes tout haut d'or pâmé sur les vélins,
Le dieu Richard Wagner irradiant un sacre
Mal tu par l'encre même en sanglots sibyllins.

It has become customary to take the 'Hommage' as a 'poetic'
version of the 'Rêverie', even to the extent that the sonnet reproduces many of the terms already employed in the prose text.[21]
However, against this tradition (which has also tended to set the
'scene' of the poem in a theatre, an argument for which I can see
little or no evidence),[22] one might also remark that the sonnet
presents a series of terms, absent from the 'Rêverie', which denote
the act (and the 'scene' for that matter) of writing: 'grimoire',
'hiéroglyphes', 'vélins', 'encre' (the site of the poem — 'mobilier',

'pilier', 'armoire' — representing therefore a study or an apartment rather than a theatre). These references take us back, not to the 'Rêverie' of the previous summer, but to the 'Hérésies Artistiques' of 1862:

O fermoirs d'or des vieux missels! ô hiéroglyphes
inviolés des rouleaux de papyrus! (*Pl.* 257)

We rediscover in 'Hommage' the essential complaint of 'Hérésies': namely, that the musical page is spared the terrible 'familiarity' (lines 6–7) with which the vulgar treats the mystery of poetry. In the poem, Mallarmé's earlier sense of outrage is tempered by humour or experience into a sentiment of resignation. How, he wonders, might we represent the mystery of Poetry in the present age? The reply comes stripped of all illusions:

Enfouissez-le moi plutôt dans une armoire. (*O.C.* 314)

The contemporary triumph is indisputably that of 'le dieu Richard Wagner' — in the face of which writing can do nothing to silence the attendant clamour. 'L'hommage est un peu boudeur', as Mallarmé was to confide in an explanatory letter to a relative, resigning himself to a seemingly admiring silence of recognition, waiting perhaps for the current wave of popularity for the latest or last god to pass .... Behind this mask of resignation, however, one may discern an expression of resistance. At the close of the poem, at the very point where Mallarmé concedes his inability to quell the trumpets of Wagner's consecration, a resistant, obstinate, contrary voice may be heard:

Mal tu p*ar* l'encre *même* en sanglots sibyllins

This barely conceals a signatory presence:

Mal ... ar ... mê ... (314)

Literally prostrate beneath 'le dieu Richard Wagner', the poet proclaims his persistence, his difference, his separation from the domain of music. The 'M' of 'Mal(larmé)' stares back across the space separating lines 13 and 14 — and fixes the 'W' of 'Wagner'. Reflect, says the gaze, upon the absolute and uncomprehending opposition of M versus W. Suddenly, in the sestet, supporting elements constellate around this antithesis:

> ... *m*aîtresses ... si*m*ulacre ... tro*m*pettes
> ... pâ*m*é ... *m*ême ...

as against:

> ... *v*ers ... par*v*is ... *v*élins

In this struggle the poet positions himself so that it is Mallarmé and poetry who will have the final and purer word. With the 'Hommage', the name 'Richard Wagner' has been uttered, and his day of glory pronounced. By contrast, 'Mal-ar-mê/Mallarmé' remains 'mal tu'. Mutely unmuted, he reserves his own glorious apparition for some future or forever virtual date. The strategic sense of playing from a position of strength allows him, seemingly sulky but quietly confident, to acknowledge Wagner's victory as merely the penultimate battle.[23]

4.2.3 What is that — Wagner?[24]

The very title of 'Richard Wagner/Rêverie d'un poète français' reproduces the opposition of names revealed at the close of 'Hommage'. Above, in bold and legible letters, the name 'Richard Wagner'; beneath, the seemingly modest anonymity of 'un poète français'. This relative positioning of the names, of 'Wagner' standing superior to an apparent 'nobody', constitutes nothing less than a trap for the composer. It suggests, by apposition, that the object of this reverie will be 'Richard Wagner': in other words, that the presently anonymous poet will muse, reflect, and speculate upon the meaning of the name 'Richard Wagner'. Yet it also implies that in the present instance the thing 'Richard Wagner' will represent no more than the stuff of (Mallarmé's) dreams. From the start, the power relationship obtaining between the bold and victorious composer and the sulky and nameless poet has in effect been twisted or turned to the latter's advantage. Should 'Wagner'

132

then trespass into Mallarmé's domain, the poet will not be held responsible for any damage or transformation it may there suffer.

The familiar reading of the 'Rêverie' admits that, while paying homage to the achievement of the German composer-conductor, Mallarmé seeks nevertheless to indicate a limit to his enthusiasm, to maintain a certain reserve. Contemporary readers of the piece had already remarked upon this effect. Henri de Régnier comments, for example, that the particular interest of the piece lay in the fact that 'tout en saluant l'avènement triomphal de l'art nouveau, le poète s'incline plutôt devant le fait magnifique que cet art représente, qu'il ne plie le genou devant sa suprématie'. He underlines 'cette réserve si significative de Mallarmé', and concludes that 'le poète apporte sa restriction' (Pl. 1593). Nobody wishes to contest the claim that a significant difference exists. But Régnier (for one) would perhaps be harder pressed to explain exactly what Mallarmé's reserve 'signified'. The reader who seeks to answer this question runs the risk of revealing the latent hostility of the poet towards his object, an aggression otherwise concealed by the veil of literary nicety.

The turning point of the text, where Mallarmé marks his reserve, occurs in paragraph twenty, a one-liner:

Tout se retrempe au ruisseau primitif; pas jusqu'à la source. (544)

From this point Mallarmé strategically turns his back on the figure of Wagner in order to evoke in the following five paragraphs his own vision of what the 'theatre' might become. This proves to be less a building, a stage, a decor, or a troupe, than simply the blank space or screen on which a certain fiction might appear. In Mallarmé's conception of the world and stage, the 'source' (or poetry) will always be situated prior and superior to the realized theatre of Wagner. So when, in the final paragraph, Mallarmé takes leave of Wagner, with a salute to the master's 'genius', it would be more accurate to say that he is in fact leaving his rival behind. Let us, however, return to the twenty-first paragraph, in order to see how the poet prepares such a separation.

The reserve has just been marked, then, with the phrase 'pas jusqu'à la source'. Now Mallarmé elaborates the difference:

> Si l'esprit français, strictement imaginatif et abstrait, donc poétique, jette un éclat, ce ne sera pas ainsi: il répugne, en cela d'accord avec l'Art dans son intégrité, qui est inventeur, à la Légende. (544)

Immediately we are confronted with a simple but apparently unbreachable distinction. On one side lies the French spirit, on the other the German mind. Invention and imagination stand opposed to a 'repugnant' reliance on legend or mythology. By implication, Wagner is portrayed as lacking the two truly 'artistic' qualities cited, and his folky source of inspiration is openly ridiculed by Mallarmé's footnote:

> Exposition, Transmission de Pouvoirs, etc., t'y vois-je, Brünnhild ou qu'y ferais-tu, Siegfried! (544)

He then proceeds to develop the distinction between the 'abstract' (which is French and inventive) and the 'real' (which is dull and German). The only 'fable' that his purely fictional conception of the theatre might allow would be 'vierge de tout, lieu, temps et personne sus'. The only 'myth' it might accept would be: 'un, dégagé de personnalité, [...] type sans dénomination préalable, pour qu'émane la surprise: son geste résume vers soi nos rêves de sites ou de paradis, qu'engouffre l'antique scène avec une prétention vide à les contenir ou à les peindre' (545). This encomium of negativity reaches a climax with the erasure of any 'real' site for the imaginary performance:

> Lui, quelqu'un! ni cette scène, quelque part [...] Est-ce qu'un fait spirituel, l'épanouissement de symboles ou leur préparation, nécessite endroit, pour s'y développer, autre que le fictif foyer de vision dardé par le regard d'une foule! Saint des saints, mais mental. (545)[25]

If one is to reach or remain at the source, one must never realize one's work. It will never have taken place. This assertion provides the basis for Mallarmé's final *dépassement* of Wagner. The ambitious composer has more or less happily realized his masterwork, which therefore has no future: the machinery of his total theatre will creak, his singers will miss notes, his orchestra will go on strike, his actors will fall into the pit … . Faced with such an achievement, in the full sense of that word, Mallarmé can only turn away with a polite but unavoidably superior smile. Which is exactly the rhetorical gesture he accomplishes at the close of the piece: the anonymous poet salutes Wagner's achievement only to surpass it. The power of the smile has all along been reinforced, however, by a second and parallel strategy — a strategy purely of the name — which throughout the text has likewise worked towards the single goal: the separation of 'Richard Wagner' from the domain of Mallarmé.

4.2.4 Charron, Richard

Alongside the argumentation of 'Rêverie', which seeks both to distinguish Mallarmé from any Wagnerian 'line' and at the same time to exclude the musician from the poet's genealogy, we may see at work a subtle and persistent attempt to transform and indeed to travesty the name of 'Richard Wagner'. The process is set in motion from the very first paragraph, where the title's opposition of the names (of 'Richard Wagner' and 'anonymous') reappears immediately in the opening sentence:

> Un poète français contemporain, exclu de toute participation aux déploiements de beauté officiels (541)

Thus we are introduced to the poet with no name. By a clever manoeuvring of syntax, however, we are given at least a hint of who that nobody might be:

> Un poète français contemporain, exclu de toute participation aux déploiements de beauté officiels, en raison de divers motifs, *aime* [. . .]

The verb, elevated by apposition into the initial M of Mallarmé, provides a shadow of the name. Once he has operated this feint and thus secured his phantomatic presence in the text, the poet then opens up the name of the musician to a fatal ridicule. He inserts, as the sentence unfolds, the following curious onomastic reference to the possible meaning of Wagner's name:

> [...] aime, ce qu'il garde de sa tâche pratiqué ou l'affinement mystérieux du vers pour de solitaires Fêtes, à réfléchir aux pompes souveraines de la Poésie, comme elles ne sauraient exister concurremment au flux de banalité *charrié* par les arts dans le faux semblant de civilisation.

Thus stand opposed, on the one hand, Mallarmé's solitary, mysterious, refined, practised but unrealizable 'Fête', and on the other, the banal, phoney but all too 'real' pomp which civilization is capable of producing at present. Needless to say, this hardly represents a very flattering way to introduce a homage to the realization of Wagner's masterwork, even if it could be argued that the musician himself does not appear directly accused *by name*. That qualification disappears if we focus our attention on the term 'charrié', which necessarily assumes an essential role in the play of onomastic antinomy as soon as we translate 'Wagner' into its French equivalent ... 'Charron'. In fact, the term 'charrié' already draws attention to itself, in as much as its usage in this instance departs from the semantic norm. We would normally expect something (here 'les arts') to be 'charrié' by some sort of current or flow (here 'le flux'). In this phrase the positions are reversed (the flow of banality being 'charrié' by the arts).[26] We soon discover, however, that the verb is reversible in another sense for, on the semantic level, whereas the primary meaning given would be 'emporter (dans son cours)' or 'transporter (une charge, une personne)', there exists also a quite different sense: 'Se moquer de quelqu'un, abuser de sa crédulité. Faire marcher. Mener en bâteau.' Now, in the context of the opening sentence of the 'Rêverie', the two meanings seem to coincide. 'The flow of banality carried/transported by the arts' takes place in a phoney civilization, whose public would thus be duped, conned, misled by a person called, logically, 'Charron'. Thus grows the weight of opprobrium that 'Richard Charron' will have to bear. Moreover, 'charrier' would also form part of that formidable cluster of verbs which in this text and elsewhere vehicle the sublime: 'emporter, transporter, enlever, exalter, etc.' By a double blow, then, Richard Wagner becomes the 'transporter' of a false sublime.

Two objections, at this point, may be raised. Firstly, from the entire flow of the 'Rêverie', why isolate this lone example of a (possible) pun on 'Wagner'/'Charron'? Secondly, how can we justify such a vast extrapolation (into the realm of the sublime) from the simple and single perception of that pun? In answer to the first point, we should consider a different passage from the text in which Mallarmé shows no hesitation in exploiting the onomastic potential of 'Richard Wagner':

> Maintenant, en effet, une musique qui n'a de cet art que l'observance des lois très complexes, seulement d'abord *le flottant et l'infus*, confond les couleurs et les lignes du personnage avec les timbres et les thèmes en une ambiance plus *riche de Rêverie* que tout air d'ici-bas [...] ou va l'*enlever* de sa *vague* de Passion, au déchaînement trop vaste vers un seul, le précipiter, le tordre (543)

We could highlight here 'vague' as adjective ('le flottant et l'infus') and as noun ('sa vague de Passion'), then 'enlever' as synonym of 'charrier', and lastly the phrase 'riche de Rêverie' as play on the forename unavoidably returning us to the title (and so to the name). Such a concentration of 'Wagnerian' elements defies coincidence. Furthermore, while only one of these terms directly refers to the derogatory pun on 'charrier', they all combine nevertheless to insist upon the name and so encourage in us a certain curiosity as to its possible meanings.[27] As for the second objection (regarding the leap from 'charrier' to the sublime), we may without difficulty reveal in the 'Rêverie' an entire sublime series, stemming from the initial 'charrié', and sustained throughout the text:

> charrié, apportée, traduire, l'apport, mobiliser, rendu (541), transports, tirée, entraîne (542), enlever (543),

intrônisée, apporterait, délivrant (544), conducteur, lever, exalter (546)

Likewise, the sublime 'flow' (which, we might suggest, has been poisoned at source) irrigates the whole piece:

> flux (541), concours, effluve/épandre (542), influence/déverser, afflux/infus/vague (543), concours (545), fontaine (546)

Having already been rejected for not 'going to the source' (or poetry), the Wagnerian sublime now finds itself ridiculed, via an attack on the name, as a false and impure flow, in whose current the public or the people would be foolish to let themselves get carried away ... . Come the close of the text, it is clear that Stéphane Mallarmé, for one, will not be transported on the conductor's cart:

> Voilà pourquoi, Génie! moi, l'humble qu'une logique éternelle asservit, ô Wagner, je souffre et me reproche, aux minutes marquées par la lassitude, de ne pas faire nombre avec ceux qui, ennuyés de tout afin de trouver le salut définitif, vont droit à l'édifice de ton Art, pour eux le terme du chemin. (546)

The argument is formal and the 'salut' definitive. Mistakenly, Wagner's work has been perceived by a group of young people as the end (the telos but also the close) of a spiritual journey called art. In Mallarmé's version of eternity, it represents merely a stage, a relative achievement, requiring on Mallarmé's part no more than a gracious and even generous acknowledgement. For him, and his career, it cannot signify an end. It will rather provide an agreeable resting place, or watering-hole, halfway up the mountain, on the never-ending or indeed illusory ascension towards the absolute:

> Cette cime menaçante d'absolu, devinée dans le départ des nuées là-haut, fulgurante, nue, seule: au-delà et que *personne* ne semble devoir atteindre. (My emphasis)

138

Beyond or beneath the mere argument, however, there appears a final onomastic twist, as if to sign off the break with Wagner. The opposition of the names re-emerges as a contrast between the elliptical 'moi, l'humble' (the anonymous poet) and the apostrophe to the 'Génie! [...] ô Wagner'. But the latter god has in the meantime been redefined as a none-too-reliable 'conductor' of the false sublime, leading his troop towards a perhaps sinister end ... for is he not also 'Ch[K]aron', the final ferryman, or mythology's ultimate 'meneur-en-bâteau'? Relative to this figure of death, Mallarmé reappears as a survivor, in the person of a singular 'personne':

> [...] au-delà et que *personne* ne semble devoir
> atteindre. *Personne!* ce mot n'obsède pas d'un remords
> le passant en train de boire à ta conviviale fontaine.
> (546)

Just as at the close of the fragment 'Sur Poe' Mallarmé had donned the modestly invisible *stephanos* in order to assume the 'couronne pour personne', so we witness here the excluded, anonymous, contemporary French poet — the 'mal-ar-mê' seemingly squeezed out of modernity by a large German reputation — reappear in the guise of the virtual 'nobody/somebody' ever striving towards the sublime. For the present, he seems happy to adopt the role of the 'passant', pausing momentarily on his journey, in order to read the *tombeau* of Richard Wagner — and move on.

4.3 Baudelaire

(Car le tombeau toujours comprendra le poète)[28]

There are many bridges one could build between the texts that rename Richard Wagner and the commemorative poem for Charles Baudelaire: first, the title itself, since the text we have come to call 'Le Tombeau de Charles Baudelaire' was originally entitled 'Hommage' (see *O.C.* 411), just like the sonnet for Wagner of 1885; secondly, the coincidence of names according to which

Mallarmé's knowledge of Wagner as early as 1862 (if only 'by name') derived directly from Baudelaire's article of the preceding year; thirdly, the discreet presence of 'Charon' in the 'Rêverie', and the name of Anubis, likewise 'conductor of souls', in the 'Tombeau'; fourthly the pair of 'temples' that appear, one 'à mi-côte de la montagne sainte' at the close of the prose text, the other, underground, at the opening of the poem.[29] One might even imagine Mallarmé's onomastic undermining of the name 'Wagner' to have been inspired by the refrain of 'Moesta et Errabunda': 'Emporte-moi, *wagon*! enlève-moi, frégate!'; and/or by these comical octosyllables from 'Le Vin de l'Assassin':

> Le *chariot* aux lourdes roues,
> Le *wagon* enragé peut bien
> Ecraser ma tête coupable

Having said that, my aim in the present section will be to separate the two homages rather than to bring them together. In section 4.2 I endeavoured to show that what has been taken for a sincere and respectful (if 'limited') homage to a kindred spirit may also be read as a discreet poetic aggression. In the case of 'Le Tombeau de Charles Baudelaire' I shall argue that what has been dubbed Mallarmé's 'hommage le plus obscur et le moins convaincant' (*Pl.* 1495) forms in fact a powerful and resonant homage to Charles Baudelaire and to poetry. The poet Mallarmé understands the poet Baudelaire, and the *tombeau* which contains his brother will accordingly express such continuity and comprehension.

'Le Tombeau de Charles Baudelaire' has been the object of a less than enthusiastic reception. Even the good Mondor expresses disapproval, in what must be the unique recorded instance of a negative remark on his part:

> Etrangement, c'est au poète des *Fleurs du mal* qui fut
> la grande admiration et la majeure influence de sa
> jeunesse, que Mallarmé a rendu, en vers, son
> hommage le plus obscur et le moins convaincant.
> (*Pl.* 1495)[30]

The unhappy reputation no doubt stems from the relatively sordid, and yet thoroughly Baudelairean, imagery of the piece: a spewing gutter; a flaming dog-face; a street-light fuelled by the gas of a putrescent corpse; a flying pubis; a prostitute-Muse; and poison ... Such an array of figures transports us to a world far removed from Mallarmé's supposed universe of elegant abstraction and spiritual reserve. The poet, however, would appear to have foreseen some trouble in the reading of his text. Just as, in 1885, he had almost pleaded with Dujardin to leave him alone and Wagnerianly unattached, so, seven years later, when the idea began to circulate of a memorial volume for Baudelaire, Mallarmé manifests a reticence bordering on discomfort. Not only does he turn down, in favour of Leconte de Lisle, the chairmanship of the committee concerned (although after the death of the latter he would subsequently have to assume the post), but he also asks of Léon Deschamps, the editor of *La Plume* and seemingly the real organizer of the memorial, not to include his name on the list of subscribers, claiming that his mere initials would suffice (*O.C.* 411). It is in the same vein of mixed feelings that Mallarmé takes on the direction of the project in 1894, hoping in vain that 'mon sonnet ne paraît pas en tête du volume', and adding this curious preface to his contribution:

> [Le sonnet] est ce qui me plaît, mais trop à côté, particulier et attaquable, pour donner le ton et, en vedette, nuirait au recueil, plutôt, vous verrez. (*O.C.* 411)

However, as Barbier and Millan remark, when the volume eventually comes out in 1896, not only does Mallarmé's name appear 'en vedette' on the title page, but also his text is made the star of the poetic contributions to the collection. Now, one might want to read these comments on Mallarmé's part as so many signs of modesty before the memory of the great predecessor; or as hints of suspicion that *Le Tombeau de Baudelaire* might turn out as disastrously as had the memorial volume for Edgar Poe; or, finally and crucially, as an expression of his concern as to how the name 'Stéphane Mallarmé' might figure and be read alongside 'Charles Baudelaire'. It is the third of these questions which I shall now address.

The present case needs to be carefully distinguished from those discussed in sections 4.1 and 4.2. The strategy adopted for Poe, in which the name had a clear role to play, aimed at once to do justice to the 'damned' poet, and to bring Poe into a French tradition, of which Stéphane Mallarmé would be the latest or ultimate avatar. In contrast to this, the objective posed and (I would argue) attained in the case of Wagner involved excluding the possibility of any such common descent, while at the same time ridiculing any lineage other than the Mallarmean. In the current instance, however, the elements of the problem present themselves differently. Firstly, by 1894, Stéphane Mallarmé has a publicly recognized claim to the succession of Charles Baudelaire. The poet will not need to engage in the kind of onomastic revisionism with which we have thus far been concerned. Secondly, although Mallarmé's *dépassement* of Baudelaire had been, from almost the beginning of his career, the driving force and inspiration of his poetic activity, the process of separation had been successfully set in motion (as I have had occasion to remark already in this study) back in the 1860s. By the time of 'Le Tombeau', the issue has been resolved and the tension of the father-son struggle dissipated. These two points largely determine the strategy of 'Le Tombeau de Charles Baudelaire', where the mature Stéphane Mallarmé, confident in the crown sported by the prince of poets, may simply pay homage to the dead poet and his living art. This he achieves by paradoxically constructing a thoroughly 'Baudelairean' text about which, however, one could never say: 'Baudelaire, s'il rajeunissait, pourrait signer vos sonnets.'[31]

Le Tombeau de Charles Baudelaire

Le temple enseveli divulgue par la bouche
Sépulcrale d'égout bavant boue et rubis
Abominablement quelque idole Anubis
Tout le museau flambé comme un aboi farouche

Ou que le gaz récent torde la mèche louche
Essuyeuse on le sait des opprobres subis

Il allume hagard un immortel pubis
Dont le vol selon le réverbère découche

Quel feuillage séché dans les cités sans soir
Votif pourra bénir comme elle se rasseoir
Contre le marbre vainement de Baudelaire

Au voile qui la ceint absente avec frissons
Celle son Ombre même un poison tutélaire
Toujours à respirer si nous en périssons (O.C. 410)

In what sense, firstly, might one describe 'Le Tombeau de Charles Baudelaire' as 'Baudelairean'? To answer this we look no further than Jean Pommier's article '"Le Tombeau de Charles Baudelaire" de Mallarmé',[32] which demonstrates just how many of the mere words of the sonnet may be traced to Baudelairean sources. The unfinished 'Epilogue', for example, to *Les Fleurs du mal* contains these lines:

Tes *temples* vomissent la prière en musique [...]
[...] tes *égouts* pleins de sang
S'engouffrent dans l'Enfer [...]
Tu m'as donné ta *boue* et j'en ai fait de l'or

'Le Vin des Chiffoniers' begins:

Souvent, à la clarté rouge d'un *réverbère*
Dont le vent bat la flamme et tourmente le verre

In 'Le Crépuscule du Soir', we find:

A travers les lueurs que tourmente le vent
La Prostitution *s'allume* dans les rues

And in 'L'Amour du Mensonge':

Quand je contemple, aux feux du *gaz* qui le colore,
Ton front pâle, embelli par un morbide attrait,
Où les torches du soir *allument* une aurore

Lastly, 'Don Juan aux Enfers':

> *Frissonnant* sous son deuil, la chaste et maigre
> Elvire

The search for sources could no doubt be extended and developed. One might also draw attention, however, to the closing lines and 'thesis', as it were, of the homage:

> Celle son Ombre même un poison tutélaire
> Toujours à respirer si nous en périssons

Does not this conclusion provide us with an emblematic representation of Charles Baudelaire which is verging on the banal? If the image seems familiar, one may wish to recall Baudelaire's own 'Le Poison', or indeed this line from the poem 'Le Voyage':

> [...] O Mort! [...]
> Verse-nous ton *poison* pour qu'il nous réconforte.

Inescapably, it would seem, the sonnet brings us back to a certain *image d'Epinal* of Baudelaire and his works, the origin of which we find in the series of journalistic pieces devoted by Théophile Gautier to his unhappy colleague. The impeccable poet develops an extended comparison between the theme and characters of Hawthorne's tale 'Rappaccini's Daughter' and his colleague's infamous 'fleurs maladives', portraying the latter as a garden of curious, but dangerous and ultimately poisonous, flowers, through which the reader wanders at his peril.[34] To give but one version of a conceit to which Gautier returned on several occasions:

> *Les Fleurs du mal* sont en effet d'étranges fleurs, ne ressemblant pas à celles qui composent habituellement les bouquets de poésies. Elles ont les couleurs métalliques, le feuillage noir ou glauque, les calices bizarrement striés et *le parfum vertigineux de ces fleurs exotiques qu'on ne respire pas sans danger.*[35]

According to Pommier, however, there exists an even more banal

144

source for Mallarmé's metaphor, since, if we turn to the transcript of the trial of 1857, we discover the following passage:

> Vers le milieu du réquisitoire de Pinard, au procès des *Fleurs du mal*, on lit: 'Croit-on que *certaines fleurs aux parfums vertigineux* soient bonnes à *respirer*? *Le poison* qu'elles apportent n'éloigne pas d'elles; il monte à la tête, il grise les nerfs, il donne le trouble, le vertige *et il peut tuer aussi*.'[36]

And yet, despite the presence of a Baudelairean vocabulary and a highly conventional representation of the poet, never could one mistake 'Le Tombeau de Charles Baudelaire' for a text signed by anyone other than Stéphane Mallarmé. Nor could one confuse the sonnet of 1894 with the 'Baudelairean' poems of the early 1860s. Thirty years of *fattura* are unmistakable. Indeed, so confident is Mallarmé of leaving his perceptible mark on the text, that he does not deem it necessary to sign the sonnet openly (as he did in the cases of Poe and Wagner) by planting his name in the *semis* of the text. He even goes so far as to mark his authorial imprint by the uniquely personal manner in which he writes into the sonnet not his own name but that of 'Charles Baudelaire'. His own presence, his signature, appears as nothing more than a shadow ('au voile qui la ceint absente avec frissons') or shadowy crown around the poet's memory.

How, then, is 'Charles Baudelaire' represented in his commemorative sonnet? Firstly, if we refer to the list of names given in the Appendix to *Les Mots anglais* (Pl. 1043), we might detect a pun in the original title ('Hommage') of the piece, since there we read: 'CHARLES, ou l'HOMME'. But Mallarmé rarely proceeds by reference alone. Thus we also find 'Charles Baudelaire' phantomatically present at the rhyme, where, in the octave, the supporting consonants clearly spell 'Ch. B.':

    … bou*ch*e
    … ru*b*is
    … Anu*b*is
    … farou*ch*e

145

    ... lou*che*
    ... su*bis*
    ... pu*bis*
    ... décou*che*

It is almost as if Mallarmé had noted Gautier's rather curious remark on Baudelaire's unique style — 'et sa marque C.B. qu'on retrouve toujours appliquée sur une rime ou sur un hémistiche' — and had then applied it, literally, as the constructive principle of the text.[37] The dominance of the paraph 'Ch. B.' is reinforced by the almost unpronounceable hemistich:

    ... torde la mè*che* lou*che*

and above all by a stubborn insistence on the B:

    ... *b*avant *b*oue et ru*b*is
    A*b*omina*b*lement ... Anu*b*is
    ... flam*b*é comme un a*b*oi ...
    ... oppro*b*res su*b*is ...
    ... pu*b*is
    ... réver*b*ère ...

A variant on the paraph (this time 'C.B.') appears in lines 2 and 4:

    Sé-pulcrale ...
    ...
    ... flam-*bé* ...

And again (perhaps more persuasively) in lines 9 and 10, where we find, successively at the fifth syllable, C and B:

    Quel feuillage *sé*-ché ...
    Votif pourra *bé*-nir ...

It should come as no surprise, therefore, that in the next line, where the name 'Baudelaire' explicitly appears, the principle of building the sonnet out of the name should be preserved:

Contre . . . *Baudelaire*

Even within the hemistich, we find a further paraph:

Contre le mar*b*re …

However, Mallarmé does not limit himself to the application of the paraph, having in this instance seemingly decided to push the onomastic principle to a quasi-cabbalistic extreme.[38] Let us consider, for example, the three terms in the text which bear a capital letter, namely '*A*-nubis', '*B*-audelaire' and '*O*-mbre', the three forming a triangular textual figure ('A-B-O') which, following the Mallarmean dogma, will not or must not be abandoned to chance. Thus, in the first quatrain, one discovers a corresponding triple figure in 'ABO':

… par l-A BO-uche …
ABO-minablement …
… ABO-i farouche …

In line 4 itself one may even read the series backwards:

Tout le mus-O flam-B comme un (ABO)-i f-A-rouche.

These triangular figures do not appear as the mere product of probability or of a simple desire for patterns and repetition. Rather, Mallarmé imbues them with an air of necessity and inevitability deriving seemingly from the name of the poem's subject, as if the figure 'ABO' stemmed quite naturally from 'Charles Baudelaire', and thus served as a secondary paraph or shorthand signature worked into the body of 'Le Tombeau':

ch-A-rles BO-delaire

Furthermore, if we now turn our attention momentarily away from the disposition of letters and towards the 'images' of the sonnet, we shall again find the onomastic desire sustained. Mallarmé takes as his inspiration an element of the name. From 'Baudelaire' he highlights 'de l'air' and then develops this feature

147

metaphorically.[39] The ghastly underground emanation comes from the name, and the aim of the poem would be nothing less than the successful sublimation of this 'recent gas' into the illusory essence or perfume of the poet. Firstly, in the octave, he overlays three possible images that the gas might form: the flaming muzzle of the dog-god; the immortal pubis of the prostitute-Muse; and the triangle-plus-wick of the streetlamp. That these three triangular figures should in turn form another triangle (thus resembling the 'ABO' figure just discussed) further reflects Mallarmé's desire for onomastic rigour. The poet then folds these images together into the final and essential 'Ombre' of the closing tercet. The triangle reappears as the mourning-veil around Baudelaire's Muse, as the commemorative halo around his absence. In order to impart a sense of inevitability to this series of apparitions, Mallarmé returns to the persuasive powers and resources of the alphabet. The image of the muzzle-pubis-lamp may be formed by placing a capital T in a capital V, and so we duly find these letters sewn into the texture of the sonnet, be it in the initial position of 'attack' in lines 4, 10, and 14:

> T-out ...
> V-otif ...
> T-oujours ...

or in other positions, liberally distributed throughout the text:

> Le T-emple ense-V-eli di-V-ulgue ...
> ... égou-T ba-V-ant ...
> T-out ...
> ... T-orde
> ... immor-T-el pubis
> Don-T le V-ol selon le ré-V-erbère ...
> ... ci-T-és sans soir
> V-o-T-if ...
> Con-T-re ... V-ainemen-T ...
> Au V-oile qui la cein-T absen-T-e ...
> ... T-u-T-élaire
> T-oujours ...

The palimpsest-like quality of the overlaying of the three images may be further illustrated by highlighting a specific change which Mallarmé made to his original manuscript. Line 10 originally read 'T-riste ...', but was then altered to the final 'V-otif ...', the V thus overshadowing the erased letter T. Now, however impressive we may find such rigour or virtuosity in the application of the name, one may still wonder why Mallarmé should elect the development of this airy triangle into 'un poison tutélaire/Toujours à respirer si nous en périssons' as the conceptual argument of the poem. I have already suggested that the figure originates from the 'de l'air' of the honoured poet's name. We could now take this point further, and argue that the triangular 'Ombre' comes to represent not just the poetry signed 'Charles Baudelaire', but all poetry and indeed poetry itself — as faithfully practised, that is, by one Stéphane Mallarmé.

The 'shadow' of the sestet, into which merge the three overlaid images of the octave, represents on one level Baudelaire's Muse: be it Jeanne Duval, Rappaccini's daughter, a certain dark mixture of exoticism, eroticism, diabolism perhaps ... . This is the conventional image of Baudelaire the purveyor of 'fleurs maladives', as we saw it traced via Gautier to the courtroom's censorial admonitions. But this sort of emblem has little resonance in Mallarmé's world, where the shadow must be given a textual role to play, and a poetic function to emblematize. The ghost must be materialized, only the better to haunt us. This final transformation Mallarmé quite simply achieves by boldly identifying the shadow, and by extension the Muse of (Baudelaire's) poetry, with the *e muet* — that most shadily absent of letters and essentially silent of syllables, whose crepuscular presence comes increasingly in the sestet to dominate the symbolic mood of 'Le Tombeau'.[40]

To be sure, we hear the sensible absence of the *e muet* in the name 'Charl(e)s Baud(e)lair(e)' itself. The supple appellation thus stretches between three and six syllables. But we should also listen to the silence of the *e muet* in line 11:

Contr(e) le marbr(e) vain(e)ment de Baud(e)lair(e).

The verse contracts to eight or expands to twelve syllables, according to the *e muet*, according to the attention we choose or fail to lend to it. In the silence, a question may be discerned: Might not the *e muet* here emblematize (as it were 'vainement') the 'elle' of line 10, and so the shadow and the Muse? The answer would seem positive, if we hearken closely to what follows:

> ... elle ...
> Au voil(e) qui la ceint absent(e) avec frissons
> Cell(e) son Ombre même ...

The play between the *e muet* of 'voil(e)' and that of 'absent(e)' (the second of which resounding, as it were, even more silently than the first) illustrates practically and graphically the image of the line. The *e muet* is precisely that 'elle' (shiveringly absent, indistinguishable from her veil), whose presence/absence Mallarmé recommends us eternally to breathe. Just before the final exhortation to inspire, we may isolate this aesthetic formula:

> ... (e) son Ombre même ...

I translate: 'the *e muet* is the very shadow of poetry'. The Muse-shadow appears, via the *e muet*, as a form of halo shining around the poet called 'Baud(e)lair(e)'. This is the indeterminate extra of language which Stéphan(e) exhorts us to breathe, or to hear breathing, in poetry. It is the *stephanos* of illusory triumph which, in the memorial gesture of 'Le Tombeau de Charles Baudelaire', he promises always to bear.

5

Conclusion

M.T. — The *e muet* of 'Stéphane' is the essential syllable of all
Poetry.
S.M. — Je dois paraître un rien cela.

Although this imaginary exchange, between myself and my
subject, has evidently never taken place, even at the most speculative moments of this study, Mallarmé's modestly dissenting
response to his portrait as 'Calixte Armel' in Camille Mauclair's
novel *Le Soleil des morts* will serve as an appropriate point of entry
to my conclusion.[1] Throughout this book I have formulated,
around and about the name of Stéphane Mallarmé, numerous
hypotheses and assertions, the accumulation of which conspires
(I would hope) to form a representation of the poet sufficiently
plausible to provoke at least the kind of qualified approbation
merited by Mauclair's efforts. To be sure, those affirmations or
descriptions have not been pulled out of a hat. I have carefully
and academically prepared my ground, first by teasing out a
theory of the name from diverse sources in Mallarmé's works,
then by arguing my way through a considerable number of cases
and types of cases in such a way as to create a semblance of lively
correspondence between, on the one hand, a fragmentary but
boldly imaginative theory and, on the other, an onomastic practice revealed at work as an open-ended sequence of 'signatures',
a winning series of seemingly contrived and wilful surprises,

151

suggestions, revelations, or doubts around the name 'Stéphane Mallarmé'. Furthermore, I have not hesitated at times to inflate my pretensions beyond such localized remarks on the name and the theory of the name, by raising the stakes to broader and perhaps more important questions in the field of Mallarmé studies (and indeed literary studies in general). When I describe, for example, the poet's evolution from lachrymose Lamartinian soul to Baudelairean ephebe to flowing Mallarmean signature, such a move implies towards biography, literary history, and the notion of 'influence' an engagement whose theoretical consequences I have not paused to reflect upon in any detail. Similarly, my reference to the discourse of the sublime (in a particular sense the greatest of all literary questions) has remained allusive, as if I were protecting myself from attack by suggesting that the special circumstances and demands of my interest in the name preclude any substantial digressions into areas (the philosophy of the name, the anxiety of influence) where in any case others have shown greater competence. In trying to formulate a conclusion to my study, then, I should be mindful of Mallarmé's cautionary phrase, since it indicates very neatly that the 'thing' I have spoken of at such length — the name — represents in a sense nothing very much at all. No more than the 'rien' epigraphically initiating Mallarmé's *Poésies*. A toque cast away in the immense ocean of literary theory, or floating along the narrow waters explored by my subject's legendary *yole*.

'Je dois paraître un rien cela.' The phrase serves also to recall an important feature of the onomastic 'strategy' whose existence this study has endeavoured to demonstrate: that each instance or appearance of the name, of Stéphane Mallarmé as his name, remains necessarily partial or virtual, seeking only ever to suggest or instil the doubt that everywhere and always there may exist a more systematic and elaborate onomastic mystery, a glimpse of which has been momentarily revealed to us in the specific operation under analysis. 'Each time an effort is made towards the signature' (I might paraphrase), 'there is nomenclature.' Despite the deliberately exaggerated air of self-confidence or self-delusion adopted at times in the preceding pages, the task befalling us in this conclusion will not be to summarize the various and diverse elements or versions of 'Stéphane Mallarmé' which I have presented, closing with a definitive and eternal name-portrait such as into Himself finally I would have changed him. The act of denomination here described appears at once as an infinite series of individual onomastic acts or performances, and also as a commitment, a fidelity, a determination, to name and rename for all eternity. The most satisfying conclusion to my book would consist in proposing its immediate reconversion into a form of introduction to a notional history of Mallarmean representations (working title: 'près d'un siècle de lecture maintenant'). Its achievement would have been to establish the position and practices of the poet himself with regard to such a venture, as well as to define the spirit if not the form in which the enterprise would need to be executed. Infinitely patient and attentive to detail, inexhaustibly optimistic in its pursuit of essences, happy to confront surprises and reversals of fate and dead-ends, and willing to humour and even understand the most far-fetched and self-deluding of truths ... Alongside the imaginary portraits of 'Mallarmé' signed by Mondor, Mauron, or Richard — in whose works the poet figures as a 'factional' representation not dissimilar to the name or character one would read in the context of a novel (*Le Soleil des morts*), a 'roman critique' (*A rebours*), or an autobiographical memoir (Regnier's *Portraits et souvenirs*, for example)[2] — I should like fraternally to align the 'Mallarmé' of Léon Bloy, Alfred Jarry, or Francis Ponge. The critical tradition would surely gain in such a transaction. Once lightened of their pretensions to historical, psychological, or interpretive truth, its members would launch out on a new and much healthier existence, where the flagrant contradictions, blind spots, and prejudices of the author would become so many sources of charm rather than exasperation.[3] The prospect of an imaginary universe where Mallarmé psychoanalysed equals Mallarmé fictionalized equals Mallarmé explicated equals Mallarmé insulted equals Mallarmé politically or philosophically or otherwise justified, and so on, strikes me as a more frequentable and indeed agreeable environment than the atmosphere often evoked by a glance through the critical bibliography. So many years of accumulated epithets — difficult, obscure, impotent, Hegelian, transcendental, baroque, obscene, Marinist, heroic, sensualist, paranoid, symbolist, schizophrenic,

153

revolutionary, happy ... — might give way to a literary glory worthy of the name.

Such a project would require a writer's light touch at the service of a scientific patience. Trusting that in the future a like intelligence may emerge, let us briefly conclude with one final scene of Mallarmé speculating on the name-of-the-poet and literary fame. In this instance it is the name, which even back in 1896 had begun to acquire a mythical dimension, of Jean-Arthur Rimbaud.[4] Written in 1896 for the North American review *The Chap-book*, on the express request of its editor, Harrison Rhodes (see *Pl.* 1587), the text has generally been passed over either as a piece of occasional journalism (a genre reputedly unpractised by our poet), or at most as evidence of Mallarmé's failure to appreciate accurately the significance of Rimbaud's lightning passage through the literary sky. Seen strictly in the light of the name, however, the letter-article (*Pl.* 512–19) will provide us with a final lesson in reading poetic destiny, and will indicate in passing that Mallarmé has proved, even in this particular instance, a more astute judge of the question than is often imagined.[5]

The first thing to remark about the article is that it is explicitly structured around the name, opening in effect and duly closing with an outspoken evocation and discussion of that very subject. The first paragraph runs:

> J'imagine qu'une de ces soirées de mardi, rares, où vous [Rhodes] me fîtes l'honneur, chez moi, d'ouïr mes amis converser, *le nom soudainement d'Arthur Rimbaud* se soit bercé à la fumée de plusieurs cigarettes; installant, pour votre curiosité, du vague. (*Pl.* 512; my emphasis)

Likewise, in the closing paragraph, the author returns to the name, wondering whether Rimbaud's sudden collapse and death immediately on touching again 'le sol natal étranger' might not be interpreted as an 'interdiction que [...] lui se retournât à la signification neuve, proférée en la langue, des quelques syllabes ARTHUR RIMBAUD' (*Pl.* 519). Much of what comes between these two appearances of the name (and the *battement* of onomastic reflection they duly excite) we might none too cruelly characterize as the rehearsal of second-hand observations and anecdotes, albeit dressed up in Mallarmé's inimitable prose and interspersed with peculiarly 'Mallarmean' touches.[6] Let us therefore concern ourselves principally and unashamedly with the name. As a first move (recalling the strategy employed in 'Sur Voltaire' and 'Whistler') Mallarmé seeks to create a certain ironic distance between himself and the question posed ('Quel, le personnage, questionnez-vous'), at once hinting at the naive and foreign origin of the latter, and suggesting that Rimbaud's reputation preoccupies Parisian literary minds less imperiously perhaps than it does the American reading public: 'du moins [the question would continue] exerce-t-il sur les événements poétiques récents une influence si particulière que, cette allusion faite, par exemple, on se taise, énig-matiquement et réfléchisse, comme si beaucoup de silence, à la fois, et de rêverie s'imposait ou d'admiration inachevée' (512). No sooner has he thus situated the problem than he unhesitatingly formulates the following imperative response: 'Doutez'! We are instructed to doubt, specifically, 'que les principaux novateurs, maintenant [...] aient à quelque profondeur et par un trait direct, subi Arthur Rimbaud'. The potential charm of the appellation appears to be rapidly diminishing, an impression confirmed by the assertion that only at our intellectual peril would we conceive of Rimbaud's contribution to French poetry as in any sense revolu-tionary, since the young rebel remained 'un strict observateur du jeu ancien', and moreover 'tout, certes, aurait existé, depuis, sans ce passant considérable'. An untroubled reading of the literary memoirs which follow would seem somewhat compromised given the severity of these opening strictures and manoeuvres. One might wonder with good cause whether Stéphane Mallarmé is really taking 'Arthur Rimbaud' very seriously at all. The suspicion persists through to the close of the piece, where Mallarmé addresses the death of the poet and, once more, his name:

> Une nouvelle inopinée, en 1891, circula par les journaux: que celui, qui avait été et demeure, pour nous un poète, voyageur, débarqué à Marseille, avec une fortune et opéré, arthritique, venait d'y mourir. (*Pl.* 517)

Arthritic: should we allow ourselves to imagine that the high seriousness of Mallarmé's name-theory has here come to conclude in a cheap pun about Arthur's arthritis? The poet immediately replies to this interrogation by confessing the uncertain loyalty he feels towards the business of biographical (and onomastic?) representation:

> Ordonner, en fragments intelligibles et probables, pour la traduire, la vie d'autrui, est tout juste, impertinent: il ne me reste que de pousser à ses limites ce genre de méfait.

The crime in my opinion should be pardoned on the strength of this confession, especially since in the remaining pages of the portrait Mallarmé does indeed push to the limits both the charm and the gravity of onomastic discourse. Two questions concerning Arthur Rimbaud (he claims) trouble at present certain literary spirits. Firstly, to know whether there might exist (as has been suggested) any previously unpublished manuscripts from the hand of the Ethiopian traveller; secondly, to imagine how the interested party himself might have reacted personally to 'la signification neuve, proférée en la langue, des quelques syllabes ARTHUR RIMBAUD'. Of these two mysteries it appears quite clear that only the former might genuinely have caused speculation on the Parisian scene, the latter stemming directly from Mallarmé's imagination and onomastic curiosity. Little wonder that the poet should judge, regarding the first question, that 'prolonger l'espoir d'une oeuvre de maturité nuit, ici, à l'interprétation exacte d'une aventure unique dans l'*histoire de l'art*' (Pl. 518; my emphasis). Rather, according to the present form of 'art-history', it seems far more important to establish 's'il avait, de retour, après le laisser volontaire des splendeurs de la jeunesse, appris leur épanouissement, parmi la génération en fruits opulents non moins et plus en rapport avec le goût jadis de la gloire, que ceux là-bas aux oasis: les aurait-il reniés ou cueillis?' In order to *trancher la question*, Mallarmé conceives for the younger poet a fairly brutal fate:

> Le Sort, avertissement à l'homme du rôle accompli,

156

sans doute afin qu'il ne vacille pas en trop de perplexité, trancha ce pied qui se posait sur le sol natal étranger.

The *arthuritic* problem is resolved with a sweep of cruel humour. Rather than waste one's intelligence hesitating over futile speculations destined, in any case, to remain without issue, better to cut oneself free from such academic constraints and simply invent an answer, or a contribution, to 'la signification neuve, proférée en la langue, des quelques syllabes ARTHUR RIMBAUD'. Fate's knife having fallen, and with that gesture having silenced Arthur Rimbaud's hypothetical reaction to his new-found fame, Mallarmé considers the matter closed, and closes his mind to further consideration. However (we recognize from sublime discourse this 'cependant' following the silence), something concerning the name remains to be said, and someone, fortunately, remains to pronounce it:

Cependant on doit, approfondissant d'hypothèse pour y rendre la beauté éventuelle, *cette carrière hautaine*, après tout et sans compromission — d'anarchiste, par l'esprit — présumer que l'intéressé en eût accueilli avec une fière incurie l'aboutissement à la célébrité comme concernant certes, quelqu'un qui avait été lui, mais ne l'était plus, d'aucune façon: à moins que le *fantôme impersonnel* ne poussât la désinvolture jusqu'à réclamer traversant Paris, pour les joindre à l'argent rapporté, *simplement des droits d'auteur*. (*Pl.* 519; my emphasis)

Having reached an apparent conclusion, Mallarmé returns, via the inevitable 'cependant', to the name and the chain of signifiers around Arthur: 'arthritique' and 'histoire d'art' rejoined by 'carrière hautaine' and 'droits d'auteur'. The notion of haughty careering doubly evokes the figure 'Arthur Rimbaud'. Firstly through the play on 'carrière', designating at once the poet's career and the path traced by this particular 'météore' (*Pl.* 512) across the French literary heavens; secondly through the element 'haut' in 'hautain' (already underlined by the meteoric pun), which is elevated out of epithetic banality by the following reminder of *Les Mots anglais*: 'ARTHUR, ou le haut' (*Pl.* 1044). In the final phrase of the text ('simplement des droits d'auteur'), the recommendation that the poet we call 'Arthur Rimbaud' should act so high and mighty in his glory finds itself expanded into a general aesthetic imperative for the poet *qua* poet and his name *qua* name. Disappearing behind such an inflation, 'Arthur le haut' emblematizes quite simply *l'auteur*. Unless we should cast that Nobody in the guise of 'le fantôme impersonnel'. An apparition of anonymity, wherein to inscribe the signature of

Notes

1 Introduction

[1] François de Mély, from an article which appeared in the *Revue Archéologique* (Paris, 1911) entitled 'Signature des primitifs. La Tradition du IXe au XVIe siècle'.

[2] See Bennington, *Dudding: des noms de Rousseau* (Paris: Galilée, 1990) and Kamuf, *Signatures, ou l'institution de l'auteur* (Paris: Galilée, 1991).

[3] Paris: Seuil, 1991. The text is two-handed. Bennington provides what he calls a 'Derridabase', that is to say a presentation of key Derridean concepts ('Remarque', 'Le commencement', 'Le signe', 'L'écriture', etc.) in the form almost of a (computer-based) critical dictionary. Below, the Philosopher writes a second text, entitled 'Circonfession', which effectively combines reflections on Bennington's work with extracts from his forthcoming publications. I should add that Derrida has recently published three related texts on the Name: *Khôra, Sauf le nom (Post-Scriptum)*, and *Passions* (all three Paris: Galilée, 1993).

[4] See 2.2 below for the importance of this concept to the development of the present argument.

[5] *Mimologiques: Voyage en Cratylie* (Paris: Seuil, 1976).

[6] See page 32, for example, where Genette argues that Socrates' rejection of the Cratylian position is an

> abandon de fait seulement assorti d'une sorte de regret de principe: 'Il subsiste donc simplement le regret de devoir aban-donner cette théorie si prometteuse'. 'Moi aussi,' dit en effet Socrates, 'j'aime que les noms soient autant que possible

> semblables aux objets; mais je crains qu'en réalité il ne faille ici, pour reprendre le mot d'Hermogène, tirer laborieusement sur la ressemblance, et qu'on ne soit forcé de recourir encore, pour la justesse des noms, à cet expédient grossier de la convention. Autrement, la plus belle façon possible de parler consisterait sans doute à employer des noms qui fussent tous, ou pour la plupart, semblables aux objets, c'est-à-dire appropriés; et la plus laide, dans le cas contraire.'

[7] The phrase cited comes from 'Toast Funèbre' (*O.C.* 242).

[8] The *Cratylus* opens with a joke by its eponymous hero, Hermogenes complaining to Socrates that, according to Cratylus, his name is not really 'Hermogenes': 'ton nom n'est pas Hermogène [dit Cratyle], même si tout le monde te le donne ...' (Genette, 23) — the point being that, although Hermes is the god of wealth, poor Hermogenes is not (onomastically?) rich.

[9] In 1992 I contacted the teacher concerned, one Madame Sipos of the lycée Jeanson de Sailly, who in turn referred me to Madame Marie-Christine Dumas of Paris VII. My enquiries continue.

[10] See 2.3.1 and 2.2.3, below, for closer discussion of these texts.

[11] See the opening lines of the 'Conférence' (*Pl.* 481), 'Sait-on ce que c'est qu'écrire? Une ancienne et très vague mais jalouse pratique, dont gît le sens au mystère du coeur.'

[12] The phrase comes from Derrida's entry on Mallarmé in Marcel Arland et al. (eds), *Tableau de littérature française*, III: 'De Madame de Staël à Rimbaud' (Paris: Gallimard, 1974), 368–79.

[13] I cannot bring myself to agree with Jean-Pierre Richard's judgement that 'peu d'auteurs même ont été plus minutieusement, et, d'une manière générale, plus heureusement étudiés que lui' (*L'univers imaginaire de Mallarmé* (Paris: Seuil, 1961), 13).

[14] Paris: Librairie des Méridiens-Klincksieck, 1986. See also: Ross Chambers, 'An Address in the Country: Mallarmé and the Kinds of Literary Context', *French Forum*, 11 (1986), 199–215; Kaufmann, *L'Equivoque épistolaire* (Paris: Minuit, 1990); Roger Dragonetti, *Un fantôme dans le kiosque* (Paris: Seuil, 1992); Marian Zwerling Sugano, *The Poetics of the Occasion: Mallarmé and the Poetry of Circumstance* (Stanford: Stanford University Press, 1992); Mary Lewis Shaw, *Performance in the texts of Mallarmé* (Philadelphia: Pennsylvania State University Press, 1993); *Dalhousie French Review*, 25 ('Mallarmé theorist of our times' special issue) (1993).

[15] Compare on this point Sugano in her Introduction and Chapter 5, 'Towards a New Poetics'.

[16] Equally there is this formula: 'L'impossibilité d'un livre total détermine, par contrecoup, le statut circonstanciel de presque tous les textes de Mallarmé' (Kaufmann, 44).

[17] For the history of this expression, one should consult Genette's article (in

Figures, I) of the same name, where he takes issue with Richard's sensualist and celebratory version of the Mallarmé myth, as expressed most famously in the following passage:

> Le vrai bonheur mallarméen, affirmons-le bien haut contre tant de commentaires tragiques et partiaux, n'est pas celui d'un vide en lequel le monde entier tendrait à disparaître; il n'est pas non plus celui d'une abstraction figée, ni d'une éternité sans forme ni saveur: c'est celui d'une vie qui jouit, en toute conscience, en tout savoir, de la seule grâce qui lui soit évidemment accordée, celle de vivre. (Richard, 601)

2 Does Stéphane Mallarmé have a theory of the Name?

[1] 'Petite philologie à l'usage des classes et du monde', *Les Mots anglais* 'par Mr Mallarmé, professeur au Lycée Fontanes', appeared in 1877. *Les Dieux antiques*, 'nouvelle mythologie illustrée, d'après George W. Cox, et les travaux de la science moderne', was published in 1880. See *Pl.* 886–1046 and 1159–1276 for texts; 1643 and 1644 for notes. For fuller studies of the works, and for information on the ratio of translation to Mallarmean addition, see respectively Jacques Michon, *Mallarmé et 'Les Mots anglais'* (Montreal: Presses de l'Université de Montréal, 1978), and Jean Seznec, 'Les Dieux antiques de Mallarmé', in *Baudelaire, Mallarmé and Valéry: New Essays in honour of Lloyd Austin*, ed. by Malcolm Bowie, Alison Fairlie, and Alison Finch (Cambridge: Cambridge University Press, 1982).

[2] Gardner Davies, in *Mallarmé et le drame solaire* (Paris: Corti, 1959), for example, having recognized that all the various myths discussed in *Les Dieux antiques* may be reduced to a solar ur-myth ('LA TRAGEDIE DE LA NATURE' (*Pl.* 1178)), goes on to interpret a suite of solar-crepuscular poems (e.g. 'M'introduire dans ton histoire') in the light of this discovery. As for *Les Mots anglais*, for which great claims have been made (e.g. Valéry: 'Le livre *Les Mots anglais* est peut-être le document le plus révélateur que nous possedions sur le travail intime de Mallarmé' ('Sorte de Préface', in *Oeuvres*, ed. by Jean Hytier, Paris: Gallimard, 1957)), Mondor strikes a note of sanity, when he says: 'Si curieuse que soit cette *Petite Philologie à l'usage des Classes et du Monde*, il y a peut-être une exagération à dire, comme l'ont fait MM. Montel et Monda "que la source de toute la poésie de Mallarmé s'y trouve en quelque sorte enfermée"' (*O.C.* 1643).

[3] See, for example, the italicized section in *Pl.* 1169, from 'Nous parlons aujour-d'hui' down to the capitalized phrase 'LA TRAGEDIE DE LA NATURE', which bears the asterisked comment: 'Note particulière à la Traduction'.

[4] Compare the following: 'Oui, maintenant comme autrefois, les poètes ne font autre chose qu'attribuer la vie à ce qu'ils voient et à ce qu'ils entendent autour d'eux. Qu'importe l'image elle-même' (1168).

[5] See 'Rêverie d'un poète français' for an explicit rejection of 'Legend': 'l'esprit

français [...] répugne, en cela d'accord avec l'Art dans son intégrité, qui est inventeur, à la Légende' (*Pl.* 544). See also 4.2 below.

[6] Hence no doubt the hollow echo heard on the few occasions when there is correspondence between *Les Dieux antiques* and the poems. For example, the reader of 'Tombeau de Charles Baudelaire' stumbles across this phrase: 'Anubis est représenté avec la tête d'un chien ou d'un chacal' (1274); the reader of 'Ses purs ongles', this: 'Quant au Phénix, emblème égyptien de l'immortalité, sous la forme d'un oiseau qui renaît de ses cendres' (1274). It is difficult to see how the reference has enriched the reading.

[7] Note that this passage comes from the final appendix to the text, added on the initiative of the translator and entitled 'Notes sur la Transcription des Noms de la Mythologie Classique'. The latter is, according to Mallarmé, 'une grave question' (1276).

[8] The former is expressed through what might be called Mallarmé's use of the big, naive question. Examples of this would be: 'Qu'est-ce que l'Anglais?' (899/1046); 'Aujourd'hui, où en est l'Anglais?' (1049); 'Qu'est-ce que le Langage, entre les matériaux scientifiques à étudier?' (901), and so on. Sometimes the question may be used as little more than a conjunction, leading the reader eagerly on: 'Est-ce tout? point: et les Noms tirés des Ecritures!' (1044); 'Quel moyen de ne pas céder à cette fatalité bizarre: en est-il un? il en est deux' (1013). As for Mallarmé's casual (not to say ironic) attitude to scientific demonstration, it shows itself frequently in the one-line paragraphs Mallarmé inserts from time to time, as if to shed a little light on such a dark accumulation of 'facts'. Examples abound: 'Tout ceci va apparaître' (901); 'Etc., etc., etc.' (901/1015); 'Quelques faits' (998); 'Trêve de détails' (1010); 'Je commence (1024); 'Voilà' (1033/1048).

[9] Compare *La Dernière Mode* for more evidence of the delight Mallarmé takes in travesty.

[10] We should not forget, however, that in spite of his 'reifying' feeling towards words and names, Mallarmé, as Derrida reminds us ('Mallarmé', in *Tableau de la littérature française*, 371), declared himself to be 'profondément syntaxier'. For an extreme example of the transformation of word into thing, consider this passage: 'Par mille interstices, il en est [des noms], se glissant dans la Langue, qui perdent l'habitude ordinaire de désigner des personnes, pour s'appliquer aux choses. RAGLAN, BROUGHAM, et MACADAM, par exemple, ce vêtement, cette voiture, ce traitement voyer.' (1045)

[11] *Oeuvres complètes de Villiers de l'Isle-Adam*, ed. by Alan Raitt and Pierre-Georges Castex, 2 vols (Paris: Gallimard, 1986–88), II, 309–12 and 1262–64 for Notes.

[12] Jean de la Fontaine, *Fables*, ed. by Jean-Pierre Collinet (Paris: Gallimard, 1991), 270–72

[13] Compare 'travaux' in line 8 of 'Les Deux Pigeons':

> ... au moins que les travaux,
> Les dangers, les soins du voyage,
> Changent un peu votre courage. (*Fables*, 270)

14 On this point, compare Vincent Kaufmann, *Le Livre et ses adresses* and Marian Zwerling Sugano, *The Poetics of the Occasion*.

15 Both phrases alluded to here come from 'Prose pour Des Esseintes', in *O.C.* 248–51.

16 *Oeuvres complètes de Villiers de l'Isle-Adam*, I, 583–96 and 1275–79 for notes.

17 G. Jean-Aubry, *Une Amitié exemplaire* (Paris: Mercure de France, 1942), 72.

18 There is perhaps even a double pun, both words meaning 'thus', around 'sic itur' and 'Igitur', suggesting perhaps that the famous 'conte' is not bound for glory.

19 *O.C.* 527–31 and 1590.

20 For evidence that Mallarmé himself would unfailingly feel the effect of a name, consider this passage from 'Hamlet' (*Pl.* 299): 'parce que Hamlet extériorise, sur des planches, ce personnage unique d'une tragédie intime et occulte, *son nom même affiché exerce sur moi, sur toi qui le lis, une fascination, parente de l'angoisse*' (my emphasis). Or again the following remark on the genesis of 'Hérodiade':

> Merci du détail que vous [Eugène Lefébure] me donnez au sujet d'*Hérodiade*, mais je ne m'en sers pas. La plus belle page de mon oeuvre sera celle qui ne contiendra que ce nom divin *Hérodiade*. Le peu d'inspiration que j'ai eu, je le dois à ce nom, et je crois que si mon héroïne s'était appelée Salomé, j'eusse inventé ce nom sombre, et rouge comme une grenade ouverte, *Hérodiade*. Du reste, je tiens à en faire un être purement rêvé et absolument indépendant de l'Histoire. Vous me comprenez. Je n'invoque même pas les tableaux des élèves du Vinci et de tous les Florentins qui ont eu cette maîtresse et l'ont appelée comme moi. (See Gardner Davies, *Mallarmé et le rêve d''Hérodiade'* (Paris: Corti, 1978), 11).

21 *Pl.* 481–510 and 1583–85.

22 We could identify this as one of the prime characteristics of Mallarmé's prose-rhythm, the one-line paragraph coming to punctuate the amazing complexity of the syntax in general. Here, examples would be: 'Simplement, on le rencontra, ce fut tout' (483); 'Je le revois' (490); 'Il se taisait; merci, Toi, maintenant d'avoir parlé, on comprend' (495); 'Je souris' (509); as well as the examples given in the text.

23 See Villiers's supposed opinion of his works: 'et ses écrits par la détresse [...] ravis comme des lambeaux [...] [Villiers] traitant cela de "devoirs français" comme au collège, parce qu'il sentait bien n'avoir pas dompté l'esprit du temps, leur gardant, à ces reliques, une secrète rancune que des événements lui en eussent imposé le hasard!' (496).

24 We may perceive a reflection of this shift in the passage (*Pl.* 498–50), where Mallarmé undertakes to describe Villiers's 'injurieux logis', but can barely refrain from turning towards a much more 'Mallarmean' interior, decorated with reminiscences of his own writing: we even find that his friend's apartment contains 'des bibelots abolis'! (*Pl.* 499).

[25] Given the argument of the preceding section, it may be indicated here that even at the opening of the lecture Mallarmé expresses considerable doubt as to Villiers's awareness of the true role and importance of the writer and writing. 'Le démon littéraire qui inspira Villiers de l'Isle-Adam', he wonders, 'à ce point fut-il conscient?' The reply is to say the least mitigated: 'par éclairs, peut-être' (481).

[26] *Pl.* 872 and 1693. As regards the title, we are unfortunately denied the pleasure of reading into it a play on 'survol', when we discover that the original text bore for a name no more than the title of its author: 'Cette réponse a été relevée sur une coupure de journal, ne portant ni nom, ni date, trouvée parmi les papiers du poète: réponse qui porte le nom de Stéphane Mallarmé imprimé comme titre et comme signature' (*Pl.* 1639). As for the date, we could make an educated guess at 1894, since not only do most of the other 'réponses à des enquêtes' date from the nineties, but, more precisely, the year would have marked Voltaire's two-hundredth birthday, and so may well have seen much of this sort of journalistic surveying.

[27] Compare this comment in Dauzat, Albert, *Les Noms de Personnes* (Paris: Delagrave, 1950), 183:

> L'anagramme a été mise à profit depuis longtemps. Qui ne sait que *Voltaire* est l'anagramme d'Arouet l.j. (le jeune), à une époque où l'*i* et le *j*, l'*u* et le *v* étaient confondus dans l'écriture? [...] Pour deux pièces satiriques, dont la seconde n'était même pas de lui, le jeune AROUET fut envoyé en exil a Sully, puis pour deux mois à la Bastille: ne désirant pas y retourner, il écrivait désormais sous le nom de VOLTAIRE.

[28] *Pl.* 532–33, 1590, and 1618–20. For the article 'The Impressionists and Edouard Manet', which survives only in the English version published in *The Art Monthly Review* in 1876, see Penny Florence, *Mallarmé, Manet and Redon* (Cambridge: Cambridge University Press, 1986), 11–18. There is not a great deal of bibliographical information available on 'Manet' and 'Whistler', beyond the following remark in the Bibliography prepared by Mallarmé for *Divagations* (1897): 'EDGARD (sic) POE, WHISTLER, EDOUARD MANET en vue de la publication, *Portraits du Prochain Siècle.*' The Bibliography is reproduced in the Gallimard edition of *Igitur/Divagations/Un Coup de Dés* of 1976, 335–38. We may safely assume, however, that the text was written after Manet's death in 1883. As regards Manet's portrait of S.M., it may be seen in the Musée d'Orsay, and is reproduced in *Mallarmé, documents iconographiques,* ed. by Henri Mondor (Vésenaz-Geneva: Pierre Cailler, 1947).

[29] See Orienti, Sandra, *Tout l'Oeuvre peint d'Edouard Manet* (Paris: Flammarion, 1970).

[30] These three pictures, according to Orienti, would represent, in Manet's own words, 'un abrégé des sujets de conversation avec l'écrivain'.

[31] The two men appear to have become friends around 1873 and remained firmly so until Manet's death in 1883 (see *Pl.* 1619–20). Mallarmé himself refers to their friendship lasting ten years (see the epigraph to this section). As regards the defence of the name, compare the following from 'The Impressionists and Edouard

Manet': 'For it was evident that the preacher [E.M.] had a meaning; he was persistent in his reiteration, unique in his persistency, and his works were signed by the then new and unknown name of EDOUARD MANET.' And again: 'But this enlightened amateur [Baudelaire] died [...] before his favourite painter had won a public name.' And lastly: 'until at length vanquished by its good faith and persistency, the jury recognized the name of Manet, welcomed it' (Florence, 12).

[32] Compare the late photograph of Mallarmé sitting beneath the portrait, cigarette in the opposite hand, legs crossed in the opposite way, body leaning in the opposite direction, as if to counterbalance his youth, or as if to present the painting, jokingly, as actual mirror rather than sign of decay (Mondor, *Mallarmé, documents iconographiques*, 45).

[33] A similar double signature appears in the woodcut frontispiece to *L'Après-midi d'un faune* (Paris: Derenne, 1876) designed by Manet that same year. On the far right-hand side of the image, we see the *M* of the artist's paraph-signature; but, if we follow the inclination of the Faun's body and eyes to the opposite bank, we also see, isolated against the bending of the reeds a second and rougher *M*, presumably marking the subject or co-author 'Mallarmé'.

[34] See Note 6 above: 'he was persistent in his reiteration, unique in his persistency [...] until at length vanquished by its good faith and persistency'.

[35] Compare the autobiographical epigraph to this section: 'J'ai, dix ans ...'. Concerning the pun on 'Manet/il reste', we may note that the painter's *ex libris* — 'imaginé par Poulet-Malassis et gravé par Bracquemond' — included the legend 'manet et manebit' ('il reste et restera') from 1874 onwards (*Manet* (Paris: Editions de la réunion des musées nationaux, 1983), 13).

[36] Concerning the name 'Manet', see Dauzat, Albert, *Dictionnaire étymologique des noms et prénoms* (Paris: Larousse, 1951).

[37] Compare the earlier version: 'Manet, when he casts away the cares of art and chats with a friend between the lights in the studio, expresses himself with brilliancy. [...] Each time he begins a picture, says he, he plunges headlong into it, and feels like a man who knows that his surest plan to learn to swim safely is, dangerous as it may seem, to throw himself into the water' (Florence, 12).

[38] Pl. 531–32 plus 1481–82, 1590, and 1603–06. See also *O.C.* 384–86 for the 'Billet' plus 480, 567, and 684 for diverse occasional gestures. For the lithograph of Mallarmé, see *Vers et Prose* of 1893; also reproduced in *Mallarmé, documents iconographiques*. Henri de Régnier recalls Mallarmé's fondness for the two portraits: 'Il y a beaucoup de portraits de Stéphane Mallarmé', he remarks, before specifying that: 'Il aimait ce double chefd'oeuvre, et se plaisait à revivre ainsi deux fois par le pinceau hardi et par le subtil crayon de deux grands artistes qui furent ces amis' (*Figures et Caractères* (Paris: Mercure de France, 1901, 139).

[39] Quoted in notes to 'Toute l'âme résumée' (*O.C.* 432), this phrase comes from the interview accorded to the *Figaro*: 'Edgar Poe a dit: "il n'est point prétexte à longs poèmes"; j'ajouterai: "nous ne pouvons chanter tout le temps".'

[40] The following passage is representative: 'l'oeuvre pure implique la disparition

élocutoire du poète, qui cède l'initiative aux mots, par le heurt de leur inégalité mobilisés; ils s'allument de reflets réciproques comme une virtuelle traînée de feux sur des pierreries, remplaçant la respiration perceptible en l'ancien souffle lyrique ou la direction personnelle de la phrase' (*Pl.* 366). On the paradox of the author signing with his absence, Derrida has the following remarks:

> Il faudrait, à l'aide de ce texte, en lui, découvrir la logique nouvelle de cette double opération; qu'on ne pourrait d'ailleurs attribuer à Mallarmé qu'en recourant à une théorie naïve et intéressée de la signature, celle-là même que Mallarmé, définissant justement ce qu'il appelait l'''opération', n'a cessé de dérouter. Un texte est fait pour se passer de références. A la chose même, nous le verrons, à l'auteur qui n'y consigne que sa disparition. Cette disparition est activement inscrite, elle n'est pas un accident mais plutôt sa nature; elle y marque la signature d'une omission incessante. (*Tableau de la littérature française*, 370)

[41] Kathleen Lochnan, *The Etchings of Whistler* (New Haven: Yale University Press, 1984), 165. In the context of exchanges between Mallarmé and Whistler, note also Mondor's comment that of those he has actually examined 'aucune n'est datée ni signée autrement que du papillon habituel à son oeuvre et à sa correspondance' (*Pl.* 1605).

[42] 'Le Whistler signifie très bien Stéphane Mallarmé'. Thus Remy de Gourmont in the *Mercure de France* in 1893 (see *Vers et Prose* (Paris: Gallimard, 1977), 172), commenting on the lithograph executed by Whistler as frontispiece to the *Vers et Prose*. The phrase could serve as epigraph for this section. Mallarmé's own reaction was equally enthusiastic:

> Whistler
>
> selon qui je défie
> Les siècles en lithographie (*O.C.* 684)

[43] Compare this creaking name-rhyme:

> Mai dont le rayon ne dure
> Pour qu'il éblouisse l'air
> Mêle l'art à sa verdure
> Et joint au printemps Whistler. (*O.C.* 684)

[44] The conceit of the poem springs from the name of the journal, *The Whirlwind* ('tourbillon'), for which Whistler had asked Mallarmé to provide a little something. Indeed, 'Whirlwind' was the poem's first title. Thus Mallarmé to Whistler in October 1890: 'Je vais, au premier jour, vous adresser, pour lui [*The Whirlwind*], un rien, combinant vos deux suggestions, de la lettre et des vers. Un petit sonnet de congratulations, avec votre nom à la rime, Ah! Ah! Ah!' (*O.C.* 385). The rather strange cackle on Mallarmé's part is echoed in Whistler's reply, a few days later: 'Oh! le sonnet! si vous saviez comme je me fais d'avance une joie de le lire! Ah! Ah! Ah!' (385). The exchange of laughter in the correspondence re-emerges in the poem with: 'Sinon rieur'. See also the anodyne occasional verse:

Leur rire avec la même gamme
Sonnera si tu te rendis
Chez Monsieur Whistler et Madame
Rue Antique du Bac 110. (*O.C.* 480)

3 What is — Stéphane Mallarmé?

[1] A detailed discussion of 'Mallarmé and the sublime' will be developed in section 3.5.

[2] In the context of *Un coup de dés*, which looms in the backgound of the passage under discussion, this tension — omnipresent in Mallarmé — between dispersal and disposition appears around the pair 'désastre/constellation'.

[3] This, incidentally, may also be called a 'paraphe'. For evidence of Mallarmé's interest in the term, consider, for example: 'Quelque symétrie, parallèlement, qui, de la situation des vers en la pièce se lie à l'authenticité de la pièce dans le volume, vole, outre le volume, à plusieurs inscrivant, eux, sur l'espace spirituel, le paraphe amplifié du génie, anonyme et parfait comme une existence d'art' (*Pl.* 367). Or again: 'Quel nom, d'arrière-exploits mémorable, vaudra le paraphe, entre des appels de splendeur, que signe avec son motif ondoyant telle grande symphonie de concerts' (*Pl.* 412). One also finds the word in the following occasional poems:

> Cette chatte humble et tendre à qui l'attache
> Porte un paraphe illustre pour moustache (*O.C.* 679)
>
> Dame au coeur clos d'une agrafe
> Tous les baisers que t'as lus
> Jusqu'ici sous mon paraphe
> Je les adresse aux talus. (681)
>
> Cet écrit, tu le porteras,
> Poste, au journal le Télégraphe,
> C'est pour Monsieur André Terras
> Un nom que la gloire paraphe. (496)

[4] See, for example the fifth plate in *O.C.*, a reproduction of 'A la nue accablante tu' as it appeared in *Pan*, April–May, 1895.

[5] Note that a complete version of the text would include, albeit as a note, the name, 'Stéphane Mallarmé', which appeared at the foot of the poem as it was first printed in *La Plume* in 1893, as well as the 'real' paraph which accompanied the manuscript of the same year (see *O.C.* 403). Kaufmann has an excellent analysis of this text on pages 44–48 of *Le Livre et ses Adresses*; see also Lucette Finas, 'Salut', *Esprit*, 441 (1974), 871–901.

[6] Note that 'Salut' served as an epigraph to *Poésies*, the poem itself therefore performing a sort of signing function (see *O.C.* 403).

[7] Compare Valéry's article on Baudelaire, 'Situation de Baudelaire', in *Oeuvres*, ed. by J.Hytier (Paris: Gallimard, 1957), 598–613.

[8] Compare this passage from 'Le Nénuphar Blanc': 'Tant d'immobilité paressait que [...] je ne vérifiai l'arrêt qu'à l'étincellement stable d'*initiales* sur les avirons *m*is à nu, ce qui me rappela à mon identité mondaine' (*Pl.* 283). Besides the inevitable, but certainly not negligeable, play on 'paressait/paraissait' (also used by Mallarmé in 'Eventail/de Madame Mallarmé' (*O.C.* 388)), we may note here how the notion of initials constituting one's signature is itself 'made naked', and then branded with the Mallarmean cachet: *s.m.*

[9] Compare the 'Eventail' dedicated to Méry Laurent (*O.C.* 374).

[10] For a more straightforward exposition of the superior quality of the blank, consider, for example: 'L'armature intellectuelle du poème se dissimule et tient — a lieu — dans l'espace qui isole les strophes et parmi le blanc du papier: significatif silence qu'il n'est pas moins beau de composer, que les vers'. (*Pl.* 872)

[11] Compare a similar figure and thematics in 'Indomptablement a dû ...' (*O.C.* 406).

[12] A phrase of which E. Lefébure, on reception of the poem, confessed: 'il y a [...] (pardonnez-le moi) deux vers que je ne comprends bien: Car un ennui, etc.' (*O.C.* 177).

[13] See *Les Fleurs du mal*, ed. by Antoine Adam (Paris: Bordas, 1990), 95–97.

[14] We may note in passing this 'intervallic' conception of the representation of the writer: 'Sans le moindre remords, apparu dans cette saison de vacance comme à son heure exacte d'apparaître, ce Journal s'interpose entre votre songerie et le double azur maritime et céleste: le temps de le feuilleter, et probablement de n'y point lire la Présentation/de Votre Serviteur/IX.'

[15] The accessory in question turns out to be a necklace, where 'Mille lettres en diamant étincellent avec l'éclat captivant d'un secret qui se montre et ne se livre pas: prénoms et noms entrelacés de celle qui porte le collier et de celui qui a fait don'.

[16] A. Dauzat, *Dictionnaire étymologique des noms et prénoms* (Larousse, Paris: 1951).

[17] See Mondor, *Vie de Mallarmé*, 14.

[18] The celebrated comment occurs in the 'Réponse sur l'évolution littéraire' (*Pl.* 866–72):

> *Nommer* un objet, c'est supprimer les trois quarts de la jouissance du poëme qui est faite du bonheur de deviner peu à peu: le *suggérer*, voilà le rêve. C'est le parfait usage de ce mystère qui constitue le symbole: évoquer petit à petit un objet pour montrer un état d'âme, ou, inversement, choisir un objet et en dégager un état d'âme, par une série de déchiffrements. (869)

[19] The sonnet served as epigraph to the text entitled 'L'Action Restreinte', which includes the following illustration, not without Whistlerean overtones, of the artist in correct posture: 'L'écrivain, de ses maux, dragons qu'il a choyés, ou d'une allégresse, doit s'instituer, au texte, le spirituel histrion' (*Pl.* 370).

[20] See Henri Mondor, *Mallarmé lycéen* (Paris: Gallimard, 1954), 270, and L.J. Austin, 'Les "Années d'apprentissage" de Mallarmé', *Revue d'histoire littéraire de la France*, 56 (1956), 65–84.

[21] See 3.4 below for a fuller reading of the signature in this text.

[22] The effect, in the earlier version (1865), is much the same: 'Et, natif, je fuirai, vainqueur de cette lutte/Les femmes qui pour charme ont aussi de beaux pleurs' (*O.C.* 183).

[23] There is also an embracing or framing signature from the first to the last line:

> M' [...]
> [...]
> Du seul vespéral de mes chars (*O.C.* 320)

The initial *M* (which reveals the 'main' ('M'in(troduire)') of the creator) is met in the bottom right corner by the other elements of the signature:

> ... al ... mé ... ar ...

[24] Compare the 'Chanson Bas' entitled 'Le Savetier', whose immortal opening verse: 'Hors de la poix rien à faire' (367) — is developed into a plea for mercy before the hammer-and-tacks hermeneutics of the literate cobbler:

> Il va de cuir à ma paire
> Adjoindre plus que je n'eus
> Jamais, cela désespère
> Un besoin de talons nus.
>
> Son marteau qui ne dévie
> Fixe de clous gouailleurs
> Sur la semelle l'envie
> Toujours conduisant ailleurs. (367)

In both instances, the desire on the poet's part would be to show a clean pair of heels to meaning.

[25] Concerning the substitution of 'Stéphane' for 'Etienne', I have read somewhere that the change of name was a precocious sign of the poet's preciosity. If such is the case, the boy must indeed have been prodigiously precocious, since, as the poem to Fanny (*O.C.* 2) indicates, he was already known as Stéphane rather than Etienne at the age of eight.

[26] *Les Contemplations*, ed. by Pierre Albouy (Paris: Gallimard, 1973), 289.

[27] The coincidence of lapidation and insult is recognized in such sayings as 'throw the first stone', etc. Both the references to lapidation that occur in Mallarmé's work seem to reflect this overlap. The first comes in the famous 'autobiographical' letter to Verlaine. The present poetic conjuncture being an interregnum, consisting in equal parts of 'désuétude' and 'effervescence', the poet can only 'travailler avec mystère en vue de plus tard ou de jamais et de temps en temps [à] envoyer aux vivants sa carte de visite, stances ou sonnet, pour n'être point lapidé d'eux, s'ils le soupçonnaient de savoir qu'ils n'ont pas

lieu' (*Pl.* 664). Aside from the self-portrait as an urbane Saint Etienne, the reader should note that Mallarmé here explicitly describes his actual poetic activity, in opposition to the chimerical work, as the occasional or intermittent emission of calling cards, which is as much as to say formalized signatures, or authorial 'apparitions'. We could hardly ask for a clearer authorization for the continuation of our project. The second comes in 'L'Ecclésiastique' of 1886. Mallarmé is wandering through the bois de Boulogne, when he stumbles across a churchman in full regalia frolicking in the vernal grass: 'total et des battements supérieurs du tricorne s'animant jusqu'à des souliers affermis par des boucles en argent' (*Pl.* 287). Should he disturb this rhythmically sublime spectacle?

> A moi ne plût […] que, coupable à l'égal d'un faux scandalisé se saisissant d'un caillou du chemin, j'amenasse par mon sourire même d'intelligence, une rougeur sur le visage à deux mains voilé de ce pauvre homme, autre que celle sans doute trouvée dans son solitaire exercice! (287)

As the suppressed smile of intelligence suggests, Mallarmé identifies his own 'sombre agitation basse' with the 'chaste frénésie' of the ecclesiastic, and thus becomes, perhaps, the ideal spectator, watching as he would wish to be watched.

[28] Such a vision is of course susceptible to the kind of sneer that we find, returning to our point of departure, in 'La Machine à Gloire'. At the climax of the tale, we read:

> Le manomètre marque tant de pression, tant de kilogrammètres d'immortalité. Le compteur additionne et l'Auteur-dramatique paye sa facture, que lui présente quelque jeune beauté, en grand costume de Renommée et entourée d'une gloire de trompettes. Celle-ci remet alors à l'auteur, en souriant, au nom de la Postérité, et aux lueurs d'un feu de Bengale olive, couleur d'Espérance, lui remet, disons-nous, à titre d'offrande, un buste ressemblant, garanti, nimbé et lauré, le tout en béton agglomoré (système Coignet). (Villiers, *Oeuvres complètes*, I, 595)

[29] The information contained in this section on the etymology and inheritance of the Greek term 'phainein' I have summarized and reproduced from Emile Boisacq, *Dictionnaire étymologique de la langue grecque* (Paris: Klincksieck, 1950). My starting point, however, was provided by the following entry in Bouffartigue and Delrieu, *Trésors des racines grecques* (Paris: Belin, 1981): '*Phanéros*, visible […] Cet élément se rattache à une racine *phan*, "apparaître", dont la postérité est abondante en français.'

[30] The alchemical reference implicit in the term 'sublimation' is hardly foreign to Mallarmé. See, for example, 'Magie' (*Pl.* 399).

[31] Barbier and Millan quote the following from a letter to Cazalis in 1865: 'Tu comprends que j'ai peu travaillé, ces temps-ci; cependant, pour me remettre aux vers et à Hérodiade, j'ai fait ces jours-ci un petit poème de la longueur d'un sonnet, mais qui n'est pas assez achevé pour que je te l'envoie'

(O.C. 193). Written in rhyming couplets and evidently not a sonnet, 'Don du poème' reads neither as an extract from the great work, nor as a genuine short poem of its own, but almost as something noted in the margin of 'Hérodiade'.

[32] For the various states of evolution of 'Les Fenêtres', see O.C. 144 and 400–1.

[33] According to Le Dictionnaire étymologique de la langue latine, A. Ernout and A. Meillet (Paris: Klincksieck, 1932), the origin of 'fenêtre', or rather that of its Latin predecessor 'fenestra', is unknown, unless we accept the following: 'On pense à un suffixe d'instrument; mais -tra est à peine représenté en latin. L'étymologie 'απο του φαιειν' [...] n'est qu'un jeu de mots. Il y a eu aussi une forme festra [...] dont fenestra est peut-être une déformation due à un rapprochement avec φαινω'. As Mallarmé has already told us (in Les Mots anglais), we should not let ourselves be troubled by a little deformation, and the fact that such a hypothetical etymology is 'only a play on words' represents more of a recommendation than it does a warning.

[34] In order to pursue this question more thoroughly, one would need to consider the rhyme-sequence and thematics of 'Le Pitre Châtié': renaître/fenêtre/traître/disparaître. (O.C. 150 and 348).

[35] One might ask whether it is the bareness of the 'deux Ls' that leaves Mallarmé ill-armed. See Brigitte Léon-Dufour, 'Mallarmé et l'alphabet', Cahiers de l'association des études françaises, 27 (1975), 321–43.

[36] On the play around 'n'être' and 'naître', we should not forget in this regard the famous correction made to line 11 of 'L'Eventail de Mlle Mallarmé', where the hand-painted original's 'Qui, de n'être éclos pour personne' cedes firstly to 'Qui, fier de n'être pour personne' and then, irresistibly, to 'Qui, fou de naître pour personne' in the definitive text (see O.C. 296).

[37] Les Contemplations (Paris: Gallimard, 1973), 275 and 276.

[38] See Les Chants du crépuscule (Paris: Gallimard-Livre de Poche, 1964), 57.

[39] Mallarmé probably also had the Hugo of Les Contemplations in mind when he wrote, in 'L'Art pour Tous' of the same year: '(Le philosophe) ne ferme pas les mains sur la poignée de vérités radieuses qu'elles enserrent; il les répand, et cela est juste qu'elles laissent un lumineux sillage à chacun de ses doigts'. (Pl. 257)

[40] Perhaps this was why, in the final correction he made to the text (O.C. 292), Mallarmé placed, as if to highlight M and S, these two commas:

Que, même sans regret et sans déboire, laisse

[41] On this point compare Mary Lewis Shaw, 'Mallarmé pre-postmodern, post-dada', Dalhousie French Review, 25 (1993).

[42] The phrase comes from the close of 'Le livre, instrument spirituel', a passage which, despite the absence of the term itself, forms surely an instance of 'Mallarmé and the sublime':

> Attribuons à des songes, avant la lecture, dans un parterre, l'at-
> tention que sollicite quelque papillon blanc, celui-ci à la fois
> partout, nulle part, il s'évanouit; pas sans qu'un rien d'aigu et
> d'ingénu, où je réduisis le sujet, tout à l'heure ait passé et repassé,
> avec insistance, devant l'étonnement. (*Pl.* 382).

[43] Louis Marvick, *Mallarmé and the Sublime* (Albany: State University of New York, 1986).

[44] An interesting discussion of this paradoxical aspect of sublime discourse may be found in Michel Deguy's essay 'Le Grand-Dire', in *Du Sublime* (Paris: Belin, 1988).

[45] See *Pl.* 261–65. The text first appeared in *L'Artiste* of the first of February 1865. However, Mallarmé later reworked it, presumably with *Vers et Prose* or *Divagations* in mind, and it was from a corrected version of the original, dating from the 1880s, that in the Pléiade edition Mondor gave us what has turned out to be an unhappily botched job. All this is explained and put right in Bonnefoy's 1976 edition of *Igitur, Divagations, Un Coup de Dés*. For our purposes, it is also worth noting, in so far as it shows how Mallarmé kept these texts on his table, that parts I and II of *Symphonie Littéraire* were radically compressed into a short text entitled 'Autrefois en marge d'un Baudelaire', which appeared in *Divagations* of 1897. Nor was part III forgotten, for as I show in this section it reappeared, in a considerably and disingenuously rejigged fashion, during the course of Mallarmé's necrological article on Théodore de Banville of 1892 (see *Pl.* 519–23).

[46] The gesture is repeated at the opening of part II with: 'L'hiver, quand ma torpeur me lasse' (263); and III: 'Mais quand mon esprit n'est pas gratifié [...] quand je suis las' (264).

[47] Thus: 'Ou ce torrent n'est-il qu'un fleuve de larmes?'; and in III: 'et les yeux pleins de grandes larmes de tendresse'.

[48] The phrase comes from the 'médaillon ou portrait en pied' of Théodore de Banville. For text, see *Pl.* 519–23; for bibliographical notes, 1587–88. Mondor omits to mention that the original version contained an extra paragraph, in which Mallarmé described to his English readers some of the other speeches that had been made upon the occasion of the erection of a monument to Banville in the Jardin du Luxembourg.

[49] Thus: 'vivant parmi la gloire oubliée des héros et des dieux' becomes 'vivant parmi le charme oublié des héros et des roses'. One is reminded of the way the religious coda to 'Symphonie littéraire, II' was cut in the later 'Autrefois en marge d'un Baudelaire' (*Pl.* 1547).

4 Writing your name into History

[1] Mallarmé wrote no fewer than four commemorative prose texts for his friend Verlaine, as well as the 'Tombeau'. See *Pl.* 510, 865, 873, and 874 for texts of the former; *Pl.* 1585, 1638, and 1639 for notes. For the poem, see *O.C.* 442–45. If I have

chosen not to discuss these texts in detail, it is in part for want of space, in part to avoid repetition (I have likewise passed over many other instances of Mallarmé's interest in diverse other names), and in part because, unlike the three figures presented in this section, Verlaine does not constitute a predecessor, or even, I would suggest, a very serious rival. None the less, one might point to the question of Verlaine's 'succession', courteously avoided by Mallarmé on *Pl.* 873; as well as the rewriting of the name ('Baonn-jaur, Maossiun Voeu-laine!') on *Pl.* 875. Similarly, one could highlight the presence of this signature in the final hemistich of the anniversary 'Tombeau' of 1897: 'calomnié la mort' giving: 'al-m-é-lam-r' and thus 'mallarmé'.

[2] See Jean-Pierre Richard's presentation of the '202 petits feuillets' which make up what I believe it would be wrong to describe as the 'text' of the so-called 'Tombeau d'Anatole'. Richard's patient and persuasive introduction might tempt us into reading these fragments in the same way as we read, for example, 'L'Après-midi d'un Faune', or even 'Hérodiade'. Since my method is already so speculative in nature, it would be foolish to engage with a text whose very existence is no more than the speculation of a critic. As regards the abandonment of the project, we need only retain Mallarmé's poignant reflection that 'Hugo est heureux d'avoir pu parler [...] moi, cela m'est impossible' (Richard, *Pour un Tombeau d'Anatole* (Paris: Seuil, 1961), 95).

[3] See the sonnet dedicated to the memory of Ettie Maspero, née Yapp (*O.C.* 280–81). It closes with the promise (made to the mourning husband by the ghost of his wife):

> Pour revivre il suffit qu'à tes lèvres j'emprunte
> Le souffle de mon nom murmuré tout un soir.

[4] The texts concerning Poe referred to here are the following: for the verse, 'Le Tombeau d'Edgar Poe' (*O.C.* 272–78), as well as the 'vers de circonstance' to be found at *O.C.* 662; for the prose, see the note on the tombeau in the Bibliography of 1894 (*Pl.* 77–78), the 'scolies' accompanying the translations of 1888–89 (*Pl.* 223–46), the 'médaillon ou portrait en pied' of 1894 (*Pl.*531) and the fragment 'sur Poe' (*Pl.* 872) reprinted in a different form by Scherer in his presentation of 'Le Livre' (page 2 of manuscript).

[5] The 'paturin' is a 'plante (graminées) qui constitue une grande partie de la végétation des bonnes prairies' (*Robert*). Its Latin name is *poa*, from the Greek meaning 'gazon, herbe, fourrage', and it has many varieties, such as *poa pratensis, poa trivialis, poa annua*, et al. Of this last it is said: 'Fleurit toute l'année même en hiver [...] Répandue par toute la terre, c'est une des rudérales les plus typiques, qui colonise, la première après les mousses, les interstices des pavés dans les rues peu fréquentées. Un botaniste du siècle dernier, Edouard le Maout, auteur d'une excellente 'Flore élémentaire des jardins et des champs', a résumé en trois mots les caractéristiques de cette espèce à la manière d'une devise: *Partout et toujours*' (Edouard Le Maout, *Flore élémentaire des jardins et des champs* (Paris: Dusacq, 1855)). I have not been able to ascertain whether Mallarmé owned a copy of Le Maout's guide, which was published in 1855, but have left

the motto nevertheless as an expression of Poe's ubiquity and perenniality in the field of poetry.

[6] 'Il est cette exception, en effet, et le cas littéraire absolu' (*Pl.* 531).

[7] On the nature of this task, note the following remark reported by René Ghil:

> Il convient de nous servir des mots de tous les jours, dans le sens que tout le monde croit comprendre! Je n'emploie que ceux-là. Ce sont les mêmes mots que le Bourgeois lit tous les matins, les mêmes! Mais, voilà (et ici son sourire s'accentuait), s'il lui arrive de les retrouver en tel mien poème, il ne les comprend pas!' (see Jacques Scherer, *Grammaire de Mallarmé* (Paris: Nizet, 1977))

[8] We might note that, faced with a comparable difficulty in the 'Hommage à Richard Wagner', Mallarmé similarly brings the name into sixth position, at the caesura.

[9] See the passage beginning 'Cependant et pour l'avouer' cited at the end of this section.

[10] In the 'scolies' to his translations of Poe's poems, Mallarmé significantly rejects the notion that 'The Philosophy of Composition' might just have been a gag: 'Ce qui est pensé, l'est', he asserts with fundamentalist gravity, before providing us with this excellent formulation of Poe's aesthetic lesson:

> A savoir que tout hasard doit être banni de l'oeuvre moderne et n'y peut être que feint; et que l'éternel coup d'aile n'exclut pas un regard lucide scrutant l'espace dévoré par son vol. (*Pl.* 230)

[11] This 'high' formula has for 'base' the hemistich 'Son siècle *ép*-ouvanté' of line 3. Via the poem Poe has been transformed from 'épouvantail' into 'E.P.', exemplary and essential poet in the future.

[12] Much material evidence could be added here in support of this statement. Firstly, the 'portrait' of Edgar Poe which appears in the octave of Mallarmé's text is largely drawn from the image of social outcast and *poète maudit* projected by Baudelaire in his 'Edgar Poe, sa vie et ses oeuvres' of 1855 (*Oeuvres complètes*, ed. by Marcel Ruff (Paris: Seuil, 1968), 319–53). More specifically, there are in the poem a number of very clear echoes of the prose sketch. Thus, within the first few pages, one finds: 'Ange', 'montre', 'angéliques', 'ce bas monde', 'sol américain', 'monstrueux', 'étrangeté', and so on. Besides these very literal echoes, one might wish to juxtapose, say, the whole of the famous sixth line with the phrase: 'parce qu'il écrivait dans un style trop au-dessus du vulgaire'. But one may also detect deeper intertextual links. For example, the prose piece opens thus:

> Dans ces derniers temps, un malheureux fut amené devant nos tribunaux, dont le front était illustré d'un rare et singulier tatouage: Pas de chance! Il portait ainsi au-dessus de ses yeux l'étiquette de sa vie, comme un livre son titre, et l'interrogatoire prouva que ce bizarre écriteau était cruellement véridique. Il y a dans l'histoire littéraire des destinées analogues, de vraies

damnations, — des hommes qui portent le mot guignon écrit en
caractères mystérieux dans les plis sinueux de leur front.

One could remark that it is from this opening passage of Baudelaire's study that
Mallarmé draws his inspiration, and takes his title, for the poem 'Le Guignon',
a hymn to 'damned' poets if ever there was one. He even takes the verse form
for this poem from the Gautier text, 'Ténèbres', which is here twice quoted by
Baudelaire. But the bizarre anecdote cited by Baudelaire suggests also something of Mallarmé's onomastic essentialism, the 'label' here ('comme un livre son
titre') bearing mysterious and influential powers similar to those Mallarmé
would attribute to the name. (And if one were to replace the tattoo *Pas de chance!*
with one reading *Manque de pot*?) As regards the specific phrase 'Que la Mort',
one may note that the three fatal words are themselves found in Baudelaire's text
on Edgar Poe. The latter, dead-drunk but not yet dead, is described as: 'non, un
corps vivant encore, mais *que la Mort* avait déjà marqué de sa royale estampille'.

[13] For an explicit statement of Mallarmé's ambitions, see the letter to Cazalis of
April 1866 (*Corr.I*, 207), in which, on the subject of 'Hérodiade', he says: 'Il me
faudra trois ou quatre hivers encore, pour achever cette oeuvre, mais j'aurai
enfin fait ce que je rêve, écrire un Poème digne de Poe et que les siens ne
surpasseront pas.'

[14] Compare the assertion 'qu'il ne serait pas malsonnant, même envers les
compatriotes du rêveur américain, d'affirmer qu'ici la fleur éclatante et nette de
sa pensée, là-bas dépaysée d'abord, trouve un sol authentique' (*Pl*. 224).

[15] The epigraph is from Flaubert's entry on Wagner in the *Dictionnaire des idées
reçues*. The texts referred to in this section are the following: 'Hérésies
Artistiques' of 1862 (*Pl*. 257); 'Richard Wagner: Rêverie d'un Poète Français' of
1885 (*Pl*. 541); 'Hommage' of 1886 (*O.C.* 314). The name 'Richard Wagner' occurs
also in these texts: 'Parenthèse' (*Pl*. 322–24); 'Solennité' (*Pl*. 334–35); 'Planches et
Feuillets' (*Pl*. 328–30); 'La Musique et les Lettres' (*Pl*. 648); 'Crise de Vers' (*Pl*.
365).

[16] Compare this expression of Mallarmé's supposed distaste for genealogy in the
reply he gave to an 'enquête sur Verlaine' in 1896: 'Si je supprimais, avec plaisir,
l'une des questions — *à qui attribuer la succession* — de Verlaine (il n'en laisse et
n'en prit aucune). Voilà qui est bien royal, convenez, d'avoir lieu par lignée' (*Pl*.
873).

[17] A very different view of the (fraternal or influential) relationship between the
two minds may be found, for example, in Suzanne Bernard's *Mallarmé et la
musique* (Paris: Nizet, 1959), 65–80 and, more recently, Bertrand Marchal, *La
Religion de Mallarmé* (Paris: Corti, 1988), 168–207.

[18] The supremacy or primacy of poetry over music is insisted upon by Mallarmé
at various points in his *Divagations*. For example: 'La Poésie, proche l'idée, est
Musique, par excellence — ne consent pas d'infériorité' (381). And again:

Le poète, verbal, se défie, il persiste, dans une prévention jolie, pas
étroitesse, mais sa suprématie au nom du moyen, le plus humble

> conséquemment essentiel, la parole: or, à quelle hauteur qu'exultent des cordes et des cuivres, un vers, du fait de l'approche immédiate de l'âme, y atteint. (389)

Or more explicitly:

> Je me figure par un indéracinable sans doute préjugé d'écrivain, que rien ne demeurera sans être proféré [...] car, ce n'est pas de sonorités élémentaires par les cuivres, les cordes, les bois, indéniablement mais de l'intellectuelle parole à son apogée que doit avec plénitude et évidence, résulter, en tant que l'ensemble des rapports existant dans tout, la Musique. (367–68).

[19] The phrase, a modest piece of self-criticism, occurs in a reply to an avuncular reader, colonel Paul Mathieu, who had expressed his curiosity as to the sense of the 'Hommage'. 'L'hommage est un peu boudeur; c'est, comme tu le verras, la mélancolie plutôt d'un poète qui voit s'effondrer le vieil affrontement poétique, et le luxe des mots pâlir, devant le lever de soleil de la Musique contemporaine dont Wagner est le dernier dieu' (O.C. 315). Even here we may see how Mallarmé's apparent modesty often barely conceals a sneer. For if Wagner is the 'latest god' (as we say 'the latest fashion') of music, then by next spring, it is implied, we'll all be dressed by Debussy. Or if, on the other hand, he is the 'last god' of music, then surely the sunrise is more correctly a twilight. Either way, the simple sincerity of the homage is somewhat impaired.

[20] Here is the actual form the request took: 'Je vous prie donc, mon cher Maître, pour que vous veuillez y songer: de maintenant au mois de Janvier prochain, ne voudriez-vous préparer un poème (si court qu'il soit!) tel que je disais, un poème extérieurement Wagnerien, — et entièrement, complètement, absolument tel que vous le voudrez' (O.C. 315).

[21] Mondor, for example, comments thus: 'l'"Hommage" [...] est, en quelque sorte, une redite [of the 'Rêverie'], utilisant un vocabulaire souvent ou presque identique; et, comme la page de prose, louant le musicien d'avoir réalisé, ou au moins approché, ce drame idéal auquel, lui, n'a cessé de rêver' (Pl. 1496). As examples of terms appearing in both the prose and the verse homage, consider the following: 'irradiant', 'simulacre', 'jaillir', 'maîtresse', 'triomphe' (542); 'précipiter', 'jaillir', 'familiers', 'Sacre' (544); 'trompette', 'parvis' (546).

[22] Thibaudet, for example, breaks the poem down in the following way:

> Premier quatrain: le vieux décor, le vieux théâtre, sur qui la poussière figure la banalité, le déjà vu. Second quatrain: la vieille poésie, qui n'est plus un chant ailé, mais une matière de bibliothèque. Tercets: le théâtre régénéré par la musique wagnerienne, dont le rayonnement transfigure aussi le livre. Le premier quatrain correspond au premier tercet (théâtre ancien — théâtre nouveau), le second quatrain au second tercet (livre mort — livre vivant) et le sonnet est construit sur les deux motifs entrecroisés du théâtre et du livre. (see Pl. 1496)

[23] Compare Serge Meitinger's analysis of the last two lines in particular:

> On peut y lire aussi plus traditionellement la gloire sans restriction de Wagner, enfin manifeste à tous; mais il faut penser que Mallarmé a tout de même voulu cette ambiguïté qui semble elle-même signalée par les tout derniers mots: 'en sanglots sibyllins'. D'où viennent ces larmes dans une gloire si évidente: de la joie? de la déception devant le mystère trop dévoilé, profané? Mais ces larmes (ces gouttes, ces notes sur les portées) sont ambigues, sibyllines, comme le sens même du poème, comme l'éloge que veut faire Mallarmé de Wagner, *ne lui accordant de louange qu'autant qu'il se sent le devoir de passer outre.* (See 'Baudelaire et Mallarmé devant Richard Wagner', *Romantisme*, 33 (1981), 75–90)

[24] In his article 'Wagner rêvé par Mallarmé' (*Romantisme*, 57 (1987), 65–73), Alain Satge has also remarked on the importance of Wagner the *name*. For example:

> Miroir tendu à chacun de ses exégètes, l'oeuvre tend à s'effacer derrière le Nom: toute l'effervescence wagnerienne pourrait n'être qu'une rêverie sur le Nom de Wagner, comme talisman, métaphore, argument ou insulte; et il n'y aurait derrière les masses des commentaires, des gloses et des pamphlets qu'une absence; un 'Wagner' qui n'existe qu'à la manière d'un personnage de fiction, et qu'on pourrait appeler, plus encore que 'l'éponyme certain de ce siècle' (Peladan), un Wagner pseudonyme: un prête-nom. (67)

And further on:

> Entre Vers et Musique, toute opposition s'abolit ici, en tant qu'ils constituent l'autre langue, l'imaginaire langue unique: 'où la Musique rejoint le Vers pour former, depuis Wagner, la Poésie': ce qui nous invite à relire une fois encore le titre de l'article, et à entendre la *Rêverie*, en taisant finalement le bruyant Nom de Wagner, comme une rêverie sur la poésie. (72)

[25] 'Lui' continues the sequence 'mythe', 'type', but has become a negative actor, as the extraordinary (and extraordinarily Mallarmean) 'negating exclamation mark' shows. A few lines later it is called 'la Figure que Nul n'est'. We should also note the following signatory paraph here, rather like the one we saw in 'Brise Marine': 'S(aint des) S(aints) M(ais) M(ental)'; but also: '(Saints des Saint)s, m(ai)s m(ental)'. Compare the double paraph noted in 'Brise Marine': 'sans mâts, sans mâts'. Would this be Mallarmé's way of proclaiming this particular and special site as his own?

[26] 'Charrier', if we take as our authority, for example, the *Trésor de la Langue Française*, means 'emporter (dans son cours)' or 'transporter (une charge, une personne)'. 'Le sujet désigne une chose, ou un groupe de personnes, assimilés à un cours d'eau.' For example: 'l'air charriait de grasses odeurs' (Sainte Beuve), or: 'le ciel charriait des nuages' (Hugo). But the subject may also be 'la rue ou la foule',

as in these examples taken from Zola: 'les boulevards charriant la foule'; 'les deux hommes étaient portés, charriés, au milieu de cette vague humaine, qui les jeta sur la route.' This both confirms and qualifies our surprise at seeing 'le flux de banalité charrié par les arts', rather than, say, 'les arts charriés par un flux de banalité'. For the examples from Zola show evidence, precisely, of such a reversibility in the term. The crowd is carried away or may itself do the carrying. Of course, in the context of a discussion of Art for the *Volk*, such a nuance is not without pertinence. Within Mallarmé's works, we find two contrasting examples of the use of the verb. In the preface to 'Vathek', for example, the tone is hardly pejorative:

> Tout coule de source, avec une limpidité, avec un ondoiement large de périodes; et l'éclat tend à se fondre dans la pureté totale du cours, qui charrie maintes richesses de diction inaperçues d'abord: cas naturel avec un étranger inquiet que quelque expression trop audacieuse ne le trahisse en arrêtant le regard. (*Pl.* 565)

At worst a little patronizing for the foreigner. In the bibliography to *Divagations*, however, we are closer to the ambiguity of our own 'charrié':

> Mobiliser, autour d'une idée, les lueurs diverses de l'esprit, à distance voulue, par phrases: ou comme, vraiment, ces moules de la syntaxe même élargie, un très petit nombre les résume, chaque phrase, à se détacher en paragraphe gagne d'isoler un type rare avec plus de liberté qu'en le charroi par un courant de volubilité. (1576)

We might also propose the following example, taken from a letter sent to Mallarmé by his friend Lefébure: 'un cordonnier fait des souliers tous les jours de sa vie, et le charron Ponsard peut s'engager à livrer tant de pièces chaque année' (Mondor, *Eugène Lefébure*, 95). It is almost as if the required translation of 'charron' would here be 'hack'. Which is hardly very flattering for 'Wagner'.

[27] If we look again at the name, we see that the 'char' was there all along in 'Richard Charron'. We may also infer that he is well rewarded (*richard*) for his labours in dodgy transportation. But there is in fact a whole series of pejorative connotations which fast irradiate from Wagner. A 'charretier', for example, is proverbially uncouth, rustic, and everything but sublime. The expression 'crier au charron' means 'crier au secours, par exemple à la vue d'un voleur'. Similarly it was, according to the *Grand Larousse de la Langue Française*, Vidocq no less who in 1837 first gave 'charrier' the sense of 'voler en mystifiant'.

[28] See *O.C.* 410–12 for text and notes of 'Le Tombeau de Charles Baudelaire'. The line forming the epigraph comes from Baudelaire's 'Le Remords Posthume'. The primary sense of the verb, given the context, is undoubtedly 'understand', but it is hard not to hear 'contain' as well.

[29] It may be noted in passing that the opening phrase of the sonnet: 'Le temple enseveli divulgue par la bouche' is a reminiscence of these lines from Racine's *Athalie* (Act Four, Scene Three):

> Hé bien! pour un enfant qu'ils ne connaissent pas,
> Que le hasard peut-être a jeté dans leurs bras,
> Voudront-ils que leur *temple, enseveli* sous l'herbe

Maeterlinck used the same words, in memory of Mallarmé or Racine or both, in the title of an essay in 1902. Given the Baudelairean context, one might also recall the opening of 'Correspondance':

> La nature est un temple où de vivants piliers

[30] One could also cite even the mere title of Austin's 1973 article '"Le Tombeau de Charles Baudelaire" by Stéphane Mallarmé: Satire or Homage?'. Nor is Gardner Davies much more enthusiastic (*Les 'Tombeaux' de Mallarmé*, Paris: Corti, 1950), 164–87. The tone seems to have been set by Mallarmé's supposed successor, Valéry, who commented to Claudel: 'Je n'aime guère "Le Tombeau de Baudelaire", et même je vous le laisse' (quoted by Jean Pommier, '"Le Tombeau de Charles Baudelaire"', *Mercure de France*, 32 (1956), 657).

[31] As Eugène Lefébure once commented to the young Mallarmé. See Henri Mondor, *Eugène Lefébure* (Paris: Gallimard, 1951), 171.

[32] *Mercure de France*, 32 (1958), 656–75.

[33] A certain amount has already been said on the subject of Mallarmé's separation from the early influence of Baudelaire. It should not be forgotten that, as early as 1867, the young Mallarmé considered the separation from his master to have already taken place, and that he saw this event as crucial to his future poetic evolution. This is clear from the following postscript to that famous letter to Cazalis of 1867 (*Corr. I.*, 244) (in which Mallarmé has just claimed no longer to be the 'Stéphane que tu as connu, mais une aptitude qu'a l'Univers spirituel à se voir et à se développer, à travers ce qui fut moi'): 'Le livre de Dierx est un beau développement de Leconte de Lisle. S'en séparera-t-il comme moi de Baudelaire?'

[34] See *Baudelaire par Gautier* (Paris: Klincksieck, 1986). The passage comparing Baudelaire's poetry to the eponymous heroine of 'Rappaccini's Daughter' appears first on 82–83, but is repeated on 96 and 108. In the final version of this theme Gautier added the following conclusion, which might be relevant to the present section: 'La muse de Baudelaire s'est longtemps promené dans ce jardin avec impunité; mais, un soir, faible et languissante, elle est morte en respirant un bouquet de fleurs.' The triteness of such a passage helps to explain why Mallarmé's conclusion, on first reading, seems so vulgar.

[35] See *Baudelaire par Gautier*, 105.

[36] See Pommier, 674.

[37] See *Baudelaire par Gautier*, 143.

[38] On the link between Mallarmé's conception of literature and the Kabbalah, see for example the fragment reproduced on page 850 of the Pléiade (or sheets 7–11 of Scherer's 'Le Livre').

[39] Michel Butor seems also to have been struck by the 'airy' element of the poet's

name. See *Histoire extraordinaire* (Paris: Gallimard, 1961), 232–34. One might also invoke in this connection Mallarmé's etymological association of 'GAS … GEIST … GHOST' in *Les Mots anglais* (*O.C.* 1036).

[40] Compare the following reflection on the singular destiny of the *e muet*:

> J'ai toujours pensé que l'E muet était un moyen fondamental du vers et même j'en tirais cette conclusion en faveur du vers régulier, que cette syllabe à volonté, omise ou perçue, autorisait l'apparence du nombre fixe, lequel frappé uniformément et réel devient insupportable autrement que dans les grandes occasions. (See *Ecrits sur le Livre* (Paris: Editions de l'Eclat, 1985), 84)

5 Conclusion

[1] *Le Soleil des morts* (Geneva: Slatkine Reprints, 1979), xi. In his preface of some years later, Mauclair explicitly claims Mallarmé as the model of Calixte Armel: 'La figure centrale de Calixte Armel est bien celle de mon maître Stéphane Mallarmé, qui fut le premier à lire mon manuscrit et l'aima' (page 8). This seems to contradict the impression given by Mallarmé's letter of June 1898:

> J'ai rapporté le *Soleil des morts* ici et l'ai lu vous devinez comme. Il assemble la légende d'un temps, et, si près, le transporte […] Il vous plut que je me sentisse en Calixte Armel, merci, et j'ai, d'un trouble aiguisé de délice, suivi cette figure jusqu'où j'y pouvais prétendre: je dois paraître un rien cela, encore que, surtout, étant un ouvrier désespéré ou malheureux, puis l'accompagnai au delà de moi vers ses proportions de rêve. Toujours est-il que si l'aspect que dégage un homme à plusieurs ne lui demeure extérieur totalement, vous êtes quelqu'un, Mauclair, qui m'aurez extraordinairement regardé. Les ans, pour peu qu'il m'en reste, ne m'excuseraient pas, littérairement, que je me contenterais, pour destin, de vous être apparu cet homme-là. (xi)

Beyond the fact that Mallarmé insists politely but stubbornly (as we have seen so many times) on marking out his essential difference, we should note here also how the signatory term 'paraître' twice occurs in this discussion of the poet's literary glory and posthumous reputation. He died four months later. As for the name 'Calixte Armel', we might gloss as follows: 'Armel' is obviously a transition of 'Mallarmé', the 'al' having drifted into the forename; 'Calixte' recalls 'calice', 'callos', and 'Calliope', while also being historically the name of three popes and a saint; the absurdity of the whole might be taken as an allegory of the misreading of Mallarmé practised by his young 'symbolisant/anarchisant' admirers, which error the poet is at pains to correct (albeit discreetly) in the letter cited above. The character itself represents Mallarmé, it is true, in a far from flattering light: brilliant but impotent, and above all out of touch with social reality, he is destined to fade in the sunrise of an unspecified revolutionary upheaval. As the editor of the Slatkine edition comments (page i):

'Mauclair a beaucoup renié, c'est vrai'; and his name has paid a high price for such 'eclecticism'.

[2] In Chapter 14 of *A rebours* we find devoted to Mallarmé several pages that might best be situated somewhere between literary criticism and the following type of dramatization of the act of reading:

> Des Esseintes approuva de la tête. Il ne resta plus sur la table que deux plaquettes. D'un signe, il congédia le vieillard et il parcourut quelques feuilles reliées en peau d'onagre, préalablement satinée à la presse hydraulique, pommelée à l'aquarelle de nuées d'argent et nantie de gardes de vieux lampas, dont les ramages un peu éteints, avaient cette grâce des choses fanées que Mallarmé célébra dans un si délicieux poème. Ces pages, au nombre de neuf, étaient extraites d'uniques exemplaires des deux premiers Parnasses, tirés sur parchemin, et précédées de ce titre: *Quelques vers de Mallarmé*, dessiné par un surprenant calligraphe, en lettres onciales, coloriées, relevées, comme celles des vieux manuscrits, de points d'or. (*A rebours* (Paris: Garnier-Flammarion, 1978), 219)

In 1884, Mallarmé writes to Huysmans in order to thank him for the appearance of his name in *A rebours*:

> Ce que je ne peux attendre, c'est non de vous remercier (parce que vous n'avez pas parlé pour me faire plaisir) mais de me dire simplement et profondément heureux, que mon nom, comme chez soi et à propos, dans ce beau livre (arrière-salle de votre esprit) circule, hôte paré de quelles enorgueillissantes robes tissées de la sympathie d'art la plus exquise! Je ne crois qu'à deux sensations de gloire, celle apprise du délire d'un peuple à qui l'on pourrait, par des moyens d'art, façonner une idole nouvelle; l'autre, de se voir, lecteur d'un livre exceptionellement aimé, soi-même apparaître du fond des pages où l'on était à son insu et par une volonté de l'auteur. Vous l'avez fait connaître celle-ci, ma foi! jusqu'au délice. (*Corr.* II, 262)

As for Regnier, his numerous recollections of Mallarmé include this anecdote of mistaken identity:

> Assidu aux concerts du dimanche, il m'arrivait souvent d'être assis auprès d'un auditeur qui ressemblait trait pour trait à l'effigie que Manet avait peint de Mallarmé et, trompé par cette ressemblance, j'étais persuadé qu'un hasard merveilleux me donnait pour voisin le poète que j'admirais. Ah! ce Mallarmé imaginaire, avec quelle curiosité, avec quel respect je le regardais à la dérobée! Que j'eusse désiré lui parler, lui dire ma ferveur de jeune rimeur, mais j'en étais empêché par ma timidité, et, à la sortie du concert, je me contentais de le suivre dans la rue pour l'apercevoir un moment encore! (*Faces et profils* (Paris: Mercure de France, 1931), 74)

³ Léon Bloy might well have laid the foundations for a new science of literary history by insult, as the following remarks would suggest: 'Qu'importe que des Jocrisses déments tel que Mallarmé soient adorés au désert par cet hébreu en plein Exode [he means Huysmans or Des Esseintes], tandis que Barbey d'Aurevilly est prétendu sadique et divagateur sacrilège?' ('Sur la tombe de Huysmans', in *Oeuvres complètes*, IV (Paris: Mercure de France, 1965), 336); 'Stéphane Mallarmé — Dessiner en marge tout ce qui peut paraître symbolique de ce qui est impénétrable. Des portes verrouillés et garnies de triples barres, des murs de clôture surmontés de culs de bouteilles; des "cartons" soigneusement cadenassés; une serrure monstrueuse fermant un tout petit endroit; une vieille fille hermétiquement boutonnée et gardée par deux dragons; etc. etc.' (*Oeuvres complètes*, XI (1963), 109); 'Arthur Rimbaud et Stéphane Mallarmé sont des poètes immobiles et solidement assis dans la même pagode d'imbécilité parfaite où le lecteur peut toujours leur décocher sûrement sa malédiction' ('On demande des malédictions', in *Oeuvres complètes*, XI, 109); 'Enfin, l'effigie de l'incroyable Mallarmé nous offre l'idée d'un raté du billard qui se serait adonné à l'absinthe dans l'espoir de rattraper ses illusions' (*Oeuvres complètes*, XV (1980), 169).

Jarry's evocation of Mallarmé occurs in Chapter 19 of *Gestes et opinions du docteur Faustroll*, entitled 'De l'île de ptyx': 'L'île de ptyx est d'un seul bloc de la pierre de ce nom, laquelle est inestimable, car on ne l'a vue que dans cette île, qu'elle compose entièrement [...] Le seigneur de l'île vint vers nous dans un vaisseau: la cheminée arrondissait des auréoles bleues derrière sa tête, amplifiant la fumée de sa pipe et l'imprimant au ciel. Et au tangage alternatif, sa chaise à bascule hochait ses gestes de bienvenue'. The piece has a note attached reading: 'Le fleuve autour de l'île s'est fait, depuis ce livre, couronne mortuaire'; this reference to the *stephanos* also appears in the obituary Jarry wrote after having attended Mallarmé's funeral in 1898: 'Le fleuve dépose éternellement, circulaire miroir de la gloire, autour de la tombe jusqu'aux pénultièmes horizons, sa couronne mortuaire' (see Alfred Jarry, *Oeuvres complètes* (Paris: Gallimard, 1988), I, 564–65).

As for Ponge, his 'Notes d'un poème (sur Mallarmé)' presents some interesting 'expressions-fixes, pour servir au coup-par-supériorité' in academic disputes:

> Mallarmé n'est pas de ceux qui pensent mettre le silence aux paroles. Il a une haute idée du pouvoir du poète. Il trahit le bruit par le bruit [...] A ceux qui ne veulent plus d'arguments, qui ne se contentent plus des proverbes en fonte, des armes d'enferrement mutuel, Mallarmé offre une massue cloutée d'expressions-fixes, pour servir au coup-par-supériorité.
>
> Il a créé un outil antilogique. Pour vivre, pour lire et écrire. Contre le gouvernement, les philosophes, les poètes-penseurs. Avec la dureté de leur matière logique.
>
> A brandir Mallarmé le premier qui se brise est un disciple soufflé de verre [...] Plus tard on en viendra à faire servir

Mallarmé comme proverbes. En 1926 il n'a pas encore beaucoup servi. Sinon beaucoup aux poètes, pour se parler à eux-mêmes. *Il s'est nommé et demeurera au littérateur pour socle d'attributs* […] Malherbe, Corneille, Boileau voulaient plutôt dire 'certainement'. La poésie de Mallarmé revient à dire simplement 'Oui'. 'Oui' à soi-même, à lui-même, chaque fois qu'il le désire'. (*Proêmes* (Paris: Gallimard, 1948), 136–38; my emphasis)

[4] One reason for choosing the case of Arthur Rimbaud to conclude with would of course be the relative proximity of the poet's centenary and the attendant cultural manifestations which the event inspired in France, as well as the thought of Mallarmé's own memorial in 1898. Whether the Minister of Culture will go so far as to pronounce in homage to the poet the name of 'Jim Morrison' (as Jack Lang did in one of his less inspired moments) remains a political question beyond the competence of the present study. The literary establishment (or at least those members of it not appearing on television with 'Rimbaud 91' merchandise to promote) did not fail to manifest its disapproval of the celebrations. Former angel in exile, Philippe Sollers, was heard to complain that 'On ne lit plus Rimbaud!' (*Bouillon de culture*, TF1, 5/1/92) and claimed that, as an experiment, he had sent the text of *Les Illuminations* in typescript to a host of Parisian publishers, who had to a man duly rejected it. Mallarmé, we know, had already observed that the public could nourish literary fame 'sans avoir lu, au besoin' (*Pl.* 530). For the sake of M. Sollers's sales figures, I trust they will not do so in his case.

[5] Mallarmé's text on Rimbaud has recently been reprinted as a plaquette (*Arthur Rimbaud* (Paris: Fourbis, 1991)). On the conjuncture of Rimbaud-Mallarmé Jean-Jacques Thomas has written a very interesting article entitled 'Porte Rimbaud … Impasse Mallarmé', *French Literature Series*, 18 (1991), 53–65.

[6] As an example of the former one might take the following: 'Avec je ne sais quoi fièrement poussé, ou mauvaisement, de fille du peuple, j'ajoute, de son état blanchisseuse, à cause de vastes mains, par la transition du chaud au froid rougies d'engelures' (513); and of the second: 'Il trafiqua, sur la côte et l'autre bord, à Aden — le rencontra-t-on toutefois à ce point extrême? féériquement d'objets précieux encore, comme quelqu'un dont les mains ont caressé jadis les pages — ivoire, poudre d'or, ou encens.' (517)

List of works consulted

1. Works by Stéphane Mallarmé

Oeuvres complètes, ed. by Henri Mondor and G.Jean-Aubry (Paris: Gallimard, 1945).

Propos de Mallarmé sur la poésie (Monaco: Editions du Rocher, 1946).

Correspondance, ed. by Henri Mondor and J.L. Austin, 11 vols (Paris: Gallimard, 1956–85).

'Le Livre' de Mallarmé, ed. by Jacques Scherer (Paris: Gallimard, 1957).

Pour un 'Tombeau d'Anatole', ed. by Jean-Pierre Richard (Paris: Seuil, 1961).

Les Gossips de Mallarmé, ed. by Henri Mondor and J.L. Austin (Paris: Gallimard, 1962).

Recueil de 'Nursery Rhymes', ed. by Carl Paul Barbier (Paris: Gallimard, 1964).

Igitur, Divagations. Un Coup de Dés, ed. by Yves Bonnefoy (Paris: Gallimard, 1976).

Vers et prose (Paris: Gallimard, 1977).

La Dernière Mode, ed. by Jean-Paul Amunategui (Paris: Ramsay, 1978).

Manuscrit autographe des 'Poésies', ed. by Jean Guickard-Meili (Paris: Ramsay, 1981).

Oeuvres complètes, I: Poésies, ed. by Carl Paul Barbier and Charles Gordon Millan (Paris: Flammarion, 1983).

Ecrits sur 'le Livre', ed. by Christophe Romana and Michel Valensi (Paris: L'Eclat, 1985).

Arthur Rimbaud (Paris: Fourbi, 1991).

2. Secondary materials

Amiot, Anne-Marie, 'Hommage ou contre-hommage à Richard Wagner: une poétique mallarmeenne de l'ambiguïté', in *Etudes et recherches de littérature générale et comparée* (Paris: Les Belles Lettres, 1974).

Assad, Maria L., 'La production du sens: "Un Spectacle Interrompu"', *Nineteenth-Century French Studies*, 12:1–2 (1983), 185–97.

Austin, J.L., *How To Do Things With Words* (Oxford: Oxford University Press, 1980).

Austin, L.J., 'Le principal pilier …', *Revue d'histoire littéraire de la France*, 51 (1951).

Austin, L.J., 'Les "années d'apprentissage" de Mallarmé', *Revue d'histoire littéraire de la France*, 56 (1956), 65–84.

Austin, L.J., 'Mallarmé disciple de Baudelaire: "Le Parnasse contemporain"', *Revue d'histoire littéraire de la France*, 67 (1967), 437–49.

Baudelaire, Charles, *Les Fleurs du mal*, ed. by Antoine Adam (Paris: Bordas, 1990).

Baudelaire, Charles, *Oeuvres complètes*, ed. by Marcel Ruff (Paris: Seuil, 1968).

Bennington, Geoffrey, *Dudding: des noms de Rousseau* (Paris: Galilée, 1990)

Bennington, Geoffrey and Derrida, Jacques, *Jacques Derrida* (Paris: Seuil, 1991).

Bernard, Suzanne, *Mallarmé et la musique* (Paris: Nizet, 1959)

Bersani, Leo, *The Death of Stéphane Mallarmé* (Cambridge: Cambridge University Press, 1982).

Blanchot, Maurice, *Faux pas* (Paris: Gallimard, 1943).

Blanchot, Maurice, *La part du feu* (Paris: Gallimard, 1949).

Blanchot, Maurice, *L'espace littéraire* (Paris: Gallimard, 1955).

Blanchot, Maurice, *Le livre à venir* (Paris: Gallimard, 1959).

Bloy, Léon, *Oeuvres complètes*, 15 vols (Paris: Mercure de France, 1963–85).

Boisacq, Emile, *Dictionnaire étymologique de la langue grecque* (Paris: Klicksieck, 1950).

Bonnefoy, Yves, 'La poétique de Mallarmé', *Critique*, 31 (1975), 1053–74.

Bouffartigue, J., and Delrieu, A., *Trésors des racines grecques* (Paris: Belin, 1981).

Bowie, Malcolm, *Mallarmé and the Art of Being Difficult* (Cambridge: Cambridge University Press, 1978).

Breunig, L.C., 'For a poetic of the pseudonym', *The Romanic Review*, 75 (1984), 256–62.

Breunig, L.C., 'Les Poètes se nomment', in *Apollinaire e l'avanguardia*, ed. by P.A. Jannini (Rome: Balzoni, 1984), 267–84.

Butor, Michel, *Histoire extraordinaire* (Paris: Gallimard, 1961).

Butor, Michel, *Les Mots dans la Peinture* (Paris: Flammarion, 1969).

Chambers, Ross, 'An Address in the Country: Mallarmé and the Kinds of Literary Context', *French Forum*, 11 (1986), 199–215.

Chassé, Charles, 'Mallarmé et l'étymologie', *Cahiers de l'Association Internationale des Etudes Françaises*, 11 (1959), 367–70.

Crow, Christine, 'Le Silence au vol de cygne: Baudelaire, Mallarmé, Valéry and the Flight of the Swan', in *Baudelaire, Mallarmé and Valéry: New Essays in Honour of Lloyd Austin*, ed. by Malcolm Bowie, Alison Fairlie, and Alison Finch (Cambridge: Cambridge University Press, 1982).

Dalhousie French Review, 25 ('Mallarmé: theorist of our times' special issue) (1993).

Dauzat, Albert, *Les Noms de Personne* (Paris: Delagrave, 1950).

Dauzat, Albert, *Dictionnaire étymologique des noms et prénoms* (Paris: Larousse, 1951).

Davies, Gardner, *Les 'Tombeaux' de Mallarmé* (Paris: Corti, 1950).

Davies, Gardner, *Mallarmé et le drame solaire* (Paris: Corti, 1959).

Davies, Gardner, 'Note on Mallarmé et Banville', *Australian Modern Languages Association*, 19 (1963), 107–11.

Davies, Gardner, *Mallarmé et le rêve d''Hérodiade'* (Paris: Corti, 1978).

Dayan, Peter, *Mallarmé's Divine Transposition* (Oxford: Clarendon Press, 1986).

Deguy, Michel, *Choses de la poésie et affaire culturelle* (Paris: Hachette, 1986).

Deldebat, Jacques, 'Execution du "Tombeau d'Edgar Poe"', *Littératures*, 9–10 (1984), 172–84.

Delègue, Yves, 'Les sourires de Mallarmé', *Romantisme*, 75 (1992), 85–94.

De Nardis, Luigi, *L'Ironia di Mallarmé* (Rome: Salvatore Sciascia, 1962).

Derrida, Jacques, *L'écriture et la différence* (Paris: Seuil, 1967).

Derrida, Jacques, *La dissémination* (Paris: Seuil, 1972).

Derrida, Jacques, *Marges de la philosophie* (Paris: Minuit, 1972).

Derrida, Jacques, 'Mallarmé', in Marcel Arland et al., *Tableau de la Littérature Française*, III: 'De Mme de Staël à Rimbaud' (Paris: Gallimard, 1974), 368–79.

Derrida, Jacques, *Signéponge* (New York: Columbia University Press, 1984).

Derrida, Jacques, *Khôra* (Paris: Galilée, 1993).

Derrida, Jacques, *Sauf le nom (Post-Scriptum)* (Paris: Galilée, 1993).

Derrida, Jacques, *Passions* (Paris: Galilée, 1993).

Dragonetti, Roger, *Un fantôme dans le kiosque: Mallarmé et l'esthétique du quotidien* (Paris: Seuil, 1992).

Du Sublime, ed. by Jean-François Courtine et al. (Paris: Belin, 1988).

Ernout, A., and Meillet, A., *Dictionnaire étymologique de la langue latine* (Paris: Klicksieck, 1932).

Faye, Jean-Pierre, *La Mode, l'invention* (Paris: Seuil, 1969).

Finas, Lucette, 'Salut', *Esprit*, 441 (1974), 871–901.

Florence, Penny, *Mallarmé, Manet and Redon* (Cambridge: Cambridge University Press, 1986).

Franklin, Ursula, *An Anatomy of Poesis* (Chapel Hill: University of North Carolina Press, 1976).

Frappier-Mazur, Lucienne, 'Narcisse travesti. Poétique et idéologie dans la "Dernière Mode"', *French Forum*, 11 (1986), 41–57.

Gardiner, A.H., *The Theory of Proper Names* (London: Oxford University Press, 1954).

Gautier, Théophile, *Baudelaire par Gautier* (Paris: Klincksieck, 1986).

Genette, Gérard, *Figures, I* (Paris: Seuil, 1961).

Genette, Gérard, *Mimologiques: Voyage en Cratylie* (Paris: Seuil, 1976).

Gill, Austin, '"Le Tombeau de Charles Baudelaire"', *Comparative Literature Studies*, 4 (1967), 45–65.

Gill, Austin, '"L'être aux ailes de gaze" dans la doctrine esthétique de Mallarmé', in *Studi in onore di Italo Siciliano* (Florence: L.S. Olschki, 1966).

Goebel, Gerhard, 'Poésie et "littérature" chez Baudelaire et Mallarmé, analyse du changement d'un concept', *Romantisme*, 39 (1983), 73–83.

Grimaud, Michel, 'Hermeneutics, Onomastics and Poetics in English and French Literature', *Modern Language Notes*, 92 (1977), 888–921.

Hambly, P.S., 'Mallarmé, Banville', *Bulletin des études parnassiennes*, 5 (1983), 1–32.

Hartman, Elwood, 'Mallarmé and Whistler: an Aesthetic Alliance', *Kentucky Romance Quarterly*, 22 (1975), 543–60.

Hartman, Elwood, 'Baudelaire, Mallarmé and Wagner: a Comparison of the German Musician's Influence on Two French Symbolist Poets', *Proceedings of the Pacific Northwest Conference on Foreign Languages*, 27:1 (1976), 27–29.

Hugo, Victor, *Les Contemplations* (Paris: Gallimard-Poésie, 1973).

Hugo, Victor, *Les Chants du crépuscule* (Paris: Gallimard-Livre de Poche, 1973).

Huysmans, Joris-Karl, *A rebours* (Paris: Garnier-Flammarion, 1978).

Le Japonisme (Paris: Editions de la réunion des musées nationaux, 1988).

Jarry, Alfred, *Oeuvres complètes*, 3 vols (Paris: Gallimard, 1988).

Jean-Aubry, G., *Une amitié exemplaire* (Paris: Mercure de France, 1942).

Johnson, Barbara, *Défigurations du langage poétique* (Paris: Flammarion, 1979).

Johnson, Barbara, 'Les Fleurs du mal armé: Some Reflections on Intertextuality', in *Lyric Poetry: Beyond New Criticism* (Ithaca: Cornell University Press, 1985).

Johnson, Barbara, 'The Liberation of Verse', in *A New History of French Literature*, ed. by Denis Hollier (Cambridge, MA: Harvard University Press, 1989).

Kamuf, Peggy, *Signatures, ou l'institution de l'auteur* (Paris: Galilée, 1991).

Kaufmann, Vincent, 'De l'interlocution à l'adresse: la réception selon Mallarmé', *Poétique*, 46 (1981), 171–82.

Kaufmann, Vincent, *Le Livre et ses adresses* (Paris: Méridiens-Klincksieck, 1986).

Kaufmann, Vincent, *L'Equivoque épistolaire* (Paris: Minuit, 1990).

Kravis, Judy, *The Prose of Mallarmé* (New York: Columbia University Press, 1976).

Kristeva, Julia, *La Révolution du langage poétique: l'avant-garde à la fin du XIXe siècle* (Paris: Seuil, 1974).

Lacoue-Labarthe, Philippe, 'Baudelaire *contra* Wagner', *Etudes françaises*, 3–4 (1981), 97–109.

La Fontaine, Jean de, *Fables*, ed. by Jean-Pierre Collinet (Paris: Gallimard, 1991).

Lawler, James R., 'Mallarmé et le "poison tutélaire"', *Australian Journal of French Studies*, 16:2 (1979), 226–32.

Le Maout, Edouard, *Flore élémentaire des jardins et des champs* (Paris: Dusacq, 1855).

Léon-Dufour, Brigitte, 'Mallarmé et l'alphabet', *Cahiers de l'association des études françaises*, 27 (1975), 321–43.

Lloyd, Rosemary, 'La Divine Transposition: Mallarmé and Banville', *French Studies Bulletin*, 9 (1983–84), 3–6.

Lochnan, Katherine, *The Etchings of Whistler* (New Haven: Yale University Press, 1984).

Longin: Du Sublime, ed. by Jackie Pigeaud (Paris: Rivages, 1991).

Longinus: On the Sublime, ed. by T.S. Dorsch (Harmondsworth: Penguin, 1965).

Manet (Paris: Editions de la réunion des musées nationaux, 1983).

Marchal, Bertrand, *La Religion de Mallarmé* (Paris: Corti, 1988).

Marvick, Louis Wirth, *Mallarmé and the Sublime* (Albany: State University of New York Press, 1986).

Mauclair, Camille, *Le Soleil des morts* (Geneva: Slatkine Reprints, 1979).

Mazaleyrat, Jean, 'La rime dans la poésie de Mallarmé', *Travaux de linguistique et de littérature*, 28:1 (1980), 437–47.

McDonald, C., 'Unsettling the score: Poetry and Music', *Romanic Review*, 77 (1986), 254–63.

McLendon, Will L., 'The Incantation of a Name: from "mal armé" to "mâle armé"', *Mosaic*, 12:4 (1979), 21–28.

Meitinger, Serge, 'Baudelaire et Mallarmé devant Richard Wagner', *Romantisme*, 33 (1981), 75–90.

Mély, François de, 'Signature des primitifs. La Tradition du IXe au XVIe siècle', *Revue Archéologique* (1911).

Michaud, Guy, *Mallarmé: l'homme et l'oeuvre* (Paris: Hatier-Boivin, 1953).

Michon, Jacques, *Mallarmé et 'Les Mots anglais'* (Montreal: Presse de l'Université de Montréal, 1978).

Millan, Gordon, *A throw of the dice* (London: Secker and Warburg, 1994)

Mondor, Henri, *Vie de Mallarmé* (Paris: Gallimard, 1941).

Mondor, Henri, *Mallarmé plus intime* (Paris: Gallimard, 1944).

Mondor, Henri, *Mallarmé, documents iconographiques* (Vésenaz-Geneva: Pierre Cailler, 1947).

Mondor, Henri, *L'Histoire d'un faune* (Paris: Gallimard, 1948).

Mondor, Henri, *Eugène Lefébure* (Paris: Gallimard, 1951).

Mondor, Henri, *Mallarmé lycéen* (Paris: Gallimard, 1954).

Morel, Jacques, 'Le "Sortilège bu" et la Pentecôte: Note sur "Le Tombeau d'Edgar Poe"', *Revue d'histoire littéraire de la France*, 83 (1983), 459–61.

Morier, Henri, 'Retour au "Tombeau de Charles Baudelaire"', in *Au bonheur des mots: Mélanges en l'honneur de Gerald Antoine* (Nancy: Presse Universitaire de Nancy, 1984).

Morris, D. Hampton, *Stéphane Mallarmé: Twentieth-Century Criticism (1901–1971)* (Mississippi: University of Mississippi Romance Monographs, 1977).

Mossop, D.J., 'Le Tombeau de Charles Baudelaire', *French Studies*, 30 (1976), 287–300.

Nicole, Eugène, 'L'onomastique littéraire', *Poétique*, 54 (1983), 233–53.

Nodier, Charles, *Dictionnaire raisonné des onomatopées françaises* (Paris: Trans-Europ Repress, 1984).

O'Neill, Kevin, 'Mallarmé's "Petit Air (guerrier)"', *Studi Francesi*, 47–48 (1972), 376–79.

Orienti, Sandra, *Tout l'Oeuvre peint d'Edouard Manet* (Paris: Flammarion, 1970).

Ossola, Carlo, 'Les "ossements fossiles" de la lettre chez Mallarmé et chez Saussure', *Critique*, 35 (1979), 1063–78.

Plato, *Ion, Ménexène, Euthydème, Cratyle*, ed. by Louis Méridier (Paris: Gallimard, 1989).

Pommier, Jean, '"Le Tombeau de Charles Baudelaire" de Mallarmé', *Mercure de France*, 32 (1958), 656–75.

Ponge, Francis, *Le parti pris des choses* (Paris: Gallimard, 1942).

Ponge, Francis, *Proêmes* (Paris: Gallimard, 1948).

Rajec, E.M., *The Study of Names in Literature: a Bibliography* (New York: K.G. Saur, 1978).

Régnier, Henri de, *Figures et caractères* (Paris: Mercure de France, 1901).

Régnier, Henri de, *Portraits et Souvenirs* (Paris: Mercure de France, 1901).

Régnier, Henri de, *Proses datées* (Paris: Mercure de France, 1925).

Régnier, Henri de, *Nos rencontres* (Paris: Mercure de France, 1931).

Richard, Jean-Pierre, *L'univers imaginaire de Mallarmé* (Paris: Seuil, 1961).

Rigolot, François, 'Poétique et onomastique', *Poétique*, 18 (1974), 194–207.

Rigolot, François, 'Rhétorique du nom poétique', *Poétique*, 28 (1976), 466–83.

Rigolot, François, *Poétique et onomastique: l'exemple de la Renaissance* (Geneva: Droz, 1977).

Rouart, Denis, and Wildenstein, Daniel, *Edouard Manet: catalogue raisonné* (Lausanne: Bibliothèque des arts, 1975).

Roubaud, Jacques, *La Vieillesse d'Alexandre* (Paris: Maspéro, 1978).

Rullaud, Norbert, 'Wagner, Mallarmé et la "Revue Wagnerienne"', *A Rebours*, 11 (1980), 35–40.

Satge, Alain, 'Wagner rêvé par Mallarmé', *Romantisme*, 57 (1987), 65–73.

Scherer, Jacques, *Grammaire de Mallarmé* (Paris: Nizet, 1977).

Scott, Clive, *French Verse-Art* (Cambridge: Cambridge University Press, 1980).

Scott, Clive, *A Question of Syllables* (Cambridge: Cambridge University Press, 1986).

Searle, J.S., *Speech Acts* (Cambridge: Cambridge University Press, 1970).

Seznec, Jean, 'Les Dieux antiques de Mallarmé', in *Baudelaire, Mallarmé and Valéry: New Essays in Honour of Lloyd Austin*, ed. by Malcolm Bowie, Alison Fairlie, and Alison Finch (Cambridge: Cambridge University Press, 1982).

Shaw, Mary Lewis, *Performance in the texts of Mallarmé* (Philadelphia: Pennsylvania State University Press, 1993).

Sollers, Philippe, *L'Ecriture et l'expérience des limites* (Paris: Seuil-Points, 1971).

Starobinski, Jean, *Les Mots sous les mots* (Paris: Gallimard, 1971).

Sugano, Marian Zwerling, *The Poetics of the Occasion: Mallarmé and the Poetry of Circumstance* (Stanford: Stanford University Press, 1992).

Thibaudet, Albert, *La Poésie de Stéphane Mallarmé* (Paris: Gallimard, 1912).

Thomas, Jean-Jacques, 'Porte Rimbaud ... Impasse Mallarmé', *French Literature Series*, 18 (1991) , 53–65.

Valéry, Paul, *Ecrits divers sur Mallarmé* (Paris: Gallimard, 1950).

Valéry, Paul, *Oeuvres*, ed. by Jean Hytier (Paris: Gallimard, 1957).

Villiers de l'Isle-Adam, *Oeuvres complètes*, ed. by Alan Raitt and Pierre-Georges Castex, 2 vols (Paris: Gallimard, 1986–88).

Wroblewski, Michael, 'Stéphane Mallarmé's "Hommage à Richard Wagner"', *Kentucky Romance Quarterly*, 27 (1980), 97–104.

Yale French Studies, 54 (Mallarmé special issue) (1977).

Index

197